Ancient Faith and Modern Freedom

Ancient Faith and Modern Freedom in John Dryden's *The Hind and the Panther*

ANNE BARBEAU GARDINER

The Catholic University of America Press
Washington, D.C.

Copyright © 1998
The Catholic University of America Press
All rights reserved
Printed in the United States of America

The paper used in this publication meets the minimum
requirements of American National Standards for Information Science — Permanence of Paper for Printed Library materials, ANSI
Z39.48-1984.
∞

LIBRARY OF CONGRESS
CATALOGING-IN-PUBLICATION DATA
Gardiner, Anne Barbeau.
     Ancient faith and modern freedom in John Dryden's The hind
and the panther / by Anne Barbeau Gardiner.
          p.   cm.
     Includes bibliographical references (p.) and index.
     1. Dryden, John, 1631–1700. Hind and the panther.
     2. Christianity and literature — England — History — 17th century.
     3. Freedom of religion — England — History — 17th century.
     4. Christian poetry, English — History and criticism. 5. James II,
King of England, 1633–1701 — Religion. 6. England — Church
history — 17th century. 7. Dryden, John, 1631–1700 — Religion.
     8. Church of England — In literature. 9. Catholic Church — In
literature. 10. Allegory. I. Title.
     PR3418.H7G37   1998
     821'.4 — dc21
     97–17714

ISBN 0-8132-0898-X (alk. paper)

To my husband, Thomas J. Gardiner

Contents

Preface

When John Dryden converted to the Catholic Church, his conversion was unabashedly public. As the preeminent living poet of his era, his action would have attracted notice even if he had remained silent. But he lost no time in writing a brave and brilliant poem of 2,500 lines to explain and justify his choice, as well as to invite his countrymen to join him in his newfound faith.

This masterpiece of religious poetry, entitled *The Hind and the Panther* (1687), was received in Dryden's day and long after with open mockery and hostility. The mockery was usually centered on the fact that the poet had represented the different churches in England as animals, and in particular had portrayed the Catholic and the Anglican Churches as the Hind and the Panther, respectively. His choice of animal speakers has long appeared to literary scholars to be at best a riddle, and at worst a proof of the poet's levity and profaneness. Since Dryden was arguably the best satirist in English literature, many scholars have dismissed the poem as an unsuccessful satire aimed at English Protestants, a work of caustic Catholic polemics written by an overzealous convert. However, as we will see, nothing could be farther from the truth.

Throughout his career the poet looked back to Jewish, Christian, and classical antiquity for his roots and forward to a flowering of religious freedom in the next age. It is no surprise, then, that his masterpiece *The Hind and the Panther* has two sides: ancient faith and modern freedom. The first two parts of this three-part poem are about ancient faith. Here he draws from a single biblical source and its allegorical commentaries to portray the Catholic Church as the spotless Hind and the Anglican Church as the Panther whose spots could easily be washed clean. The third part of his poem, exactly equal in length to the first two parts combined, is about modern freedom. Here Dryden looks forward to a time of civil and religious liberty in England after the repeal of the Test Acts. These Test Acts, passed by parliament only recently during the Restoration, were laws that the poet regarded as inhuman and unjust because they excluded from public employment, both civil and military, all those who would not take an oath to deny the Catholic Real Presence in the Eucharist and then conform to the national church by kneeling to receive her Communion.

On the side of ancient faith, Dryden has composed a poem that is like a great cathedral constructed according to a ravishing design and filled with noble imagery. No one has ever penetrated the structure so deeply before as to realize that it is all of a piece. Dryden's two Churches in dialogue, his animal figures, his story line, and his splendid imagery—all are derived from only eight chapters of the Bible. But what chapters! They make up Solomon's Canticle of Canticles, the song that was thought to reveal in melting terms the immeasurable height and breadth of Yahweh's love for his Bride Israel, the Church.

From the Canticle of Canticles and the many allegorical commentaries written about it from antiquity to the seventeenth century, Dryden drew the entire design of his masterpiece. All the animals he used in his poem to represent the Catholic Church and various Protestant sects had been discovered long ago in Solomon's Song by Church fathers and other interpreters, and their reading of the Song was still current in the seventeenth century. Thus, the poem is no riddle after all. It had only been turned into a riddle by its early, hostile critics. No incongruity had ever been thought to exist before Dryden's day between the great theme of Christ's love for his Church and the animal figures believed to represent the Jewish Church and the Church drawn from the Gentiles in the Canticle of Canticles.

On the side of modern freedom, Dryden devotes half the lines in his poem to a plea for the repeal of the Test Acts. These were parliamentary statutes behind which the Anglican Church had found security after her restoration as the national church in 1661. No one has noted before that the precise political context of Dryden's poem is the repeal campaign mounted by a handful of bold spirits from 1685 to 1688. The Quaker William Penn was in the forefront of these highly vocal opponents of the Test Acts. It should be no surprise that Dryden surpasses himself in wit and eloquence when he targets laws like these, parliamentary statutes that turn the Eucharist, as he puts it, into a political shibboleth and a spiritual poison.

When *The Hind and the Panther* is read in conjunction with the lively pamphlets of the repeal campaign, pamphlets almost completely ignored by historians of liberty of conscience, it becomes clear that the poet engaged his poetic gifts with bold, uncompromising courage on the side of repeal. Ironically, the very same arguments that Dryden and his fellow repealers conceived against the Test Acts were resurrected in 1786–1790 in another repeal campaign and were used yet again to finally overthrow the Test Acts in 1828. It is high time that Dryden and Penn were praised for having articulated a modern ideal of religious and civil freedom almost 150 years before it was enacted by the parliament of England.

In the past ten years I have traveled to many research libraries here and abroad to read the manuscripts and printed works left by Restoration Catholics and their opponents, so as to learn from these primary texts the background of Dryden's conversion and the actual context of *The Hind and the Panther*. As a result of this study, a picture of the Restoration emerges in these pages that is not found in the usual accounts of the period. Modern scholars, for example, tend to ignore the torrent of mockery against the Real Presence in the Eucharist that provides the underpinning for the Test Acts and the Revolution of 1688. Historians usually do not take seriously the many treatises and sermons that defame Catholics as people worse than heathens for their idolatry of the Eucharist, that is, as people completely undeserving of civil or property rights. Yet in the late seventeenth century religious doctrine was as potent an ingredient of politics as xenophobia. An accusation with such strong biblical resonances as that of damnable idolatry was potent indeed to arouse the hatred of the mob and the utter contempt of the educated class. As Dryden shows, this charge put the mark of Cain on Catholics and seemed to justify all that their enemies did to them.

Surely the charge of idolatry thundering against him from the pulpits across the nation in 1685–1688 contributed much to driving James II, the last Catholic king of England, out of his three kingdoms. It was the weapon of choice to defend the Test Acts just at the time when the Catholic king wanted to suspend these laws and summon a parliament to repeal them. And, as we will see, it was above all to acquit the Catholic Church of the imputation of idolatry raised by the champions of the Test Acts that Dryden came forward to confess his faith publicly in *The Hind and the Panther*. In the course of his poem, he revealed that the words of Jesus Christ about his Real Presence in the Lord's Supper had been the catalyst for his conversion to the Catholic Church. And surely, in the context of the pervasive charge of idolatry, it took heroic courage for the poet to avow meekly and repeatedly in *The Hind and the Panther* that he—the leading man of letters of his day, a man widely acclaimed for his superior wit and judgment—firmly believed in and adored the Real Presence of the Body of Jesus Christ in the Sacrament of the Altar.

Acknowledgments

My research for the second part of this book began in 1988, when a grant from the National Endowment for the Humanities enabled me to travel to Great Britain, visit the British Library, and read manuscripts and pamphlets related to the struggle for liberty of conscience waged between 1660 and 1688. I am grateful for this grant and for a number of other grants from the Research Foundation of the City University of New York that allowed me to visit research libraries.

I am deeply obligated to the staffs of the following libraries where I gathered the materials for my book: the Vassar College Library, the Beinecke Library of Yale University, the William Andrews Clark Library of the University of California, the Bodleian Library of Oxford University, the British Library, and the Quai d'Orsay Archives in Paris. Helpful, too, were the staffs of the Archbishop Corrigan Library in Dunwoodie, New York, and the Warburg Institute of London.

I wish to express my deepest appreciation of my husband Thomas J. Gardiner's unfailing assistance and encouragement during the researching and writing of this book. I also wish to thank friends and colleagues for giving my manuscript a careful reading and making many good suggestions, in particular Thomas H. Clancy, S.J., George McFadden, David M. Vieth, Patricia Bruckmann, and Robert Trisco. My appreciation also goes to Jerry Leath Mills and Robert P. Maccubbin for reading parts of my manuscript, and to Stanley Jaki, O.S.B., for his heartening friendship and inspiring example. My thanks, finally, to those at The Catholic University of America Press who have helped me give final shape to this book: David J. McGonagle, Susan Needham, and Philip G. Holthaus.

PART ONE

Ancient Faith

CHAPTER I

Introduction

John Dryden (1631–1700) is one of the handful of writers who form the first rank of England's literary pantheon. Indeed, his literary status is on a par with that of Chaucer, Spenser, Shakespeare, and Milton. His works, which fill twenty volumes in the modern University of California Press edition, are characterized by intellectual daring and vigor, as well as by imaginative splendor and stylistic polish. Besides setting his indelible mark on the English language itself, Dryden excelled in a great variety of genres, including drama, satire, and lyric poetry. He has been rightly called the father of English criticism and has been justly celebrated for his noble, spirited translation of Virgil.

Besides all this, Dryden wrote what is arguably the greatest poem of all times about the Catholic Church and certainly one of the most deeply reflective poems in English literature. This work, *The Hind and the Panther* (1687), was the result of his conversion to Catholicism in his mid-fifties, probably the best known conversion in English history, apart from that of Cardinal Newman. To honor his newfound church as the immortal Bride of the heavenly Bridegroom, Dryden composed his longest original poem and still the least understood of all his major works.

There was no human security or public esteem to be gained by his conversion. Samuel Johnson conceded that Dryden suffered for it the "persecution of critics" and the "importunities of want," a judgment with which contemporary scholars agree, one of them concluding that he sacrificed "his worldly fame" for it.[1] Although the poet joined the church with the largest number of adherents in Europe, he became a member of a despised and scapegoated minority in England. True, a Catholic king was seated on the throne, but James II was perceived as a man with only a few years to live; and besides, in 1686, the year Dryden converted, the heir apparent was Princess Mary, raised a Protestant, married to the staunch Protestant William of Orange, and very unlikely to give English Catholics patronage or relief from the Penal Laws that restricted them. Indeed, Dryden lost his positions as poet laureate and historiographer royal when William and Mary ascended the throne. From the time his conversion became public, he began receiving a volley of printed invectives such as no other poet in English history ever had to endure. One scholar characterizes these pieces as "painfully dull reading," and another observes that "no one is likely to question the sincerity of his motives today, or to deny that his change of religion was a matter of intellectual conviction."[2] Yet some critics still think the poet was insincere and merely trying to save face by not repudiating his conversion to Catholicism during the last twelve years of his life, despite the fact that he endured the loss of office and income; separation from his three sons, who went to live abroad, one to be a priest and the other two to serve as retainers to the pope; and unremitting attacks on his good name.[3]

Dryden's poetry is informed throughout by an Olympian view of history. For him, history is not just a sequence of events wrought by chance or human choice; rather, it is God's opus, the grand epic of humanity which he composes according to a master plan as the ages unfold. Past, present, and future coexist in Dryden's greatest poetry because he sees time as mysteriously subsumed in an eternal present in the design of Providence. Each of his major works may be seen as a paradigm of history

1. Samuel Johnson, *Lives of the English Poets*, 2 vols., ed. Arthur Waugh (London: Oxford University Press, 1961), 1:283; Arthur W. Hoffman, *John Dryden's Imagery* (Gainesville: University of Florida Press, 1968), 131.

2. James M. Osborn, *John Dryden: Some Biographical Facts and Problems* (New York: Columbia University Press, 1940), 155; Phillip Harth, *Contexts of Dryden's Thoughts* (Chicago: University of Chicago Press, 1968), 227.

3. Charles Ward, *Life* (Chapel Hill: University of North Carolina Press, 1961), 238; Stephen Zwicker alleges that Dryden spent his entire life "in the pursuit and use of strategy and disguise," in *Politics and Language in Dryden's Poetry* (Princeton, N.J.: Princeton University Press, 1984), 159.

as a divine art. No matter what form he turns his hand to, he introduces something of the epic into it, so as to ponder the ultimate cause of the rise, preservation, or ruin of a church or a nation. In effect, he combines his two public offices of historiographer royal and poet laureate to act as England's poet of history.

In *The Hind and the Panther* Dryden uses the Canticle of Canticles, also known as the Song of Songs (hereafter referred to as "Canticles" or "Song") as a key with which to decode God's artistic design in sacred history. This was an inspired choice, for the Jews had long employed Canticles as a key with which to decipher their travails through time, from their exile in Egypt to their last return to Israel. In addition, Christians had long read Canticles as the metahistory of their Church, finding in this song the Bride's beginning out of the Bridegroom's wounded side, her break with the Jewish Church, her afflictions from the pagans, and her growth to an eschatological worldwide extension. From antiquity to the seventeenth century, Canticles was read as a sublime work occurring in an eternal present, yet containing all time past, present, and future within a single design.

Dryden pondered not the existence of God, but the nature of his providential rule over history. He lived in a rationalist age, when the belief in miracles was already under attack. And yet, in many of his works written before *The Hind and the Panther,* he defended miracles as signs of God's real presence and of his direct participation in history. For example, in the last act of *Tyrannick Love* (1670) he brought an angel onstage to break the wheel on which St. Catherine of Alexandria was to be tortured. In *Threnodia Augustalis* (1685) he showed Charles II reviving briefly from death at God's command to complete the transfer of government to his brother (114–16), and in *Religio Laici* (1682) he affirmed his belief that a special Providence had kept the Bible from being corrupted as it was handed down through the ages (296–300).

Dryden distinguished a general from a special Providence. In *The Hind*, God strikes out the "mute creation" with a "careless beat" but kneads up humans by hand (1:253–75). Dryden expects Providence to act personally in human history; and within human history he believes God's special care is reserved for the elect, whose very hairs are counted. In the dedication to *Annus Mirabilis* (1667), he remarks that virtuous individuals sometimes end unfortunately on earth and are rewarded after death, but entire communities that are good are rewarded within time because "Providence is engag'd too deeply" to allow "any vertuous Nation" to end unfortunately. In many of his writings Dryden treats the story of the Christian people as a grand, unfolding design shaped directly by the hand of an always present God. Indeed, the action of several of his heroic plays shows Providence enlarging the bounds of Christianity without any significant help from the Christians: in *The Indian Emperour* (1667), *Tyrannick Love* (1670), and *The Conquest of Granada* (1672) we see pagan Mexico, imperial Rome, and Moorish Spain, respectively, all yielding to Christianity, not because Christians are stronger or better as individuals, but because God paves the way for the spread of the Christian faith by giving wondrous signs and by breaking down the old orders from within.[4] This does not mean that Dryden regards non-Christians as reprobates, as many others did in his day. On the contrary, in *Religio Laici*, he affirms his belief that by the "secret paths of *Providence*" and the "transcending Goodness" of God, the merits of Christ's sufferings may be extended even to those who never heard his name; thus, pagans who have "lifted high their *Natural Light*," that is, have obeyed the law written in their hearts and received a baptism of desire, like Socrates, may indeed be saved (186–211). His plays abound with good Muslims and good pagans.

In *Britannia Rediviva* (1688) the poet envisions God as "He walks the round" of his Providence, looking on the "Rise of Empires, and their Fall" with his "usual Eye," that is to say, dealing with secular governments according to a general plan for history, but responding directly and personally to the cry of his suffering Church in Hungary and raising a miraculous "Sign" to eclipse the "Moon" of the Ottoman armies (75–81). Dryden means that the Christian victories in Eastern Europe in the 1680s, like those of Constantine in the fourth century, reveal God to be intimately involved in the survival and expansion of Christianity.[5] This idea of a special Providence for Christians is the groundwork of the poet's attack

4. The seventeenth-century idea is well illustrated in *Sermon sur la Providence* (1656), where Bossuet compares Providence to a cylindrical mirror that gathers a maze of apparently confused lines and colors (in paintings done for this purpose) into a beautiful design. See *Oeuvres*, 11 vols., ed. Abbé Velat et Yvonne Champailler (Paris: Migne, 1857–1875), 7:22–35.

5. *Poems 1685–1692*, ed. Earl Miner and Vinton A. Dearing, in *The Works of John Dryden*, ed. H. T. Swedenberg, Jr., et al., 20 vols. (Berkeley and Los Angeles: University of California Press, 1956), 3:212. Hereafter the Swendenberg et al. edition will be referred to as "California edition."

on state-imposed conformity in religion in *The Hind and the Panther*. Since the Christian faith is under God's present care and is destined by Christ's promise to a worldwide extension, its survival does not and should not depend on coercive parliamentary laws.

In *The Hind and the Panther* Dryden finds inspiration in an ancient faith (figured as the Hind) which, in the opening line, he calls "immortal and unchang'd."[6] He hints that God has preserved this faith from natural aging by a special Providence. On the other side, he portrays the Anglican Church (figured as the Panther) as much "declin'd" in years (2:150) to hint that she exists under general Providence or second causes, and so has a mortal cycle of growth and decay. Indeed, for Dryden, it is a sign of the sustaining hand of Providence when a government of immemorial origin enjoys unabated life from age to age. In his time, both Protestants and Catholics claimed to be faithful to the ancient foundations of Christ's Church. Similarly, both royalists and parliamentarians claimed to be faithful to an ancient, unwritten British constitution. Few questioned (at least in public) the sacredness of foundations or the value of remaining faithful to immemorial constitutions in religious or civil government. In the case of Christianity, both Catholics and Protestants charged each other with "innovations," which meant a lack of fidelity to Christ's teachings. The Protestants accused Catholics of innovating during the Middle Ages, while the Catholics charged Protestants with innovating at the Reformation, their favorite question being, Where was your church before Luther?

A few years before his conversion Dryden began to complain about parliamentary innovations in religion, comparing the "Factious Croud" in parliament to ancient Jews prone to idolatry: "Gods they had try'd of every shape and size / That God-smiths could produce, or Priests devise" (*Absalom and Achitophel*, 49–50). What he condemned in particular was the novelty of a sacramental test enacted by the "Common cry," that is, the clamor of the House of Commons, to bar Catholics and other nonconformists from secular employment: "the common Cry is ev'n Religion's Test" (*The Medall*, 103). Paradoxically, it is within the context of reverence for ancient foundations that the poet employs the second half

6. *Poems 1681–1684*, ed. H.T. Swedenberg, Jr., and Vinton A. Dearing (California edition, 1972), 2:7, 46; *Poems 1685–1692*, 3:133. Hereafter, I will cite *The Hind and the Panther* in my text.

of *The Hind and the Panther* to attack the sacramental test, the contemporary statutory law which he sees as impiously flouting Britain's ancient constitution in church and state. As we will see, the writings produced in the years 1685–1688 against the Test Acts provide an illuminating political context for the second half of his poem.

When Dryden joined in the campaign to repeal the Test Acts, he engaged himself to attack religious prejudice. One scholar fittingly describes *The Hind and the Panther* as "a poem directed against religious bigotry"; another observes shrewdly that it was always in character for Dryden to treat the "bigot" as his foe and to hold fast "to the sense of inclusive charity that at all times marked his religion," for "liberty" was his "highest political value"; still another notes that the poet traces in this work the "patterns" of "religious tolerance and intolerance."[7] Dryden's childhood upbringing among Protestant nonconformists should not be overlooked as the source of this value of tolerance. Indeed, his contemporary biographer fills in many valuable details about the poet's early years spent listening to "Puritan preaching" and living "among the Puritan country gentry."[8] Although as an adult Dryden distanced himself from Calvinist predestination and professed a universal call to salvation in *Religio Laici* (1682), he consistently maintained the nonconformist principle of liberty of conscience even when he was a conformist. He believed that the state could not coerce subjects into uniformity of exterior worship, but could ask of nonconformists only that they conduct themselves peaceably. When *The Hind and the Panther* is studied, as it is in the second part of this book, in conjunction with the pamphlets produced in 1685–1688 by a small group of Catholics, Independents, and Anglicans opposed to the Test Acts, it becomes evident that the poet employed the same half-dozen arguments for repeal of those Restoration statutes that others, like the Quaker William Penn, used in that campaign.

This book, then, fills a gap. It will show that Dryden's poem has a

7. David Hopkins, *John Dryden* (New York: Cambridge University Press, 1986), 100; George McFadden, *Dryden the Public Writer, 1660–1685* (Princeton, N.J.: Princeton University Press, 1978), 217, 224; Alan Roper, *Dryden's Poetic Kingdoms* (London: Routledge and Kegan Paul, 1965), 112. In addition, George Myerson, in *The Argumentative Imagination,* sees Dryden as having given a model here of how to argue charitably and open-endedly about religion (New York: St. Martin's Press, 1992), 85–87.

8. James Anderson Winn, *John Dryden and His World* (New Haven, Conn.: Yale University Press, 1987), 1, 26.

grand and unified design that has hitherto gone unnoticed. The design of the work is a seamless garment: the imagery, the plot, the animal characters, and the arguments against the Test Acts all form a single whole, for they are drawn from a single biblical book, the Canticle of Canticles. For centuries Dryden's poem has been unfairly ridiculed for its alleged lack of unity. Samuel Johnson insisted on the poem's "original incongruity" of design,[9] but Johnson failed to see that the animals in Dryden's fable are not Aesopian mirrors of human weaknesses but great mythical constructs. As will be shown, Dryden drew these animals from ancient commentaries on Canticles. His animals look godward, not manward, and are windows into the divine attributes of the Church as divine Bride.

Other students of the poem have alleged that Dryden's design in *The Hind* is "discontinuous" or "unsystematically handled," and that his poem is a "risk-taking failure" in which he tried "to do too many things at once."[10] One of them notes that "no one has been able to speak of its mixture of beast fable and polemics as a unified whole."[11] This book will try to do precisely that. It will attempt to show that Dryden's beast fable is the groundwork for his defense of ancient faith and his plea for modern freedom.

The last years of Dryden's life were all of a piece, too. Throughout the reign of William and Mary the poet remained in England, serene and undaunted, waiting for Providence to restore the rightful royal line. Faithful to his outlawed monarch, he composed veiled Jacobite verse, such as "Lady's Song"[12] and the prologue to *The Prophetess* (1690), and satirized the 1689 settlement in a coded way in the plays *Don Sebastian* (1690), *Cleomenes* (1692), and *Love Triumphant* (1693), and also in his essays and translations. Furthermore, he demonstrated his loyalty by seeking only the patronage of men who were in opposition to the government, as, for example, the Marquis of Halifax, who had initially welcomed William of

---

9. Samuel Johnson, *Lives of the Poets*, 1:316.

10. James Kinsley, "Dryden's Bestiary," *Review of English Studies*, n.s. 4 (1953): 331; D. W. Jefferson, "The Poetry of 'The Hind and the Panther,'" "*Modern Language Review* 79 (1984): 34; Earl Miner, *Dryden's Poetry* (Bloomington: Indiana University Press, 1967), 199; Winn, *Dryden and His World*, 423, 427.

11. Sanford Budick, *Dryden and the Abyss of Light* (New Haven, Conn.: Yale University Press, 1970), 163.

12. The young printer William Anderton was executed for treason in 1693 merely for publishing his *Remarks upon the Present Confederacy* that year; Dryden made the same points in a subtler, coded language.

Orange but was in serious trouble at the time Dryden chose to honor him with a dedication.[13]

In the service of his ancient faith he also composed another religious poem, entitled *Eleonora* (1692), in which he delineated the pattern of a Catholic saint. Sir Walter Scott, in his life of Dryden, considers the poet, at the end, to have been something of a Catholic saint himself: "If we are to judge of Dryden's sincerity in his new faith, by the determined firmness with which he retained it through good report and bad report, we must allow him to have been a martyr, or at least a confessor, in the Catholic cause."[14] A modern biographer notes far more cautiously that "it would be difficult to cite any evidence in his published work" after *The Hind and the Panther* "to show that he ever regretted the step he had taken or that his commitment to the Roman Catholic faith was less than total."[15]

The poet's idea of his faith as a great gift is indicated in a letter he sent his cousin Mrs. Steward in 1699, a year before his death. He writes, "I can neither take the Oaths, nor forsake my Religion, because I know not what Church to go to, if I leave the Catholique; they are all so divided amongst them selves in matters of faith, necessary to Salvation: & yet all assumeing the name of Protestants. May God be pleasd to open your Eyes, as he has opend mine: Truth is but one; & they who have once heard of it, can plead no Excuse, if they do not embrace it."[16] In these words, written twelve years after *The Hind and the Panther,* Dryden confesses that his faith came to him as sight to a man born blind; it opened his eyes to "see" the universality of Christianity, so that he cannot now believe that Christ's Church could be divided into independent national churches. In this letter to Mrs. Steward, Dryden echoes the very words of St. Peter,

13. Halifax resigned from office in February 1690, spoke out to defeat an abjuration oath against James II, and was soon implicated in a Jacobite conspiracy. By June 1691 the government was considering whether to charge him with misprision of treason while he was seeking permission to travel abroad. This was the time Dryden dedicated to him. See my essay "Dryden's Patrons," in *The Age of William III and Mary II,* ed. Robert P. Maccubin and Martha Hamilton-Phillips (Williamsburg, Va.: College of William and Mary, 1989), 327.

14. Scott, *The Life of John Dryden,* in *The Works of John Dryden,* 18 vols. (London: William Miller, 1808), 1:320.

15. Charles Ward, *Life,* 222.

16. "Letter 67, Dryden to Mrs Steward," in *The Letters of John Dryden,* ed. Charles E. Ward (Durham, N.C.: Duke University Press, 1942), 122–23.

who refused to depart with those Capernaites "scandalized" by Christ's teaching on the Real Presence. Speaking for the Apostles, St. Peter asked the same question Dryden does here: "To whom shall we go, if we leave you?" (Jn 6:68). The letter to Mrs. Steward is also about the poet's principled stand on freedom of conscience: he confesses that his "Conscience" will not let him take a religious test for office and renounce outwardly the faith he inwardly professes.

Finally, this study will challenge T. S. Eliot's statement that Dryden lacks "profundity" and "insight."[17] At the deepest level of design, *The Hind and the Panther* is a rapturous epithalamium for the wedding feast of God and redeemed humanity. When a good measure is taken of this achievement, it will be seen to be poetry as deep as Sheol and as high as heaven (Eph 4:9–10). Indeed, the mystical beauty of Canticles informs every part of Dryden's *The Hind and the Panther*, conferring on it a grandeur of scale, a prophetic depth, and a richness of imagery perhaps unparalleled in the English language. One scholar observes rightly that Dryden replaces metaphor here with a "dazzling monstrance of mystery."[18] If by "profundity" Eliot meant a racking uncertainty about being saved or a piercing anguish about the adequacy of a private faith, then indeed that kind of profundity is lacking in *The Hind and the Panther*, for Dryden celebrates with undisguised joy his having left behind just such a private faith to enter the great seagoing "vessel" of the public, universal faith of Christ.

More than any other English writer, then, Dryden was the conscious heir of a great literary and spiritual tradition. Ancient Jews, Greeks, Romans, medieval Britons—these were all his forefathers. When he converted to Catholicism, he became even more keenly aware than he already was that he had received the *depositum* of the ages and a corresponding obligation to improve, adapt, and transmit it faithfully to posterity. As much a great intellectual as an originating genius, Dryden remains the poet who above all teaches us to look at history as divine art, who instructs us to see in the temporal sphere wondrous glimpses of God's eternal design.

17. T. S. Eliot, "John Dryden," in *Selected Essays of T. S. Eliot* (1932), reprinted in *Dryden: A Collection of Critical Essays*, ed. Bernard N. Schilling (Englewood Cliffs, N.J.: Prentice-Hall, 1963), 16.

18. Budick, *Dryden and the Abyss*, 235.

CHAPTER 2

The Two Church-Brides in Canticles

The great theme of *The Hind and the Panther* is the mystery of the nuptial union of Christ and his Church, a divine marriage begun on Calvary, continued through history, and consummated at the Last Judgment. Like St. Paul in his letter to the Ephesians, Dryden in this poem dwells on the Church as Christ's visible spouse on earth. He shows her as forming one mystical body with her hidden Bridegroom and sustained in her undeviating course from the day of his visible departure in the Ascension to the day of his Second Coming.

As a recent convert to the Catholic faith, John Dryden knew from personal experience that his Protestant countrymen denied that the Roman Catholic Church was the Bride of Christ. He knew that many English books and sermons printed since Elizabethan times had accused Catholics of committing idolatry. For example, in the homily on idolatry recommended in Article 35 of the Church of England, it was asserted that Catholics had all been drowned in abominable idolatry for eight hundred years before the Reformation.[1] It was not only because of their use of crucifixes and statues of Mary and the saints that Catholics had been called idolaters. Some prominent Anglican bishops of the past century,

---

1. "The III Sermon against Perill of Idolatrie," in *Certaine Sermons or Homilies Appointed to Be Read in Churches* (1623), 2 vols. in 1, introd. Mary Ellen Ricke and Thomas B. Stroup (Gainesville, Fla.: Scholars' Facsimiles and Reprints, 1968), 57.

like Jewel, Downam, and Bilson, had joined Puritans in condemning them for the supposed idolatry of adoring Christ in the Sacrament of the Altar.[2]

Imitating ancient prophets such as Jeremiah and Hosea, who said that Israel had forsaken her Bridegroom Yahweh and gone whoring after foreign lovers when she committed idolatry, many English Protestants alleged that the visible Church had divorced Christ by her idolatry and had become the whore of the Antichrist, as depicted in Apocalypse 17. Some, like Milton, said the divorce had occurred in the first century, after the apostolic age; others said that it had occurred in the fourth century, in the age of Constantine; and still others said in the eighth century, when the Second Nicene Council encouraged the use of images, or in the eleventh century, when the Church defined transubstantiation in opposition to Berengarius, a precursor of Zwingli. To answer this grave charge, Dryden creates a poem comprising about 2,500 lines of rhymed poetry, beginning with a figurative account of English history from Henry VIII's separation from the Catholic Church to the end of the English Civil Wars. He then shapes a dramatic dialogue about Christ's Church supposed to occur in the reign of James II between the Anglican and Catholic Churches, with each one taking the form of an animal symbolizing Christ. Throughout both the narration and the dialogue, Dryden argues that the nuptial union between Christ and the visible Church was always by its very nature indissoluble. There could never have been a divorce, for the marriage was always under God's intimate care. To prove his point, the poet takes as his paradigm the Canticle of Canticles, the immortal marriage song of Christ and redeemed humanity, then thought to represent the whole of sacred history from the time of the Crucifixion.

While modern readers tend to regard Canticles as a sensuous wedding song about mortal spouses, the prevailing view among seventeenth-century Englishmen was that this text revealed the abiding love of Christ for his Church. For this reason, the poet draws his characters, his dramatic plot, his dialogue, his imagery, and even his animal symbolism from a text which his countrymen, whether Puritan, Anglican, or Catholic, generally consented to read as an allegory of Christ's love of the Church. As we will see, Dryden uses as his groundwork not only the actual text of

---

2. Edward Stillingfleet, *A Discourse Concerning the Idolatry Practised in the Church of Rome*, 2d ed. (London: Henry Mortlock, 1672), Preface, B⁺.

Canticles but also a line of allegorical commentary passed down from the Church fathers through the medieval expositors to the Protestant interpreters of his own day.

Canticles provides the model for a dramatic dialogue between two Church-Brides. From third-century Alexandria to seventeenth-century England, there was a line of interpretation that saw two Church-Brides speaking in this song—a Bride confined to a single nation and a Bride embracing all peoples. The first Bride was the Jewish Church and the second Bride was the Church called forth from the Gentiles. The "legal" or Jewish Bride found shelter under man-made laws, saw only shadows of what was to come, and was confined to one people. The "evangelical" Bride, the one drawn from the pagan nations, found shelter under the Cross, leaned on the Bridegroom's own body, and went forth to spread the Gospel to all nations. Dryden follows this paradigm of the two Church-Brides in his poem: he depicts the Anglican Panther as the one-nation Jewish Bride who relies on human laws, has a shadow of the Real Presence, and does not proselytize, while he shows the Catholic Hind as the Bride who goes forth to all nations, has the Real Presence of Christ in her sacrament, and relies on Christ's promise of a special Providence to sustain her. In earlier poems, such as *Absalom and Achitophel* (1681), Dryden had portrayed the English as the Jews *before* Christ, the chosen race living in the midst of idolaters. Now he shows the English as the Jews *after* Christ, jealously trying to repress by man-made laws the infant Church that bears the universal scepter in matters of faith.

In the commentaries attributed to Cassiodorus and Bede, among others, we observe two Church-Brides speaking each in turn from the very first lines of Canticles: the Jewish Church expresses her yearning for the Incarnation of the Messiah in the initial phrase "Let him kiss me," and the Church of the Gentiles calls out to the Bridegroom right after her, "Draw me."[3] Similarly, the marginal notes of the English Geneva Bible reveal that the idea of two Church-Brides conversing in Canticles was widely accepted in England. The Geneva version was the most popular version of the Bible in England before the Restoration, and in the 1615 authorized edition we find notes for Canticles 8:1 and 8:8 that mention two Church-Brides as speakers: "The Church called of the Gentiles speaketh thus to

3. Richard Frederick Littledale, *A Commentary on The Song of Songs, from Ancient and Medieval Sources* (London: Joseph Masters / New York: Pott and Amery, 1869), 14.

the Church of Jerusalem" and "The Jewish Church speaketh this of the Church of the Gentiles."[4] The idea of a pair of Church-Brides in dialogue is also found in seventeenth-century English commentaries on Canticles. For example, the Anglican Thomas Brightman echoes the ancient idea that in Canticles 3:6 the Church of the Law exclaims in wonder at the progress of the Church of the Gospel, and the Puritan Thomas Wilcox interprets Canticles 7 and 8 as being about the Jewish Bride and the Bride called from the Gentiles, respectively.[5]

Besides the dramatic personae of two Church-Brides, Dryden draws from Solomon's Song the chief elements of his plot. It may come as a surprise to readers of *The Hind and the Panther* that there actually is a plot undergirding this argumentative poem. Indeed, in the first half of the poem, Dryden creates a dramatic plot consisting of two strands: the estranged National Bride is summoned home but refuses to return, and the Universal Bride ascends in three steps from persecution to peace. This was the double story which, as we will show, a line of exegetes had found in Canticles from Christian antiquity to the seventeenth century. They had seen the Sulamitess of Canticles 6 as the alienated Jewish Bride summoned four times to "return, return, return, return" to the inclusive *figura* of *sponsa universalis*. In their allegorical reading, they said that the Sulamitess had estranged herself from the Bridegroom under the Cross, and she was now summoned to return again to a marriage grown worldwide since her exile.[6]

Inspired by the allegory of Canticles, Dryden frames all of his poem as a call to the Panther to "return, return" to the Universal Bride. Accordingly, much of the dialogue between the Hind and the Panther is an attempt to woo the one-nation Bride into the multination Bride, to gather England into the New Jerusalem from which she has strayed. This is why Dryden paradoxically calls the Panther "estrang'd" in 1:337 and 1:564, and again "Stranger Dame" in 2:671, even though she dwells in her own native land. As in Ezekiel 16:3, where sinful Jerusalem is called a "foreigner,"

4. *The Bible* (London: Robert Barker, 1615).

5. Thomas Brightman, *A Commentary on The Canticles or The Song of Salomon* (London: Henry Overton, 1644), 1011, 1057–58, 1071–75. Printed in Latin in 1614, this work is bound with Brightman's commentary on the Revelation of St. John. Also, *The Work of That Late Reverend and Learned Divine, Mr. Thomas Wilcocks* (London: John Haviland, 1624), 72, 84. The dedication of the section on Canticles is dated 1585.

6. On the Sulamitess, see Littledale, *Commentary,* 297–300.

the child of an Amorite and a Hittite, so in this poem the Anglican Church has become a foreigner since taking the oath of supremacy. To confirm this, Dryden rebukes her for her "wandring heart" in 1:338, a phrase that evokes Jeremiah 14:10 about Israel's going forth to seek foreign lovers instead of staying home with her Bridegroom Yahweh.

Although the Panther refuses the call at the end of her "hour of Grace" (3:893), all is not lost, for the Panther herself surmises that her daughter "Lavinia"—that is, a future generation of Anglicans—will marry the returned "Aeneas" (3:776). Here Dryden alludes to Virgil's idea of a thousand-year plan (from the time of Aeneas to that of Augustus Caesar) for the rise and growth of Pax Romana, hinting that Divine Providence also has such a plan for England and the world. When the English resume their place in the Universal Bride, they will inaugurate that worldwide spiritual peace that is the Bride's eschatological destiny. Dryden believes a special Providence is shaping the events of James II's reign to set them on this path of a Pax Britannia. The poet may have known the following prediction of Nostradamus, mentioned at the end of Brightman's annotations of Canticles, "That *Rome* shall be ruled by her old *Britonish* head."[7] Whereas Brightman interprets this prediction to mean that the British will someday conquer Catholic Rome in the name of Protestantism, the poet envisions instead an era of peace to be inaugurated by a British Constantine. In *Britannia Rediviva*, written the following year, he hints that James II is that new Constantine bent on establishing peace: "Now view at home a second *Constantine*; / (The former too, was of the *Brittish* Line)" (88–89).

Since Dryden assigns the Panther the role that Christian commentators had ascribed to the "legal" Bride in Canticles, it is appropriate that he shows her as adorned with Jewish "*Phylacteries*" (1:399) rather than with the Christian "seal," and as relying for her survival on "humane laws" like the Test Acts, rather than on the "solid rock" of Christ's promise that he will be a Providence for his Church even before "th'infernal gate" (1:490–96). He also points out that the Anglican Panther has left the "meat" of her Eucharist for a "shadow," that is, a figurative sacrament like the ancient Jews' manna (2:49). Here he alludes to St. Paul's remark that the Church of the Law received only a "shadow" of good things to come (Heb 10:1). Dryden hints that the longer the Panther depends on man-made laws for

7. Brightman, *Commentary*, 1088.

survival, the farther she wanders from the pasture and garden Christ has made in the wilderness of history. She is slowly being transformed from a "well-bred civil beast" (1:569) into a confirmed "Salvage" (3:358), a wild "*Pardelis*" or leopard, by her recent, secret adultery with the Wolf. In literary tradition, the panther was a tameable creature, while the leopard was a ferocious animal resulting from the mating of a panther with a dog.[8] In the narrative part of *The Hind and the Panther*, Dryden tells us that the Presbyterian Wolf is descended from a dog run wild, who was once within the Church-Ark. Later, in the dialogue, the Hind warns the Panther that the Wolf-Dog's secret mating with her during the Restoration is driving her wild and causing her to be more deeply estranged from the Universal Church.

In the plot of *The Hind and the Panther*, Dryden not only shows the English Bride as being summoned home to the worldwide marriage and refusing the call, but he also shows the Universal Bride in England going from the darkness of persecution to the sunshine of peace. In the allegorical interpretation of Canticles there were three ascents of the Bride, each punctuated by the question, Who is this? In the first ascent (3:6), the Bride came forth as a single pillar of smoke from the wilderness, to the amazement of the Daughters of Jerusalem. In the second ascent (6:9), she came forth like increasing light, first resembling the dawn, then the moon, and finally the sun. In the third ascent (8:5), she emerged from the desert leaning on the arm of her Beloved, revealing her full conjugal union with him by using the first person plural to speak about a younger sister, a newly planted church.

Dryden borrows this plot line and shows the Protestant onlookers three times "amaz'd" at the sight of the English Catholic Church emerging almost miraculously from the depths of persecution in the years 1678–1682 into the full liberty granted by royal prerogative after 1685. They are astonished that Providence has allowed the Hind not merely to survive the pelting storm but to rise again glorious after her affliction. In the first ascent, she comes forth from hiding to reveal her "heavenly hiew" before a chorus of "amaz'd" English sects at the royal watering place (1:530–48); in the second ascent, after inspiring the Panther to seek for

8. Albert the Great, *Man and the Beasts*, trans. James J. Scanlan, M.D., *Medieval and Renaissance Texts*, vol. 47 (Binghamton: State University of New York Press, 1987), 171.

the Bridegroom's hidden dwelling place, she announces to the "amaz'd" Panther that hers is truly the voice of the Beloved (2:394–400) and then confirms her identity by a series of signs conveyed to the Panther as ever-increasing light (2:517, 527, 650); in the third ascent, she reveals her full conjugal union with the Bridegroom by inviting the once-again "amaz'd" Panther (2:714) to enter into her little shed where the Divine Shepherd is often "receiv'd." Thus this word "amazed" punctuates each stage of the Hind's ascent, just as the question "Who is this?" marks each stage of the Bride's ascent in Canticles. At each stage a veil is removed and a divine aspect is revealed in the Bride.

A distinctive motif that Dryden borrows from Canticles is that of the dewdrops of the night. When the Hind invites her to take shelter, the Panther is drenched with "dews," "dew drops," and the "rough inclemencies of raw nocturnal air" (2:664, 684–87). In Canticles 5, at the center of the eight chapters of Canticles and at the heart of the allegorical narrative, the "dew" and the "drops of the night" are mentioned just when the Bridegroom summons the Bride. In those verses the Bridegroom laments that his head is chilled, his hair filled with the dewdrops of the night. In the Douay version of 1615 he says: "Open to me my sister, my love, my dove, mine immaculate: because my head is ful of dew, and my lockes of the drops of the nights." In the allegorical readings these dewdrops are sometimes said to represent the imperfectly obedient churches afflicting the head of Christ. In Dryden's poem the Hind commiserates with the Panther because of the dewdrops and invites her into her shed. She also mentions the dangers that the sectarians pose in the night as a reason the Panther should enter in. When the Panther is in her outer room, the Hind gives her hospitality and then tries to persuade her to stay forever. After the Panther's refusal, the Hind retreats into her sanctuary where the Panther cannot follow. Thus, just as Canticles has three places—the garden, the cellar (a place for eating), and the bedroom—so in *The Hind and the Panther* there is the royal garden where the Churches come to drink of the royal bounty, the bower where the Hind and the Panther eat, and the inner place where the Hind withdraws for rest and heavenly contemplation.

Upon first entering the Hind's "shed," the Panther is "pacify'd" (2:720), a word evoking Canticles 6 because the name *Sulamitess* was thought to derive from *salem* or peace. The temporarily peaceful Panther

—peaceful because James protects Catholics by his royal prerogative—finds an "hour of Grace" (3:893) in which she might leave behind temporal security for the shade of the Cross. Although the Bridegroom is not visible in Dryden's poem yet, as the Anglican Richard Sibbes observes in his collected sermons on Canticles published in 1648, Christ's "ministeriall knocking" can be heard in the words of his Bride the Church, since "he that heareth you, heareth me" (Lk 10:16).[9] Paradoxically, the Bridegroom is present in the poem both in the loving welcome of his Universal Bride and in the affliction of his One-Nation Bride, who is chilled by the hostility of the English sects.

It is Canticles, then, and its rich legacy of commentaries that provides Dryden with the idea of two Church-Brides walking, resting, and talking in a pastoral setting till the breaking of dawn. Yet, one may ask, why did Dryden portray these Church-Brides as archetypal animals? The animal symbolism of *The Hind and the Panther* is traceable both to Canticles and to the ancient bestiary *Physiologus*, in part a Christian commentary upon Canticles. One should note that no book of Scripture mentions so many animals as Canticles. The chief animals of Dryden's poem are either named in this biblical text or have been read into it by allegorical interpreters. And as we will show later, ancient commentators long ago noticed a link between Canticles and *Physiologus*, where both the roe and the panther are conceived to be distinct images of Christ.[10]

Inspired by the way *Physiologus* interpreted Canticles, Dryden conceived the Hind as the Bride of Christ-the-Roe, and the Panther as the intended Bride of Christ-the-Panther. Though spotted by sin, the Panther can easily be washed bright, and she has a potentially irresistible perfume of words with which to draw the wild herd after her. There will be no loss of identity when the Panther re-enters the Universal Church: she will simply increase in fragrance and brightness until the rebellious sects follow her willingly. She will then fulfill the role which God keeps in abeyance for her as "Pan-Thera." This universal role is foreshadowed by the name which in Greek means "all animals" and which evokes the shepherd-god Pan.

---

9. Richard Sibbes, *Bowels Opened; or, A Discovery of the Near and Dear Love, Union and Communion betwixt Christ and the Church*, 3d ed. (London: John Clark, 1648), 126–27.

10. Anon., *Physiologus*, trans. Michael J. Curley (Austin: University of Texas Press, 1979), xvi.

Since Christian tradition taught from of old that there was no literal level in Canticles, Dryden draws from the ancient bestiary *Physiologus* to supply a literal level for his poetic adaptation of Canticles. He creates a drama in which two archetypal animals represent churches, each mirroring different attributes of the divine Bridegroom. This animal fable is a veil over the mystery of the immortal marriage bed, the *thalamus* celebrated in Canticles and in this poem. Dryden envisions the coming embrace of Hind and Panther in one communion as an eschatological event, a meeting of sun and moon. He thinks justice and peace will kiss at this final ingathering of the Jews, that is, the chosen English, into the walls of the New Jerusalem.

On 25 March 1686, James II gave permission for Catholic books to be printed in England for the first time in over a century. Under the protection of the king, the poet seized this unprecedented moment to create a public dialogue between the Anglican Church and the Catholic Church.[11] He looked to Canticles for his double-layered plot: for the estranged Bride being wooed to return to the inclusive Universal Bride, and for the infant Church ascending with miraculous speed from the horror of persecution to the civility of peace. Further, he looked to Canticles for an imagery and a rhetoric consecrated from antiquity, a spiritual sword to vindicate his newfound Church against the defamations printed since the days of Henry VIII.

CHAPTER 3

Commentary on Canticles, Ancient Jewish to Early Modern

Ancient Jewish commentaries long ago interpreted the Song of Songs as a story about the marriage of Yahweh and Israel. The text was read at Passover, a feast celebrating the Exodus as the start of Yahweh's conjugal love for Israel. Canticles was thought to be related to the prophecy of Hosea, where Israel is figured as the Bride who has wandered after foreign lovers; Yahweh declares that he will lead his Bride back into the wilderness and she will call him "husband" (2:4–16). In the Talmud there is mention of an ancient dispute about whether Canticles belonged in the canon of Scripture. Rabbi Aqiba, a contemporary of Emperor Hadrian, defended the Song with these words: "[T]he whole world was not worthy of the day in which this sublime Song was given to Israel; for all the Scriptures are holy, but this sublime Song is most holy."[1] He implied here that Canticles was a poetic counterpart of the Holy of Holies, the inner sanctuary of the Temple of Jerusalem, the place of Yahweh's presence.

The Talmud and the later Targum, a Chaldee paraphrase of Scripture,

---

1. Christian D. Ginsburg, *The Song of Songs and Coheleth, Translated from the Original Hebrew, with a Commentary, Historical and Critical* (New York: KTAV, 1970), 25. My remarks on the Talmud, the Targum, and Rashi are all taken from pp. 25–43 of this book, which first appeared in 1857.

both agreed that the "Beloved" or "Bridegroom" in Canticles was Yahweh, and that the "Bride" was the Congregation of Israel. However, the two approached the text differently: the Talmud saw it as mystical drama, the Targum as cryptic history. The Talmud viewed Canticles as revealing a Bridegroom's love hidden beneath the rigorous Mosaic law. The Targum, written down at the start of the Middle Ages, interpreted the text as a cryptic account of the great plan of Providence: it outlined the travails of the Jews from the Exodus to the end of the Diaspora, from Moses to the final ingathering in Israel at the end of sacred history.

According to the Targum, the "Gentile nations" have a small listening role in the Song; they are the "daughters of Jerusalem" addressed in Canticles 1:5. In that verse, Israel the Bride confesses to the Gentiles that she became swarthy with sin when she made the Golden Calf, but grew comely again by repentance. Later on, in an eleventh-century commentary on Canticles, R. Solomon ben Isaac, called Rashi, consoled his fellow Jews by arguing that the Bride of Canticles is wandering like them in strange lands. In his account the forsaken Bride of Canticles confesses her guilt and resolves to return to her first husband, after having been led astray by false lovers under the figure of wolves. In Dryden's poem, too, the Wolf misleads the Panther, so that she is further estranged and exiled. Following the lead of the Targum, Rashi gave the Gentile nations the listening role of "daughters of Jerusalem" and paraphrased the Bride's lament to them in 1:5—"If I am swarthy, like the tents of Kedar, which are discolored by the rain, in consequence of their being constantly spread out in the wilderness, I shall easily be washed, and be as beautiful as the curtains of Solomon"—in such a way that her swarthiness of skin appeared as the spotting and discoloration caused by rain, not by the sun. There were Christian exegetes throughout the Middle Ages who read the estranged Bride's discoloration in the same way. As I will show, Dryden envisions the Panther's discoloration or spotting as caused not by excess but by deprivation of light.

Beginning with St. Theophilus of Antioch, a fragment of whose second-century commentary survives, ancient Christian exegetes embraced the idea also found in the Talmud that Canticles has no significant literal level. Origen, Athanasius, Augustine, and Jerome agreed that it was a song celebrating the divine marriage between Christ and the Church. With the exception of Theodore of Mopsuestia, whose views were condemned at the Fifth General Council, there was consensus on this point among Christian exegetes until the Reformation. In England, the allegorical view was preferred well into the nineteenth century.

In the third-century commentary of Origen, the Bride was the Church taken either collectively or individually, either as *sponsa universalis* or as *sponsa particularis*. There was no contradiction between these levels, for the Bride's threefold ascent could refer to the rise of the Church or to the soul's mounting the ladder of love. It became a high art form in the twelfth century to contemplate the individual soul's bridal ascent to Christ. On the eve of his death, St. Bernard of Clairvaux wrote eighty-six exuberant sermons just on the first two chapters of Canticles.[2] The idea of the Bride of Canticles as the mounting *anima* still permeated religious poetry and mysticism into the sixteenth and seventeenth centuries, as we see in St. John of the Cross's *Spiritual Canticle* and in Francis Quarles's *Sion's Sonets*, an English Protestant paraphrase of Canticles (1625). Quarles speaks of Solomon's Song as truly "mysticall, the divinest of subjects." For him the Bride is sometimes the Church, as when Christ the Bridegroom says of her sacrament "Come taste her Vyands, and bee deified," and sometimes the individual soul, as when she remarks how "my weak flesh," a "wall of sin," keeps out the divine Lover at communion "and bolts me in."[3] In the lines on his conversion incorporated into *The Hind and the Panther*, Dryden depicts his soul as *sponsa particularis* joined at the moment of communion with both the Bridegroom and the Bride: he receives the body of Christ and is joined in one body with the Church-Bride.

And besides *sponsa universalis* and *sponsa particularis*, there was also *sponsa singularis*. Catholic expositors from the twelfth to the eighteenth century envisioned the Bride of Canticles as the Virgin Mary. She is the *sponsa singularis* of Rupert of Deutz, Denys le Chartreux, and Louis de Montfort. All these mystical approaches to the Bride were welcome, but Christian expositors before the Reformation generally avoided a merely historical or literal sense. They thought the main point of this text could not be the celebration of a human marriage or a love affair.

2. *Sermones super Cantica Canticorum.* See *On the Song of Songs*, 4 vols., trans. Kilian Walsh and Irene Edmonds, in *The Works of Bernard of Clairvaux* (Kalamazoo, Mich.: Cistercian, 1971–1980).

3. *Sions Sonets. Sung by Solomon the King and Periphras'd by Fra. Quarles* (London: W. Stansby for Thomas Dewe, 1625), unpaginated. See sonnets 7 and 14.

In the sixteenth century Sebastian Castellio shocked Geneva by persisting in his view, against all of Calvin's arguments to the contrary, that Canticles was an obscene song about one of Solomon's love affairs and the Bride nothing more than a candidate for the king's seraglio. This was the main reason Calvin banished him from Geneva. In a certificate he gave Castellio about their separation, Calvin said Canticles had the same theme as Psalm 45 [44], the only difference between the two songs being that Solomon celebrated the beauty of his bride, pharaoh's daughter, in a different style in Canticles. In effect, he agreed with Castellio that Canticles had a historical sense, but he claimed that the text celebrated a lawful marriage between Solomon and the Egyptian princess, not an impure love affair.[4]

Neither of the literal levels debated in Geneva in the sixteenth century seems to have been generally acceptable to English Protestants in the seventeenth century. In 1685 the Anglican controversialist Dr. Simon Patrick, in a work on Canticles dedicated to Henry Compton, bishop of London, calls it an absurdity to read the text as relating to an individual woman, whether an Egyptian princess or a member of the seraglio. No single woman, he argued, can reasonably be compared to many cities and armies as the Lady of Canticles is, so she has to be "a Body or Society of men." Dr. Patrick cites Theodoret, the ancient bishop of Cyrrhus, as saying that the Bride is both singular and plural in Canticles, both a garden and gardens, because she is simultaneously the entire Catholic Church and the parts thereof. He also points to St. Paul's use of the words "Church" and "churches," singular and plural, for a Christian assembly in a given locale.[5] John Wesley repeats virtually the same argument in the middle of the eighteenth century. If Dryden knew Dr. Patrick's work, he found confirmation there for his idea of two Church-Brides—a single, national Bride estranged from a plural, inclusive Bride.

Whether they were Anglican, Puritan, or Independent, and whether they were living in Britain or in the colonies, Englishmen throughout the seventeenth century held on to Origen's third-century teaching that Canticles was an allegory about Christ's nuptials with the Church or with the

4. Ferdinand Buisson, *Sebastien Castellion*, 2 vols. (Paris: Hachette et Cie, 1892), 1:198–99. The Latin manuscript of this certificate survives.

5. Symon Patrick, *A Paraphrase upon the Books of Ecclesiastes and the Song of Solomon* (London: Richard Royston, 1685), 22, 147, 150.

soul. The chapter headnotes of the 1611 King James version and the marginal notes of the 1615 Geneva version of the Bible both interpret Canticles as dealing with the marriage of Christ and his Church. The headnotes in the King James text, however, do not mention the second Bride until Canticles 8, when the "little sister" is identified as the Bride drawn from the Gentiles. So presumably, in the King James version, the marriage song concerns only one Church-Bride until chapter 8, the Jewish-Christian Church. As I will show later on, whether we read such Anglicans as Richard Sibbes, George Sandys, and Simon Patrick, or such Puritans as Thomas Wilcox and William Guild, or such Independents as Henry Ainsworth and John Cotton, we find that they all share a common ground: they all insist on an allegorical reading of Canticles. In this respect, the English of the seventeenth century were still the heirs of Origen, Bede, and Bernard of Clairvaux. Some of them, like Thomas Brightman, also read Canticles as cryptic sacred history, in the manner of the Targum. They saw it as a code for the entire plan of Divine Providence for the chosen race of the elect. Brightman drew a historical chart matching the three ascents of the Bride to the progress of Protestantism from the Waldenses to the Lutherans, and he even used Canticles to predict that Rome would fall in 1620, the Jews convert soon afterward, and the Ottoman empire then go down shortly in defeat.[6] Such a reading of Canticles as the plan of Providence for Christian history had already been attempted by Nicholas De Lyra before the Reformation and earlier yet by Aponius. Likewise, Dryden uses Canticles as prophetic history, as Divine Providence's utterance in hieroglyphs of the future glory of English Catholicism.

Dryden would have known, then, that Solomon's Song was a biblical text about which the English consented to follow ancient and medieval interpretations rather than private judgment. They regarded it as too obscure a text to study without the help of inherited annotations, whether Jewish or Christian. And Dryden might well have reasoned that since his countrymen generally agreed with him that Canticles depicted Christ's love for his Church, this text was an excellent foundation on which to erect his great defense of his newfound church as the Universal Bride.

In 1682, John Lloyd, the vicar of Holy Roods, laments that his fellow Protestants in Europe have reduced Canticles to a literal sense. He prefaces

6. Brightman, *Commentary,* 1077–79.

his pindaric paraphrase of the Song with the complaint that Theodore Beza's trochaic version of Canticles echoes Catullus and the "softest of Heathen Poetry," and that Hugo Grotius has unjustly called it a "Formal piece of Courtship to an *Aegyptian* Mistress."[7] He may also have known that Luther had called the Bride a figure for Solomon's government, and Canticles itself an "encomium of the political order." Luther was inconsistent, however, for elsewhere he reverted to the allegory of Christ's presence with his Church-Bride.[8] The secular view of Canticles slowly made its way into England, too, as we see in the clergyman Samuel Croxall's *Fair Circassian* (1720), a play in which Canticles is turned into a temporal love story. And now, in the late twentieth century, the literal sense so prevails that modern commentaries no longer convey how Canticles, for Dryden and his contemporaries, was a golden tabernacle containing the divine mysteries. Whereas the great idea of a ladder of human love, which was drawn from Canticles in the high Middle Ages, took its last stand in the heroic plays of John Dryden in the 1670s, the idea of a ladder of divine love found in Canticles, the romantic ascent of the mortal Lover, that is, redeemed humanity, to the call of the divine Beloved, prevailed for two more centuries.

It is just possible that while he was at Cambridge Dryden might have heard a lecture on the cabalistic interpretation of Canticles. Ralph Cudworth developed an interpretation of the Song of Solomon that included elements of the Kabalah and left a strong impression on Simon Patrick, who was at Cambridge in 1650 when Dryden arrived. In the preface to his 1685 annotations, Dr. Patrick remembers Cudworth's lectures on Canticles and gives favorable notice to his idea that the Bridegroom of Canticles is Tiphereth, the name of the sun in the Kabalah, while the Bride is the moon Malcuth, and their marriage feast in the upper world is the hidden design of Canticles.[9] Since Dryden seems to draw his idea of Christ as Pan from Cudworth, it may well be that some of his sun and moon imagery also glances at this astronomical myth.

7. John Lloyd, *The Song of Songs; Being a Paraphrase upon the Most Excellent Canticles of Solomon in a Pindarick Poem* (London: For Henry Faithorne and John Kersey, 1682), A4 of the Preface.

8. "Lectures on the Song of Solomon" [delivered 1530–1531], trans. Ian Siggins, in *Luther's Works*, vol. 15, ed. Jaroslav Pelikan (St. Louis: Concordia, 1972), 195.

9. Patrick, *Paraphrase*, vi–vii. Dr. Patrick received his B.A. in 1647–1648 at Cambridge and his M.A. in 1651.

More likely, though, the poet discovered a treasure trove of commentaries on Canticles in two books he acquired in 1680 from the library of the Catholic earl of Digby. T. A. Birrell's list of Dryden's purchases at that book auction in April 1680 indicates that at the time he wrote *The Hind and the Panther* the poet owned two of the great medieval annotations of Canticles: the seven-volume *Opera* of Cardinal Hugo of St. Cher, a thirteenth-century expositor of the Bible, in a 1502 edition, and the five-volume *Enarrationes* of Denys le Chartreux, a fifteenth-century expositor, in a 1548 edition.[10] Cardinal Hugo's notes would have provided Dryden with the entire narrative line in the allegorical reading of Canticles: the two Brides, one Jewish and one Gentile, engaging in dialogue; the wooing of the estranged Bride to return to her first Bridegroom and re-enter a marriage now become worldwide; and the triple ascent of the the Universal Bride. Dryden probably used Cardinal Hugo as an entry to other patristic and early medieval interpreters. The Carthusian annotator whom Dryden purchased at the same auction was called the "Ecstatic Doctor," and he emphasized the Virgin Mary as *sponsa singularis* of Canticles. This Marian approach to the Bride of Canticles seems to inform Dryden's *Eleonora*, an elegy about a saintly Englishwoman.[11] Besides these works, Dryden might have had access to other commentators, for as poet laureate and historiographer royal he would have had access to the royal library and, as a convert writing in defense of the Church, he would surely have been welcome to use the library of any Catholic peer. According to one tradition, *The Hind and the Panther* was composed at Ugbrook, at the home of the Catholic Lord Clifford.

Although modern biblical commentaries are generally of little help in recapturing the awe with which seventeenth-century readers looked on Canticles, the Anchor Bible's volume on the Song is exceptional in this respect. After printing a series of modern notes for each section of Canticles, this work appends in smaller print some representative passages

---

10. T. A. Birrell, "John Dryden's Purchases at Two Book Auctions, 1680 and 1682," *English Studies* 42 (1961): 197. Cardinal Hugo and Denys le Chartreux were purchased at the Digby sale, 19 April 1680. I have used Cardinal Hugo's commentary found in a later edition, in *Opera Omnia* (Venice, 1754), 3:106–38, in the Archbishop Corrigan Library, Dunwoodie, New York.

11. Dryden's Eleonora nurses the sick and poor with her own hands, personally distributes food to the hungry, educates her children in holiness, and dies on Pentecost Sunday at age thirty-three, the same age as Christ, dressed in white for the eternal wedding feast.

from ancient and medieval commentators who interpreted Canticles as an allegory. These passages in the Anchor Bible are all taken from Richard Frederick Littledale, an Anglican who made a remarkable compilation of the many allegorical readings of Canticles, verse by verse. His classic work is entitled *A Commentary on The Song of Songs: From Ancient and Medieval Sources* (1869). Littledale includes not only ancient commentators but medieval ones, like Cardinal Hugo and Denys le Chartreux; and he even cites Cornelius Lapide, a seventeenth-century Jesuit. Like the Anchor Bible, this study will rely greatly on Littledale's exhaustive compilation for the basic outline of the allegorical interpretation of Canticles which prevailed from antiquity to the seventeenth century. The reason for using him is that this is not a study of the poet's particular sources, but rather an attempt to prove—in the teeth of three hundred years of criticism to the contrary—that *The Hind and the Panther* has a well-unified design drawn from a vast, rich, exquisite literary tradition grounded on Canticles. This tradition Dryden inherited from both East and West, from ancient Jerusalem and Alexandria, from Athens, Antioch, and Rome, as well as from medieval France and Britain.

Since he revered ancient genres of poetry, Dryden may also have been moved to take Canticles as his model by the high literary esteem in which the Song was held in his day. In terms of dramatic poetry, Canticles was regarded as the Hebraic counterpart to the works of Aeschylus. In *The Reason of Church Government* Milton praises the Song for its literary form: "The Scripture also affords us a divine pastoral drama in the song of Solomon, consisting of two persons, and a double chorus, as Origen rightly judges."[12] Very likely Dryden noticed how this idea of Canticles as an ancient, biblically sanctioned drama had helped poets like Grotius and Milton to publish Hebraic-style dramas in the face of Puritan hostility to the theater. No doubt, too, Dryden saw how the design and imagery of Canticles permeated some of the greatest religious literature of seventeenth-century England, particularly the contemplative love poetry of John Donne, George Herbert, and Richard Crashaw.

---

12. *The Reason of Church Government Urged against Prelaty,* book 2, in *John Milton: Complete Poems and Major Prose,* ed. Merritt Y. Hughes (New York: Odyssey, 1957), 669.

CHAPTER 4

The Divine Attributes Shared
between Two Brides

The distinctive attributes that the poet gives to the Catholic Church in *The Hind and the Panther* clearly belong to the Lady of Canticles. Nevertheless, he also keeps some of the key attributes belonging to the Lady of Canticles in reserve for the Anglican Church. By dividing the attributes of the Bride and keeping some in abeyance for the Panther, as if these attributes were always ready to be reclaimed by the English Church, Dryden implies that the Panther is an estranged particular church called to return to her place within the Universal Bride. If she returns, she will be one dove again instead of a flock of pigeons; she will be a bright, powerful moon instead of a spotted, half-captive moon.

In Canticles, according to the interpretation that prevailed from antiquity to the Middle Ages, the Bride is all of the following: she is the doubly unspotted spouse of the beloved, a humble shepherdess loved by a shepherd, a princess betrothed to a great king, a clear sun, a pure fountain growing into a great stream of water and nourishing many places, an enclosed garden, a plant yielding sweet fruit, a building with a sure foundation, a tower of defense, a resting place for the Bridegroom, and a valiant army marching under flying banners.

It is no coincidence that these unique attributes of the Bride in Canticles

—so thoroughly elaborated in the allegorical commentaries—are the very ones Dryden gives to the Hind in *The Hind and the Panther*. She is the doubly unspotted spouse of the Beloved (1:1–4, 2:519); the shepherdess who is a resting place for the Divine Shepherd *Pan* (2:709–11); the heiress crowned with "spiritual Royalty" on her "wedding-day" (2:487–525); a "streaming blaze" of light in darkness (2:650); a "deathless plant" producing "dying fruit" and "sanguin seed" (1:17–24, 2:8–9); a "limpid stream" of tradition from a single fountain running a "lineal" course through the centuries, growing into "wealthy Tides" and watering all shores (2:551, 614); an impregnable building founded on rock (1:124, 2: 588–90, 612); a tower of defense (2:365–66); and a valiant marching army (2:294).

But the Bride of Canticles also has several attributes that Dryden reserves for the Panther. First, she is a dove who finds refuge in the clefts of the rock, allegorically the wounds of Christ. The Douay version of Canticles contains this verse: "My dove in the holes of the rocke, in the holow places of the wal, shew me thy face" (2:14). Dryden keeps this special name of "Dove" for the English Church, provided she re-enter the Universal Bride. In the Hind's tale the single "Dove" represents the original English Church, while the plural "Pigeons" represent the disunified Church since the time of Henry VIII (3:946–1288). The Dove is such an important aspect of the Lady of Canticles that the Anglican preacher Richard Sibbes, in his collected sermons on Solomon's Song published in 1648, devotes the entire seventh sermon to it, bringing together much dove lore from the Bible and *Physiologus*.

In Sibbes, as in Dryden, we have a literary and symbolic rather than a naturalistic view of animals. Both writers draw from the ancient Alexandrian author of *Physiologus*, whose zoology had a life of its own in Western literature, art, and heraldry, and whose influence can be traced through medieval bestiaries to seventeenth-century literature. According to this tradition, God created the animal world as a set of mystical hieroglyphs about himself. Each animal was placed in Creation as a ray of light to teach us about an attribute of God. Sibbes finds this idea of animals appealing, as we see when he observes concerning Canticles that "there is no Creature but it hath a beame of Gods Majesty, of some attribute."[1] This idea also derives from another ancient Alexandrian, Origen, who

---

1. Richard Sibbes, *Bowels*, 167. Sermon VII on the dove is thirty pages long.

taught that "each earthly thing has an image and likeness of heavenly things," especially animals, who "still have the forms and images of incorporeal things by which the soul can be instructed to contemplate also those things which are invisible and heavenly."[2]

Dryden reserves a second attribute of the Bride of Canticles for the Panther: she is "spotted" or discolored, but can easily be made bright again. In some ancient Christian commentaries the Bride in the opening verses of Canticles is the Church before the coming of Christ, spotted or discolored by sin. In fact, the Bride declares in the Vulgate version "Quia decoloravit me sol" (1:5).[3] The allegorical meaning, as seen in Rashi and in Hugh of St. Victor, is that the Bride is spotted by a diminishment of light. It is intrinsic to Dryden's design that the spots of the Panther should be linked to the discolorations of an obscured moon, to which she is also compared. It is not surprising that the poet would read the word "discolored" in Canticles 1:5 as "spotted" because the two words were still interchangeable as late as 1755, when Samuel Johnson defined "spot" as a "mark made by discoloration."[4] Hugh of St. Victor comments that the heavenly Bridegroom sees his estranged Bride as a mirror that cannot reflect his light fully because of her "spot": "Thou hast some spot upon thy face, thou art foul, and bearest another image than Mine, cleanse it, therefore, that *We may look on thee*" (RFL, 299). Once the Bride reunites with the Bridegroom, he cleans her so that she has "not a spot" and can thus reflect his full glory (4:7). Dryden draws on this allegorical reading when he depicts the Hind-Bride as doubly "unspotted" and the Panther-Bride as doubly "spotted," yet easily made bright again (1:3, 329).

As Dryden conceives them, neither the Hind nor the Panther can fully reflect the divine attributes of the Bridegroom at the start of James II's reign. In the case of the Hind, the divine image has been darkened by years of defamation. In the case of the Panther, the divine image has been darkened by sin and separation from the Universal Bride. And so both these Brides can say for different reasons "I am blacke but beautiful"

2. Hans Urs von Balthasar, *Origen, Spirit and Fire: A Thematic Anthology of His Writings*, trans. Robert J. Daly, S.J. (Washington, D.C.: The Catholic University of America Press, 1984), 44–45.

3. *Canticum Canticorum*, in *Biblia Sacra, Vulgatae Editionis*, 3 vols. (Milwaukee, Wis.: Bruce, 1955), 2:807.

4. Samuel Johnson, *A Dictionary of the English Language* (New York: Arno Press, 1979).

(Canticles 1:4), for this verse was read allegorically in both these ways: either the Bride was in mourning because she was persecuted, or she was in darkness because she had sinned and fallen from the sunlight of grace (RFL, 21–25).

A third key attribute of the Bride that Dryden reserves for the Panther is that of being as fair as the moon (Canticles 6:9). In the first part of his poem, he wishes ardently that the Panther might rise high in the Church-sky and be a bright, clear moon again:

> Then, as the Moon who first receives the light
> By which she makes our nether regions bright,
> So might she shine, reflecting from afar
> The rays she borrow'd from a better star:
> Big with the beams which from her mother flow
> And reigning o'er the rising tides below.
>
> (1:501–6)

Note that the sun here is figured as a female, a "mother," which is very unusual in the European literary tradition, where the sun is usually portrayed as male and the moon as female. In Philo of Carpasia's commentary on Canticles 6:9, however, the Universal Bride is pictured as a female sun that mirrors a "perfect likeness of Christ" and is "flooded with divine light." This imagery is closely related to the idea of two distinct Brides as speakers in Canticles, because Honorius comments on verse 6:9 that the sun is the Church radiating the full light of the Gospel, while the moon is the old Jewish Church clinging to human laws (RFL, 285–86). The image of a half-captive moon who is "Rul'd while she rules" (1:509) is thus related to the idea of the Panther as a Church half-fallen to earth, spotted by reliance on man-made laws for survival. The Panther will regain her true identity when she reflects the light of her "mother" the Universal Church, who can be called the "Sun" because, as the Bride, she is one with her Bridegroom, the "Sun of Righteousness." The poet grieves that English laws divide the Moon from the Sun and thus cause a discoloration and weakening of spiritual authority.

The poet draws a fourth distinguishing mark from Canticles and gives it to the Panther: that her mother was deflowered under a tree (Sg 8:5). In the Vulgate version of Canticles, which St. Jerome translated directly from the Hebrew text in A.D. 398, we read "Sub arbore malo suscitavi te: Ibi corrupta est mater tua, Ibi violata est genitrix tua." The Douay version translates this passage as "Under the apple-tree I raysed thee up: there thy mother was corrupted, there she was defloured that bare thee."[5] This striking passage is not found in the English Protestant versions, which are based on the post-Christian Masoretic pointings of the Hebrew text. Indeed, the verse in the King James version is as follows: "there thy mother brought thee forth; there she brought thee forth that bare thee." Ancient commentators usually applied this passage about the mother raped under a tree to Eve, seduced by the Serpent under the Tree of the Knowledge of Good and Evil in Eden (RFL, 354). Milton takes the key word "deflowered" from this traditional idea of Eve's fall and uses it in Adam's lament in *Paradise Lost* (9:901): "How art thou lost, how on a sudden lost, / Defac't, deflourd, and now to Death devote?"[6] But some Christian expositors also applied the word "deflowered" to the estranged Bride, the ancient Jewish mother who found shelter behind man-made laws when she strayed under the Tree of the Cross.

Dryden alludes to this verse of Canticles, concerning an illicit and forced sexual act under a tree, when he describes the start of the English Reformation as a kind of original sin: "A *Lyon* old, obscene, and furious made / By lust, compress'd her mother in a shade" (1:351–52). The woman who was "compress'd" here was the ancient mother, the former Church in England, the original of the present Panther. She was deflowered "in a shade" when Henry VIII forced her clergy in convocation, in 1529, to call him the supreme head of the Church. The Catholic Church in England, in 1687, is only a small mission sent from Rome, an outreach of the Universal Bride—and this is why the Panther can dismiss the Hind as a "foreign intruder" like Aeneas, an exile trying to return to the ancient mother. However, Dryden insists that it is the Panther who is the "wanderer" and the "stranger," because she is the one exiled from her true home in the Universal Bride.

The first epigraph of the poem, "Antiquam exquirite matrem," or "Seek your ancient mother" (*Aeneis*, 3:96), seems to have two applications: in one way it fits the English Catholics and in another way the Anglicans. On the one hand, the Hind seeks her ancient mother deep within

5. "Salomons Canticle of Canticles Which in Hebrew Is Called Sir Hasirim," in *The Holie Bible . . . by the English Colledge of Doway*, 2 vols. (Doway: John Cousturier, 1615), 2:345. All the biblical citations in this book are from the 1615 Douay version.

6. Milton, *Complete Poems*, 399.

the Panther so she can stop being a mission church and find herself home in England. On the other hand, the Panther is summoned to leave her insular "labyrinth" and go back to her ancient mother the worldwide Church. Throughout the poem the Hind and the Panther are both called to welcome the other, to receive and be received, in the equality of love, neither having to fear a loss of identity when they join into one Bride.

The Independent Henry Ainsworth, who relies much on the Targum in his annotations on Canticles published in 1623 and 1642, points out that the ancient Jews also identified the Sulamitess in Canticles 6 as the Bride Israel estranged from Yahweh and summoned to return to him. Ainsworth then links the Sulamitess to the Prodigal Son in Jesus' parable, the wandering sinner coming home to the Father.[7] Like Ainsworth, Dryden links the welcome awaiting the Panther when she re-enters the inclusive Bride to the great feast that the father in Christ's parable prepares for the son who had suffered "famine" in foreign lands (2:639–41). The poet casts the Panther as the Sulamitess-Prodigal Son because he conceives that Providence reserves a special role for her when she comes home. He images the return of the English into the Catholic Church as the prophesied, final ingathering of the Jews in Israel near the end of sacred history.

7. Henry Ainsworth, *Solomons Song of Songs in English Metre: With Annotations* (N. pl.: N. publ., 1642), unpaginated, but the annotations follow after each of the eight chapters of the Song. This was first printed in 1623 and profoundly influenced John Cotton, who also wrote a commentary on the Song.

CHAPTER 5

The Names "Hind" and "Panther"

Excusing himself for having "peopl'd" the British Isles with many "Beasts unknown," Dryden confesses at the beginning of part 3 that he had "those great examples" of Aesop's *Fables* and Edmund Spenser's *Prosopopoia; or, Mother Hubberds Tale* to lead him (3:1–11). This self-protective remark, however, is no declaration of the models the poet used in shaping the Hind and the Panther. For there is nothing quite like this Alexandrian zoology in Aesop or Spenser. And besides, Dryden's remark is prefaced to part 3, where, as he says, he descends to "the Common Places of *Satyr*." But even as he argues against the Test Acts in the second half of the poem, the last 1,298 lines on modern freedom, he navigates in the waters mapped out in the first half of the poem, the 1,294 lines on ancient faith.

In another place Dryden observes that he follows the rules of architecture when he composes poetry and buries the foundation of his literary edifice below ground.[1] Thus he intends the groundwork of his artistic construct to be below the sightline of the reader. And this is what he has done in the grand design of *The Hind and the Panther*: he has lodged deep in the subterranean part of his poem all his borrowings from Canticles and from the Alexandrian bestiary *Physiologus*. His animals are not mirrors

---

1. For example, Dryden refers to the plot of a literary work as the underground, unseen foundation in "The Grounds of Criticism in Tragedy," prefixed to *Troilus and Cressida* (1679), California edition, 13:234.

of Restoration or Reformation history, but instead a form of symbolic speech drawn from antiquity and the Middle Ages. These creatures look not only earthward, but heavenward, to divine attributes and a metahistory of God's people on earth. Even though they engage in a dialogue that appeals to our rational faculties, the Hind and the Panther are hieroglyphs of Christ and his lordship over history. As such, they reach to a level of reality where discursive language cannot go.

It is likely that Dryden gives the Universal Bride the character of a hind because in Canticles she is visited by the Bridegroom in the form of a roe. In the Douay version the Bride declares "my beloved is like unto a roe, and to a fawne of harts" (2:9), and at the end of Canticles she urges her Beloved to flee like a roe to the mountaintops, a passage that was applied to the Ascension. Dryden's portrait of the Hind answers well to this hieroglyph of Christ-the-Roe as the Bridegroom of Canticles. There are other representations of Christ as roe or stag in the Middle Ages, as in the Chad Legend, but this imagery also originates from Canticles and its long history of medieval interpretations.[2] In the third century Origen stated that Christ was well represented by the roe of Canticles because he comes to us in contemplation and destroys serpents (RFL, 88). Dryden's Hind faithfully mirrors these two attributes of Christ, for she is a contemplative and also a valiant defender against spiritual foes.

For Christian commentators from antiquity to the seventeenth century, the roe who comes "leaping in the mountains, leaping over the litle hills" to speak to his Bride is Christ. The roe stands in darkness outside, looking at his love through a glass: "Behold he standeth behind our wall, looking through the window, looking forth by the grates. Behold my beloved speaketh to me" (2:8–10). The marginal notes in the early seventeenth-century Douay version—which Dryden may well have owned after he became a Catholic—explain that the visit of the roe reveals Christ's intimacy with his Church on earth: though he is not visible, yet the Church "resteth secure" and "reposeth in him," so that feeling his assistance, she "confesseth, and preacheth boldly his Ghospel and truth against al Pagans and Heretikes." Guillaume de Saint-Thierry, who in the twelfth century gathered all the scattered comments in St. Ambrose concerning Canticles,

---

2. "The Hind and the Legend of Saint Chad," in Budick, *Dryden and the Abyss of Light*, 181–217. The key elements of this legend seem to be drawn from Canticles and the commentaries on it.

writes that the roe's keenness of sight and swiftness of pace relates to the divine name "Deus," a word decoded as "I see, I run."[3] The roe and the hind, then, are hieroglyphs for the divine Beloved and the Bride made immortal by his love, that is, Christ and redeemed humanity.

Some expositors link the roe's standing behind the wall near his Bride to the Lord's Supper. And this is one of those places in Luther's 1530 commentary on Canticles where he puts aside his thesis about the Song's being an "encomium" on "the present state of the realm" and returns to the allegory of Christ's nuptials with his Church. Concerning Canticles 2:9 he writes, with a glance at Zwingli for his denial of the Real Presence during their Marburg Colloquy of 1529, "Christ is present to His church through the Word and sacraments, but He is not perceived by the eyes."[4] In his annotations to the second chapter of the Song, the Independent Ainsworth also sees the roe's standing behind the wall as "a more neere communion with Christ." Likewise, Dryden's Hind, alluding to the sacrament, speaks of her Beloved as a hidden presence that is often "receiv'd" in her little shed.

The name "hind" occurs also in the King James version of Canticles in the repeated oath "I charge you, O ye daughters of Jerusalem, by the roes, and by the hinds of the field" (2:7). The Douay text translates this verse as "by the roes, and the harts." Luther's comment on this oath is that the hinds represent "saintly prophets" and "Christ Himself as the Head of all the saints."[5] This is how Dryden conceives of the Hind, too, as the visible communion of saints where Christ is the hidden head. Moreover, in Proverbs 5:19 a wife faithful from youth to age is called "a hinde most deare," a text which supports Dryden's idea of the Hind as the ever-chaste Bride. And finally, the hind in Scripture represents the poor of Yahweh, the *anawim* who discern the traps of the wicked and fly swiftly to the mountaintops when persecuted (2 Sm 22:34). Dryden's language for the Hind evokes the *anawim,* for he shows her flying from

3. William of St. Thierry, *Exposition on The Song of Songs*, in *The Works of William of St. Thierry*, 2 vols., trans. Mother Columba Hart, O.S.B. (Shannon, Ireland: Irish University Press, 1970), 2:124. See also *Song of Songs*, in *The Anchor Bible*, trans. and annot. Marvin H. Pope (Garden City, N.Y.: Doubleday, 1977), 121. Marvin Pope mentions this twelfth-century commentator's debt to St. Ambrose.

4. Luther, "Lectures on The Song of Solomon," 218.

5. Luther makes virtually the same comment on the oath each time it recurs; see "Lectures," 216–17, 224, 256.

English hunters, from "Scythian shafts" and "hounds," and discerning the well-laid "snare" (1:5–8, 2:1–9). The Panther, who relies for safety on human laws, mocks the Hind for her defenselessness and fleetness of foot (2:10–7).

The name "Panther" can also be traced to Canticles. The name was thought to be implied in Canticles 4:8, when the Bride is called forth from the mountains of the leopards. In this verse, she is called "my spouse" for the first time. As the tameable cousin of the leopard, the Panther-Bride is summoned to leave her wild companions and to be docile. St. Epiphanius says she is called to leave behind her those "variegated and powerful sins" represented by the leopard and to embrace the "poverty of Christ" (RFL, 167). This fits well with Dryden's design: in the extended invitation at the end of part 2, the Hind likewise summons the Panther to come forth from the temptations to "pomp" and "gain" and to embrace the poverty of a humble "shed" where the divine "Pan" abides, "Pan" being the first part of the Panther's name and one of the names of Christ in this poem (2:712–13).

In the ancient bestiary *Physiologus*, Christ is imaged not only as the roe, but also as the panther of Canticles. When the Bridegroom draws the Bride of the Song toward him by his fragrance, the author of *Physiologus* sees the hieroglyph of the divine Panther, whose attribute is irresistible perfume, which by synesthesia is also ravishing music. He adds that "Our Lord Jesus Christ who is the true Panther draws to himself all humankind" by a "fragrance" which is also the irresistible melody of the Word, the ravishing voice of the new Orpheus, who can tame the savage beast. Commenting on Canticles 4:10, "the fragrance of your oils is more than all other spices," the same author states that Christ-the-Panther draws all men by a sweet-scented music: "What else can the oil of Christ be but his commands spiced beyond all others? For just as a strong kind of spice gives off a sweet fragrance, so too the words which issue from the mouth of the Lord rejoice the hearts of men who hear and follow him." In *Physiologus*, too, we read that the Bride of Canticles embodies his attribute and also draws the Bridegroom to herself by her own perfumed eloquence.[6]

Dryden would have known *Physiologus* or works derived from it, since this text was translated into many languages and adapted into many bes-

6. *Physiologus*, 42, 45.

tiaries. As we saw, a seventeenth-century clergyman like Richard Sibbes would still refer to *Physiologus* in a sermon on the Lady of Canticles as a dove. The Panther-Bridegroom is as much a hidden presence in Dryden's pastoral drama as the Roe-Bridegroom. The panther and the roe mirror two distinct attributes of Christ: the irresistible fragrance of his Word, and the mighty valor of his Passion. The English Panther is being wooed to return and be part of the all-inclusive Bride again, because she is needed to embody worldwide the fragrance of the Bridegroom.

In *Physiologus* we learn that the panther represents Yahweh in the Septuagint, a Greek translation of the Hebrew Scriptures dating from around 100 B.C. The panther is an image of how Yahweh deals with those outside of the Jewish Church: "I became . . . like a panther to the house of Ephraim" (Hos 5:14).[7] Guillaume Le Clerc, in his thirteenth-century bestiary, interprets this passage in Hosea as revealing the great design of Divine Providence: Christ would draw his Bride from the Gentiles in the same way the panther draws wild animals, not by harsh laws but by a sweet fragrance of breath, that is, by irresistible words.[8] In Dryden's poem the divine Panther of Canticles is the heavenly form which the English Panther is called to mirror, a form she now reflects only in a spotted, discolored way because she was deflowered by Henry VIII. The poet implies that if she regains the attributes of the divine Panther, the Panther will Orpheus-like draw the English sects after her by the fragrant fervor of her preaching, without the use of coercive laws.

We see by this imagery that Dryden regards great preaching as an irresistible perfume and proposes it as the chief means of ensuring the growth of Christianity in Britain and throughout the world. The poet mourns that his nation exports to far distant shores, instead of the Christian message, the stench of crime and viciousness:

> Our sayling ships like common shoars we use,
> And through our distant colonies diffuse
> The draughts of Dungeons and the stench of stews;
>
>   (2:568–70)

Although the Panther has received Christ's command to spread the Gospel to the ends of the earth, she allows a line of ships like sewage

---

7. *Physiologus*, 42.

8. *Le Bestiaire: Das Thierbuch des Normanischen Dichters Guillaume Le Clerc*, ed. Dr. Robert Reinsch (Leipzig: O. R. Reisland, 1892), 313–14.

pipes to carry from England the worst pollution of dungeon and brothel to "some far *Indian* coast." Here Dryden implicitly contrasts the foul stream disembogued by English ships to the Hind's "wealthy Tides" watering all shores with the Gospel (2:548–51). He alludes to St. Francis Xavier, the Jesuit missionary who preached the Christian faith in India and Japan. Indeed, at the time he wrote *The Hind and the Panther,* the poet may have already begun translating the life of St. Francis Xavier from the French of Dominique Bouhours, a work he dedicated to Queen Mary Beatrice of Modena in 1688.[9]

Dryden exclaims that when the Anglican Panther is cleansed of her "stains," she will be "too good to be a beast of Prey" (1:330). This is not Aesop's realm, where animals can never change their spots and nature. On the contrary, this is a world where a "Salvage" beast can be transformed by one spiritual washing into a docile creature, where a predator can suddenly lie down peaceably side by side with its former prey. Throughout the first two parts of his poem and in the tales of part 3, Dryden draws on the kind of animal symbolism found in the Bible, in *Physiologus,* and in the medieval bestiaries derived from these two sources. In such works, the attributes of Christ are embodied in diverse beasts like the lamb, the lion, the roe, the panther, the phoenix, the eagle, the pelican, and the dove. An animal may be likened to Christ because of a single attribute, such as sweetness of breath. In Dryden's poem, when the Hind rebukes the Panther for repeating the Wolf's slanders against the Catholic Church, she draws her clinching argument from *Physiologus*: "The Panther's breath was ever fam'd for sweet" (2:228).

In *Physiologus* the panther's very name points to Christ, for *Pan-thera* is interpreted to mean one who gathers or befriends all wild animals except the hellish dragon.[10] As we will see, Dryden portrays Christ as Pan in his poem because he is no hunter but rather a friend of all animals, even the wild ones beyond his sheepfold. In heraldry, the panther's sweet breath was pictured as flames issuing from the head,[11] an appropriate

---

9. *The Life of St. Francis Xavier* (1988), California edition, vol. 19.

10. *Physiologus,* 43.

11. In British heraldry the panther is "invariably found flammant, i.e., with flames issuing from the mouth and ears," to represent its sweet breath; sometimes it has a horned head and clawed feet like a griffin. See Arthur Charles Fox-Davies, *A Complete Guide to Heraldry* (London and Edinburgh: Nelson & Sons, 1929), 193–95.

image to represent intelligence and eloquence. Should the Panther return and fully reflect her original form, she would both guard her own flock and befriend the "spotted" herds in Britain. Like Pan and Orpheus, she would draw these wild ones to follow her by the perfume of her song, not hunt them and frighten them out of their lairs.

CHAPTER 6

The Hind as Spouse, Shepherdess, and Queen

In Canticles the name "my beloved" belongs to the Bridegroom (2:8–10, 17; 6:1–2), while the name "my spouse" belongs to the Bride (4:8–12). These distinctive names are often echoed in later religious poetry. Thus, in *The Hind and the Panther,* when the Hind calls Christ "her belov'd" and herself "his unspotted spouse," she alludes to Canticles. "Behold," she says, "What from his Wardrobe her belov'd allows / To deck the wedding-day of his unspotted spouse" (2:518–20). Here the names "spouse" and "beloved" are carefully chosen with an eye on Canticles, for they are connected explicitly to the Church's "wedding-day," and the Song of Solomon was interpreted to be the epithalamium for the wedding day of Christ and his Church. In all of Dryden's poetry the words "spouse" and "beloved" occur only three and four times, respectively; they are found only in this passage and in the *Aeneis* (1697). While he uses the coarse name of "mate" for the Wolf, the Panther's new lover (1:449), Dryden uses the word "spouse" to imply that the Hind is bone of the bone of her "beloved," as Eve was of the first Adam (Gn 2:24). Indeed, St. Paul reflects that the Church forms one body with Christ, which he nourishes as his own flesh: "He that loveth his wife, loveth himself. For no man ever hated his owne flesh: but he nourisheth and cherisheth it, as also Christ the Church: because we be the members of his body, of his flesh and of his bones" (Eph 5:28–30). It is this theme of conjugal union that Dryden ponders when he invites the reader to enter with him into the great "vessel" where "our Saviour" is "Pilot" (1:131–32), that is, into the Mystical Body of the Church where Christ is head.

The pastoral element is prominent both in Canticles and in *The Hind and the Panther*. At the start of Canticles a shepherdess asks that her beloved shepherd "draw" her to the pasture where he feeds his sheep at midday. In reply, the beloved tells the shepherdess to come and follow "the steps of the flocks" so as to "feed thy kids beside the tabernacles of the pastours" (1:1–8). A short time later the two come upon a little bed in a green place (1:17). The Septuagint has two readings, "our shady bed" and "thou art a shadow to our bed," while the Vulgate has "our little bed is flowery." Since he sees the Church itself as the bed of Christ, Origen says it is *our* bed because the Bride's "members" belong to the Bridegroom and he himself is her shade. Nicolaus of Argentina thinks that the "little" bed of the Vulgate is the "bed of the Cross," the bridal couch of Christ and his Church (RFL, 52–54). Regarding the first chapter of Canticles, the English Independent Ainsworth remarks that a bed is an altar of sacrifice in Isaiah 57:7, and so "our bed" implies an altar. Dryden makes the "shed" of the Hind mirror all these aspects of the "bed" in Canticles, for it is at once a resting place for the Divine Shepherd, the Tree of Life, and the altar for the Sacrifice of the Mass.

In Dryden's poem the Hind's leafy dwelling resembles the shepherd's shady couch of Canticles, for hers is "a shed / With hoary moss and winding Ivy spread" (2:697–98). This "shed" (a word derived from *shade*) turns out to be a place where the shepherd Pan often returns to lie down as her guest. When the Panther enters, the Hind adjures her not to despise her humble retreat:

> . . . for this poor aboad
> Has oft receiv'd, and yet receives a god;
> A god victorious of the stygian race
> Here laid his sacred limbs, and sanctified the place.
> This mean retreat did mighty *Pan* contain. . . .
>
> (2:707–11)

The phrase "oft receiv'd, and yet receives," in connection with a divine guest who triumphed over death and hell and "sanctified" a place, cries out to be applied to the Sacrament of the Altar. In Samuel Johnson's *Dictionary* of 1755, the word *receiver* still denotes, in the third place, a partaker of the Lord's Supper. Earl Miner rightly sees in this passage an affirmation that the "celebration of the mass involves the so-called Real Presence of Christ whenever enacted."[1] The Hind has received and still receives the shepherd Pan, for he has laid and still lays "his sacred limbs" in her inner room (2:697–722). Dryden in part borrows from St. Paul, who calls Christ the Great Shepherd of the sheep who rose from the dead (Heb 13:20), but he also adds to this Origen's idea about the Church as the "bed" of Christ. He echoes other expositors of Canticles, too, among whom are St. Ambrose, who says the Church makes herself "a resting place for the Word" who once had nowhere to lay his head (RFL, 128). The nuptial bed or *thalamus* is what is celebrated in an epithalamium, and so it is no surprise if Dryden, who makes the ancient wedding song his paradigm, celebrates the nuptial bed as the central mystery of the Church. Thus, in answer to the Protestant charge that Christ divorced his visible Church many ages ago, Dryden tells the reader about the hidden marriage bed of Christ and the Church, a bed continuously present at the heart of sacred history since the death of Christ.

It is interesting that when Dryden and the Hind name the Bridegroom in *The Hind and the Panther*, they usually call him by the affectionate title of "our Saviour" (1:131; 2:163, 397, 481; 3:305). Only once does the Hind call him "Christ," and that is when she is showing how Protestants compare him to Moses (2:132). The Panther uses the names of "Christ" and "our Saviour" only once each in the entire poem (2:299; 3:216), but not to refer to his abiding presence with her, but rather to speak of the *text* of his preaching. There is, however, another name for Christ in this poem: twice Dryden calls him "Pan."

Dryden would have known that Edmund Spenser, Ralph Cudworth, and Milton had used the classical name of "Pan" for Christ. Spenser used it in *The Shepheardes Calender* (1579), in the May eclogue where a pair of clergymen, a Catholic and a Protestant, engage in a dialogue. In a note, Spenser explains that the name "Pan" befits Christ as "the very God of all shepheards, which calleth himself the greate and good shepherd," for "Pan signifieth all, or omnipotent, which is onely

---

1. Earl Miner, *The Restoration Mode from Milton to Dryden* (Princeton, N.J.: Princeton University Press, 1974), 332.

the Lord Jesus."[2] Cudworth likewise names Christ "the great Pan" in
The True Intellectual System of the Universe (1678), a book to which
Dryden refers in his translation of Virgil's *Aeneid*. Cudworth finds the
name "Pan" appropriate for Christ because of Plutarch's saying that
spirits were heard moaning that "the great Pan was dead" in the reign of
Tiberius, around the time of Christ's death. He interprets the name
"Pan" to mean Logos and Providence combined: it is "that divine wis-
dome which diffuseth itself through all things," and the "rational and
intellectual principle" of the universe "presiding over it." In addition,
the name "Pan" seems to him appropriate for the God who became
flesh to die for mankind: "Pan being used not so much for the naked
and abstract Deity, as the Deity as it were embodied in this visible cor-
poreal world, might therefore the better signify God manifest in the
flesh, and clothed with a particular human body (in which respect alone
he was capable of dying)."[3] Milton, too, sees the name as evoking the
Incarnation, for he calls Christ "mighty Pan" in his "Nativity Ode" (89).
Cudworth observes that Pan was "clothed with the skin of a libbard,"
but his leopard spots were spots of light, indeed stars, because the night
sky itself draped Pan's shoulders. Thus, the ideal form of the English
Panther could well be the great Pan of the Incarnation, the Good Shepherd who befriends all wild animals while keeping his own flock, and
who governs all from a lofty place in the sky. Curiously, Pan and Panther are matched in another sense as well, because according to Plato's
Cratylus Socrates thought Pan irresistible for eloquence, just as the author of *Physiologus* thought the panther was.

Since Pan was a feeder-god, and since Dryden gives the name Pan for
Christ's Real Presence in the Hind's inner room, the name might conceiv-
ably evoke *Panis, Pain,* the bread of life, where pastor and pasture, feeder
and food are one. Revealing his newfound belief in the Real Presence in
the Sacrament of the Altar, the poet speaks not only of Pan's placing his
"limbs" in the Hind's "shed" but uses an especially Catholic rhetoric to
hint that Christ not only contains the mysteries but is in some way contained there, too: "This mean retreat did mighty *Pan* contain" (2:711).

2. *The Complete Poetical Works of Spenser*, ed. R. E. Neil Dodge (Boston:
Houghton Mifflin, 1908), 27.
3. Ralph Cudworth, *The True Intellectual System of the Universe*, 3 vols. (London:
Thomas Tegg: 1845), 1:582–85.

In another place Dryden speaks of Christ as "blessed *Pan*" for still another reason, that he left his Bride an example of how to deal with misbelievers. He did not go out to discover and kill wolves in the wild; he simply defended his own sheep:

> Not so the blessed *Pan* his flock encreas'd,
> Content to fold 'em from the famish'd beast:
> Mild were his laws; the Sheep and harmless Hind
> Were never of the persecuting kind.
>
> (1:284–87)

If the Panther fully mirrored the divine Pan, then, she would protect her flock without tracking nonconformists into their hiding places. She would renounce civil penalties for religion, leave the nonconformists in peace, and teach her own flock well.

The poet depicts the pastors of the Catholic Church as continuing this defensive work of guarding the sheepfold and the vineyard from wild intruders (2:365, 535, 612). Later on, in the *Fables* (1700), Dryden returns to this important theme in "The Character of a Good Parson," adapted from Chaucer. Dryden's Parson is vigilant to prevent heretics from seizing his sheep, but he does not hunt them down in their own wilderness; according to Dryden, the Good Parson "from the prowling wolf redeemed the prey, / And hungry sent the wily fox away" (72–74).[4] Ironically, the story of the Good Parson is set in the reign of Henry IV, when heretics were for the first time burned at the stake in England under the statute *de haeretico comburendo*.[5] Before that law was enacted, heresy in England was not punished so severely. The Good Parson seems to ignore the new law imposing a death penalty on Lollards and does not report them to civil authorities for punishment. Instead, he follows Christ-Pan's model of shepherding and minds his own sheep. Drawing an implied parallel between Henry IV and William III as two usurpers using persecution to steady their thrones, the poet hints that pastors would do well to imitate the Good Parson in 1700 by guarding their own flocks instead of enforcing the harsh new laws against Catholics.

4. Scott, *The Works of John Dryden*, 11:397. The *Fables* (1700) volume has not yet appeared in the California edition.

5. Sir Matthew Hale, *Historia Placitorum Coronae*, 2 vols. (London, 1736), 1:395–97. The law 2 H. 4 cap. 15, to which Commons assented, provided for burning heretics, or Lollards. Judge Hale says that before the usurpation of Henry IV, the penalty for heresy was only confiscation and seizure of goods.

Dryden images his Church as a cultivated bower in the wilderness, a place where the special Providence of Christ as Divine Shepherd ensures that the flock will always be protected from spiritual predators and will always be fed. In *The Hind and the Panther* he reveals that the two main motives of persecution are these: spiritual famine, in the Wolf's case, and insecurity, in the Panther's. Both involve a loss of faith in a special, miraculous Providence that sustains the Bride in history. Both lead to a reliance on coercion, whether psychological or civil—an internal certainty of supralapsarian predestination or an external array of coercive statutes.

Just as the humble shepherdess of Canticles turns out to be a "prince's daughter" at the wedding feast (7:1), so likewise the lowly shepherdess in Dryden's poem turns out to be high born: she raises her eyes to her "kindred sky" (2:396), "ascends the throne" on her marriage day (2:498), and compares herself to "ancient heirs of Eastern kings" (2:521). She tells the Panther that a "crown" was given her by the Beloved and its "annex'd condition" is infallibility in spiritual matters, "Immunity from errours." However, this "spiritual Royalty" is no cause for pride: it is rather a "glorious weight" to bear for others, like the Cross. For in Canticles 3:9–11, the nuptial crown is allegorically the Crown of Thorns, and the palanquin or portable bed, the Cross.

Dryden uses the word "weight" to interconnect the Church's authority with the titanic weight of the crown of Redemption which her Beloved placed on his head at the heavenly conclave. The Bride's crown parallels that "pondrous proffer'd crown" at which all the angels shuddered, but which her Beloved took up graciously as his own:

> And the whole hierarchy with heads hung down
> Submissively declin'd the pondrous proffer'd crown.
> Then, not till then, th'eternal Son from high
> Rose in the strength of all the Deity;
> Stood forth t'accept the terms, and underwent
> A weight which all the frame of heav'n had bent,
> Nor he Himself cou'd bear, but as omnipotent.
>   (2:508–14)

Just as the angels at the great parliament despaired of saving humanity because of their weakness, so the false Brides now despair of guiding humanity unerringly. And just as the angels "Submissively declin'd" the crown of Calvary, so these Churches "shrink" at and "shun" the crown in spiritual matters. The Hind is the valiant Spouse, the *Mulier fortis* of Proverbs 31:10, who receives the great burden gladly; she takes up as hers alone the promises of unfailing assistance from her Beloved. Dryden's image of the immortal Bride and Bridegroom as bearing a colossal weight above their heads for the sake of humanity identifies them as the foundation stonework of the City of God, the New Jerusalem. The poet alludes here to Ephesians 2:20, where St. Paul calls the Apostles and Prophets the foundation of the Church and Christ himself her cornerstone. He may also glance at Eusebius, who describes the crown of the Bridegroom in Canticles 3:11 thus: "behold the crown of living stones which is the Church itself, set on the head of Christ by love" (RFL, 142).

In another image of her "spiritual royalty," the poet compares the Church to Jove stopping the earthborn Giants' rebellion. The Universal Bride resolves religious controversies from age to age by convening councils and casting down from the Church-sky the thunderbolts of her decisions: "with paternal thunder vindicates her crown" (2:538). The word "paternal" implies that she uses apostolic traditions recorded by the Church fathers to strike down errors. Thus the Hind defends her sacred mysteries without descending to fight a ruinous "civil war" on level ground with the rebels below. These rebels would be only too glad to marshal ranks of biblical texts and engage in interminable civil war with ranks of other texts presented by the Church. Dryden sees the Hind's "sceptre" not just as a rod of punishment but also as one of healing, for Moses could end as well as summon plagues with his rod, and the Apostles were "Physicians" who cured the plagues of religious error from a distance with authoritative words (2:336, 367, 542).

In contrast to the Hind's heavy crown, the Panther's authority in religious controversies is lightweight: her "wild belief" is tossed on waves and turned by changing winds like a "weathercock" (1:430, 465). The Panther's "magick wand" resembles the rods of the Egyptian sorcerers, who could raise but not stop a plague, and who finally capitulated to Moses when they saw the "dishonest sore" on their own faces (2:538–47). In other words, the Panther cannot heal the "spotted kind" in Britain because she herself is afflicted with their spots. As "mock Queen" and "crown-gen'ral of the land," she is in the position of the usurper Cromwell, enforcing outward conformity (1:498, 2:410) by coercive laws but not exercising the kind of fragrant, melodious innate authority embodied in Pan and Orpheus.

CHAPTER 7

The Hind in Three Ascents
from Persecution to Peace

Besides borrowing the attributes of shepherdess and queen from Canticles, Dryden also borrows the idea that the Bride rises in three rapid
steps from persecution to peace. The first ascent is the one from the
wilderness, in Canticles 3:6, where the Daughters of Jerusalem exclaim
in amazement "What is she, that ascendeth by the desert, as a little rod of
smoke . . . ?" Some commentators saw in this verse the Christian Church
arriving after ten Roman persecutions to a peaceful haven under Constantine. The column of smoke denoted the martyrs on the altar of sacrifice (RFL, 124).

At the end of part I of *The Hind and the Panther,* the royal Lion roars
to signal an end to the persecution of the Hind. The Lion represents
James II, whom Dryden compares in *Britannia Rediviva* (1688) to Aris-
tides and Constantine, two paradigms of justice in literary tradition. The
Lion commands the Hind to come forth unafraid and bring her
"younglings" to the public watering place for the first time in more than a
century. The wild sects are stunned at the sight of the Hind and stand
"mutely still," staring and wondering why she does not have ten horns on
her head like the Beast in Revelation, as the Panther and Wolf told them
she had (1:534–35). Their wonder increases as they look more closely:

>   . . . but nearer when they drew,
> And had the faultless object full in view,
> Lord, how they all admir'd her heav'nly hiew!
>   (1:541–43)

Soon the Independents lose all fear and begin to frisk about the Hind. At this point, the Puritan or Presbyterian Wolf falls mute because the Hind has caught his eye: he "cou'd not howl, the *Hind* had seen him first" (1:552). In medieval bestiaries derived from *Physiologus*, the Wolf was unable to howl if he was caught first by a man's gaze.[1] Since the Hind's legendary attribute is sight, she perceives the Wolf first and silences him with her manly, valorous eye. The point is that she will neither flatter nor hunt the Presbyterian Wolf, but only awe him with intrinsic spiritual authority.

At the Bride's second ascent in Canticles 6:9, someone exclaims: "What is she, that cometh forth as the morning rysing, fayre as the moone, elect as the sunne . . . ?" Some ancient expositors put these words in the "mouth of the repentant Synagogue," to whom the Panther is paralleled in Dryden's poem (RFL, 285). Having emerged from utter darkness, the Bride of Canticles quickly increases in brightness, first as the dawn, then as the moon, and finally as the sun. In accordance with this pattern, Dryden's Hind makes a second ascent in part 2, rising from a predawn glimmering to a noonday brilliance. She is *ecclesia docens* teaching *ecclesia discens*, or the Panther asking to be taught. For indeed the Panther asks a series of probing questions in part 2.

In ancient times the plot of Canticles was believed to begin with the Bride's search for the Bridegroom, culminating in her discovery of him in 3:5. Dryden may have wrought this motif into the design of part 2, for the Panther seeks the Bridegroom by asking the Hind several times where the infallible living guide, the new "mighty *Moyses* of the chosen crew," is to be found. The Hind finally responds with Christ's own words in Gethsemane when the mob came to arrest him before dawn, except that now the pronoun is "she": "she whom ye seek am I." At these words, the Panther is struck down just as the mob was in John 18:6. She is "no less amazed" than they were. Therefore, the poet implies that she is thrown back to the earth, as when Christ "own'd his Deity" in the phrase "I am he," which is

1. Albert the Great, *Man and the Beasts*, 156. Also see T. H. White, *The Bestiary: A Book of Beasts, Being a Translation from a Latin Bestiary of the Twelfth Century* (New York.: G.P. Putnam, 1960), 58.

literally the meaning of *Yahweh* (2:396–400). The word "amazed" links this predawn theophany to the earlier one at the watering place. The Panther is now overcome with awe, just as the sects became "mutely still" (1:535) when they sensed a divine presence in the Hind's extraordinary rise from persecution to glory.

The light then increases as the Hind describes the four marks of the universal Church in the Nicene Creed (one, holy, catholic, and apostolic) as the "rays" with which her Bridegroom adorns her head on her wedding day: "Behold what heav'nly rays adorn her brows" (2:518). She uses the image of a single light to depict her unity with the Bridegroom: her faith is "one solid shining Diamond, / Not sparkles shatter'd into sects like you" (2:527–28). But most of all, she speaks of her faith as the "sun" which has been, in the past, only partially and briefly eclipsed. The ancient heretics darkened her light by the same "errours which new sects maintain":

> And we can point each period of the time,
> When they began, and who begot the crime;
> Can calculate how long th' eclipse endur'd,
> Who interpos'd, what digits were obscur'd:
> > (2:606–11)

She implies that modern errors, like ancient ones, are doomed to a brief ascendancy and can only darken a few "digits" of her light.

At the end of the second ascent, there is a great burst of light as the Hind expresses her love for the English people. Suddenly it is brilliant day as she renounces all claims to church lands and declares she wants only to "feed" them. The light of her love banishes the dead spirits still haunting Britain:

> A streaming blaze the silent shadows broke:
> Shot from the skyes a chearfull azure light;
> The birds obscene to forests wing'd their flight,
> And gaping graves receiv'd the wandring guilty spright. . . .
> > (2:650–53)

This is a kind of exorcism. Dryden's phrase "silent shadows broke" in the above lines echoes the "fleeing shadows" of Canticles 4:6, which in the allegorical reading were the shadows of the Law being expelled by the light of the Resurrection (RFL, 159). It is this noonday love that mortifies the

Panther and causes her to be drenched with the dewdrops of the night, like the Bridegroom of Canticles, so that she quietly accepts the Hind's hospitality and enters her "shed."

In Canticles 8:5 the Bride's third ascent reveals her as one perfected in love and closely united with her Beloved: "Who is this, that cometh up from the desert, flowing with delights, leaning upon her beloved?" This is the third and last exclamation of wonder at the progress of the Bride in Canticles. Likewise, Dryden shows the Panther as "amazed" once again as she observes how the Hind relies on her Beloved day by day, and how she cherishes the counsels of perfection, such as the monastic vow of poverty. When the Panther enters the Hind's shed, she is "amaz'd to see / Contempt of wealth, and wilfull poverty" (2:714–15). It is at this point that the Hind tells her about the shepherd Pan who comes to lay his "limbs" and often be "receiv'd." Thus Dryden uses the word "amazed" for each of the three showings of the Hind (1:534; 2:399, 714) and echoes the triple cry of "Who is this?" in Canticles. The poet shows that the shaping hand of Providence is not confined to the external world but can also touch human hearts. For example, at the end of *Absalom and Achitophel* (1681), God imparts majesty to the weak king's voice so that his subjects can be moved with awe and recognize "their Maker in their Master" (936–38). Similarly, in the triple "amazement," Dryden implies an act of Providence moving the hearts of the English to receive the Hind.

Each part of Canticles was thought to end in the mystical repose of the Bride: she rested bodily while her heart stayed alert for love of her Bridegroom. It is no surprise, then, if the two halves of Dryden's poem both end with the Hind's going into a state of bodily repose, first by lying trustingly at the side of the Panther (2:722) and second by retreating into her inner room, the sanctuary of the Real Presence (3:1295–96). The reader glimpses the eschatological destiny of the Hind in the last lines of the poem, where she enters her mystical repose:

The Dame withdrew, and, wishing to her Guest
The peace of Heav'n, betook her self to rest.
Ten thousand Angels on her slumbers waite
With glorious Visions of her future state.

(3:1295–98)

In the eighth-century hymn "Urbs Ierusalem beata," the Church is described in just this way, as surrounded by angels like a bride with her maids: "et angelis coronata, / ut sponsata comite."[2] Cardinal Hugo of St. Cher thought the repose of the Bride in Canticles 8:4 was a foretaste of the Church's future blessedness (RFL, 348).

Thus, in the dramatic plot of Dryden's poem, the Panther has witnessed the Hind's three ascents and has seen her reflecting the light of her Bridegroom. Dryden adds that he, too, saw a light in the sky in 1685, and he read it to mean that James II's victory over the Duke of Monmouth was a special Providence, a divine intervention to show that the Catholic king's rule was part of a larger plan for England (2:654–62). A year later, in *Britannia Rediviva,* the poet mourns that the English are like the Jews in Exodus, not trusting that Providence will sustain them, but wanting to go back to the slavish security of Egypt under coercive laws in religion: "The Manna falls, yet that Coelestial Bread / Like *Jews* you munch, and murmure while you feed" (65–66). He warns his countrymen that if they rebel against James II, they will have to "wander in the Wild," as they did in 1641–1681, for another forty years.

2. *Latin Hymns Sung at the Church of Saint Hugh Letchworth,* arranged and translated by Adrian Fortescue (Harrison, N.Y.: Roman Catholic Books, n.d.), 122. This volume is a reprint of a 1913 edition.

CHAPTER 8

The Hind as Fruitful Plant
and Unspotted Spouse

In the allegory of Canticles, the Bride is the enclosed orchard where the Bridegroom goes to enjoy his "fruit" (5:1, 7:13). She is the pomegranate tree whose fruit he eats and drinks. Similarly, in Isaiah 5:1–2, Israel is the "choicest vine" of Yahweh's vineyard, but when he goes to taste the fruit he is disappointed to find that it tastes wild and sour. When Dryden characterizes the Hind as a "deathless plant" that bears "dying fruit" (1:24), he glances at this rich biblical imagery about a divine husbandman coming to taste the fruit of the plant he has cultivated and watched over.

The image of a "deathless plant" with "dying fruit" and "sanguin seed" evokes at once the pomegranate tree in Canticles 4:13 and the Tree of Life, which was identified by expositors with the Sacrament of the Altar. The phrase "dying fruit" denotes the Sacrifice of the Mass, where Christ's death on Calvary is offered up in union with the sufferings of his saints and martyrs. Dryden has the Panther herself speak of the Catholic priests executed in the Titus Oates Plot as victims offered up on the altar of sacrifice, saying that "all" the Hind's "priestly calves" were laid as "sacrifices on their Altars" (2:8–9). This glances at the summer of 1679, when eight priests whose only crime was their priestly vocation were executed under the 1585 statute.[1] Dryden's rhetoric in the opening lines of the first two parts of *The Hind and the Panther* begs to be applied to the Mass, where Christ, joined in one mystical body with his martyrs, is both priest and victim, vine and dying fruit.

In the phrase "deathless plant" with "dying fruit," Dryden also glances at the words of Christ: "I am the Vine, you are the branches. He that abideth in me, and I in him, the same beareth much fruite" (Jn 15:5). In this Vine, God's husbandry no longer occurs from outside the mystical plant, as in Isaiah, but from within it. The special Providence of God has become one with his Real Presence; the Vine-dresser is one with the Vine. Dryden hints at this hidden Presence within the "deathless plant" which generates fruit or offspring resembling Christ. For he shows the martyrs' "vocal blood" in 1678–1681 praying for pardon on their "perjur'd foes" (1:15–16), just as Christ's sacrificial blood prays "Father, forgive them" from the altar.

The Hind rejoices as well as mourns over her English martyrs. She rejoices because she knows their blood is "sanguin seed" that increases her "sacred breed" (1:17–18). Dryden alludes here to the ancient Christian proverb "Semen ecclesiae sanguis est martyrum," the blood of martyrs is the seed of the church. He parallels the multiplication of the Church during persecution to the growth of "Captive *Israel*" under Pharaoh's oppression. The poet expects the reader to recall that Yahweh promised Jacob he would be present with Israel in Egypt, would cause the Israelites' numbers to increase greatly, and would eventually secure their freedom (Gn 46:2–4). Israel increased in number under Pharaoh's persecution because Yahweh the husbandman was there, multiplying the "sanguin seed" from "dying fruit." The phrase "sanguin seed" also evokes the pomegranate in Canticles 4:13. Rabbi Ibn Ezra saw the pomegranate of Canticles as alluding to temple sacrifices. Similarly, Christian expositors like St. Athanasius and Philo of Carpasia saw this fruit full of seeds as the symbol of martyrs, because these produced a great many spiritual children (RFL, 292, 184).

Although the Bride of Canticles is not called "mother," yet since she is "my spouse" who produces "fruit" that resembles the "beloved" on the "deathless plant" which is herself, she is in a sense a mother. The Douay

---

1. John Kenyon called the summer of 1679 the "great holocaust of the Plot" in *The Popish Plot* (London: Heinemann, 1972), 178–82, 272.

version has a note next to the place where the "Beloved" comes into his garden to enjoy his "fruit" (5:1), stating that "the spouse condescending to God's will, is well content to suffer persecution." This is how Dryden uses the word "fruit," too, alluding to those who were martyred during the Oates Plot and who brought about conversions such as his: their souls became "immortal" while their "bloud" turned into the "seed" of converts. Indeed, there is a link between the English martyrs of the Oates Plot and Dryden: Dom James Corker, who received Dryden into the Catholic Church, was chaplain of two martyrs executed for their faith in 1680 and 1681, Thomas Howard Lord Stafford and St. Oliver Plunket. Corker published Lord Stafford's *Memoirs,* a detailed account of this peer's death, while Dryden paid a moving tribute to this sainted kinsman of his in the marriage song for Anastasia Stafford.

The image of the Church as mother pervades Dryden's poem. Indeed, the Hind is surely "milk white" rather than "snow white" because she offers nourishment to the English in their "famine," the word "milk" connecting her food to the divine "milk" that flowed from the Creator's breast in Dryden's exquisite account of Adam's birth:

But, when arriv'd at last to humane race,
The god-head took a deep consid'ring space:
And to distinguish man from all the rest,
Unlock'd the sacred treasures of his breast.

(1:256–59)

A few lines later, the meaning of "breast" is made clearer by a reference to divine "milk": "Thus kneaded up with milk, the new made man / His kingdom o'er his kindred world began" (1:274–75). In Canticles 4:10, but only in the Catholic translations, the Bride praises the "breasts" of the Bridegroom. In the allegorical readings, this word "breasts" is interpreted to mean the "milk" of doctrine, a better nourishment than the "wine" of the Law (RFL, 173). Dryden would have known, of course, that the panther was associated with wine in mythology, for this motif is found in the popular *Topsell's Beasts.*[2]

The poet himself, when he refers to the speakers in the dialogue, repeatedly designates the Hind as the "Matron," that is, the mother (2:147, 401;

---

2. Edward Topsell, *Topsell's Histories of Beasts,* ed. Malcolm South (Chicago: Nelson-Hall, 1981), 154.

3:68, 277, 420, 892), but he never names the Panther "Matron." Nor does he call the Panther simply "Dame," but "stranger Dame" and "Salvage Dame" (2:671, 3:422), always insisting that she who regards the Hind as a foreigner is herself an exile. Dryden calls the Hind "mother" four times (1:21, 505; 2:10, 497), and calls the Panther "mother" once, but only to show her as an "indulgent" rather than a "true" mother: "No mother more indulgent but the true" (1:451). He also has the Hind tell the Panther that there are "cheats" among her clergy who falsely call her "mother" (3:153).

The Panther herself acknowledges the Hind to be a tender mother, but makes fun of her for being helpless when her young are martyred (2:8–14, 3:615–17). The Hind, on the other side, warns the Panther that she is surrounded by "pretended" sons who "call" her "mother" but who wish her "dead." They inquire into her "years" in their eagerness to inherit her "grandame gold," that is, to squander her precious reserves of the ancestral English faith (3:144–59). That the Panther appears as a "grandame" in a "muff" hints that she is growing aged and cold, and that she is a branch too long severed from the "deathless plant" and from the Divine Husband exercising his providential husbandry from within.

In Canticles, the Bride is motherly in the nurturing sense of being a "fountaine of gardens" and a "wel of living waters." She is water falling from a mountain and becoming a reliable stream for many gardens (4:12–15). This passage was often linked with Ecclesiasticus 24:30, "my brook became a river, and my river became a sea," and with Ezekiel 47:1–12, where waters issuing from the Temple grow into a "mighty torrent" bordered with fruitful trees. In his poem, likewise, Dryden gives the Hind the strikingly biblical attribute of starting as one source and growing into a great flow of water encompassing the earth: she begins as "A limpid stream drawn from the native source" and grows until her "tides" are "unconfin'dly spread" to water every shore (2:551, 614–17). After his conversion, Dryden would surely have sung the medieval hymn "Jerusalem et Sion filiae" that celebrates the Church as just such a stream from the one source of Christ's wounded side:

> Hanc sanguinis et aquae munere,
> dum penderet in crucis arbore
> de proprio produxit latere Deus homo.[3]

3. *Latin Hymns*, 126.

St. Augustine liked to repeat this point, that the Church, like Eve, was born from the pierced side of her Spouse, in the water and blood streaming into her sacraments. Sts. Gregory the Great and Bede made similar comments on the Bride of Canticles, as pouring down "waters of Baptismal grace and Apostolic teaching" upon the earth (RFL, 191–92).

Besides all the bridal, pastoral, agricultural, royal, fructifying, and maternal imagery he draws from Canticles and its commentaries, Dryden also finds there the idea that the Church is the twice-unspotted Spouse: "Thou art al fayre o my love, and there is not a spot in thee" (Sg 4:7). The phrases "al fayre" and "not a spot" are a repetition of the same praise. Likewise, the poet begins *The Hind and the Panther* with doublets indicating that the Hind is "unspotted":

A milk white *Hind*, immortal and unchang'd,
Fed on the lawns, and in the forest rang'd;
Without unspotted, innocent within,
She fear'd no danger, for she knew no sin.

(1:1–4)

He says twice that she is outwardly pure—"milk white" and "unspotted"—and twice that she is inwardly pure—"innocent" and "sinless." Besides Canticles, another biblical text produces such doublets about the Church as the unspotted Bride: in Ephesians 5:27, St. Paul reiterates that Christ has a "glorious church, not having spot," a Bride "holy and unspotted."

Perhaps the Hind is doubly unspotted because she is the Church's eternal glory made present, a kind of realized eschatology. She is the Church Triumphant glimpsed at the heart of the Church Militant. Indeed, later in the poem Dryden plainly links the Hind's lack of spots to the eternal wedding feast: "Behold . . . What from his Wardrobe her belov'd allows / To deck the wedding-day of his unspotted spouse" (2:517–19). This is the consummation of the marriage of the Lamb in St. John's revelation, when the Bride is clothed in unspotted white for the works of her saints (Rev 19:7). But, on another level, Dryden's Hind is unspotted because she is the Church Militant washed continually in the Bridegroom's blood. The entire dialogue in the second part of the poem can surely be construed as the Hind's defense of her perennial unspottedness, that is, her intimate union with the Bridegroom for over sixteen hundred years. This view of the Bride as doubly unspotted, within and without, follows a line of allegorical commentary on Canticles 4:7. St.

Justus of Urgel says that "even the Church Militant is *all fair* in her Bridegroom's sight, fair in all the ranks and orders of her Saints, great and small; not only in her Martyrs, Confessors, and Virgins, but in her temperate, almsgiving, and penitent members." Moreover, St. Bernard of Clairvaux sees the Church as "fair within and fair without, in the beauty of the sacraments, the manifold ranks of the hierarchy, in supernatural gifts of grace." Denys le Chartreux likewise finds the Bride doubly fair, in "claritas" and "caritas," in her contemplation and in her zeal to serve God and neighbor. And finally, the seventeenth-century Jesuit Lapide repeats this point, that she is unspotted also as Church Militant because "daily penitence keeps her free of mortal sins and removes the stains of venial guilt" (RFL, 163, 143).

The poet laments that his Protestant countrymen hold a far different opinion of the Catholic Church. They claim that all their "erring ancestours" were "Drown'd in th' Abyss of deep Idolatry" for over seven centuries (2:633). This passage echoes the sermon on idolatry recommended in Article 35 of the Church of England. The Rheims New Testament of 1582 makes this comment on Ephesians 5:29: Protestants claim that Christ "divorced" his Church and that for her idolatry she became "a very whoore."[4] Indeed, it was a short step, once they denied the Real Presence in the Sacrament of the Altar, for Protestants to call those who adored Christ in the sacrament "idolaters." It was another short step to say that Christ had divorced his Church for this idolatry of bread and wine in the fourth century, the epoch when the Church first emerged from concealed worship. As the *Encyclopedia of Religion and Ethics* notes, eucharistic worship "in the course of the fourth century," attained "in most localities that form which is known as 'Catholic.'"[5] The Hind mourns that "Disdain of Fathers" first began the "daunce" (3:407), alluding to the view held by many English Protestants that Church fathers of the fourth century had been asleep, like the Bride in Canticles 3, when Catholic worship came in. In reply to the Panther's charge that there are "dreadfull gaps" between the Apostles and the traditions found in the fourth century, Dryden has the Hind defend these traditions as a heavenly "*Jacob's* ladder"

4. "Annotations to Chapter V," in *The New Testament of Jesus Christ, Translated Faithfully into English* (Rhemes: John Fogny, 1582), 522–23.
5. J. Vernon Bartlet, "Worship (Christian), Particularly Eucharistic, in the Ancient Church," in *Encyclopedia of Religion and Ethics*, 13 vols., ed. James Hastings (Edinburgh: Clark, 1921), 12:765–67.

between Christ and the Church fathers. In part 2 the Hind glances at a favorite argument Catholics used in the seventeenth century to defend the Church of the fourth century: they challenged the Protestants to find a single lawful general council or any approved Church father in the first five centuries who agreed with them that the Church had fallen into idolatry in the fourth century.[6] This is what the Hind refers to when she speaks of "ancient ages" being "accused":

> You must evince tradition to be forg'd;
> Produce plain proofs; unblemish'd authours use
> As ancient as those ages they accuse;
> Till when 'tis not sufficient to defame:
> An old possession stands, till Elder quitts the claim. . . .
>   (2:233–37)

The Hind contends that if the Panther cannot find corroboration in antiquity that fourth-century worship was corrupted, then her accusation has no merit, for what she calls idolatry in the adoration of the sacrament is authentic worship handed down to those Church fathers from the Apostles.

After defending her ancient traditions, the Hind reminds "Madam *Panther*" tartly that her "Adulterer" the Wolf has quite dismissed all the ancient traditions as "toys" (2:232–51). Her word "adulterer" hints that the infidelity is all on the accusing Panther's side, and the word "toys" hints that for the Wolf there is not even a step remaining between the Apostles' teachings and the written testimony of the fourth-century Fathers. Indeed, the Puritan Wolf sees nothing trustworthy handed down to the fourth century except the bare biblical text, without glosses. He conceives of original Christianity as something that can be re-imagined by solitary individuals reading the New Testament at sixteen hundred years' distance, armed only with the "private spirit."

Besides seeing her traditions as steps that remained unbroken through the centuries, by God's Providence, the Hind also sees them as defensive weapons and bulwarks. She compares them to the sword of Goliath (2:600), with which David defended himself from the persecution of

6. Basile [Dubois] de Soissons, *Défence invincible de la vérité orthodoxe de la Présence Réelle de Jésus-Christ en l'Eucharistie* (Paris: Pierre Compain, 1680), 6. In this book Father Basile collects the sermons he gave in the Queen-Mother's Chapel in London, while serving in the late 1660s as Queen Henrietta's chaplain.

King Saul (1 Sm 21:9), and to a great wall that prevents the "entrance" of error and behind which, "safe entrench'd," she defies the encircling foe (2:366). In Canticles 4:4 the neck of the Bride is compared to "the towre of David, which is built with bulworkes," on which hang the arms of valiant warriors. Ancient commentators wrote that this tower denoted the Apostles and the Doctors of the Church combating heresy (RFL, 152–53). In the hymn "Aeterna Christi munera," attributed to St. Ambrose, the Apostles are called the victorious leaders and warriors of heaven, "belli triumphales duces, / caelestis aulae milites." Dryden's adaptation of this hymn emphasizes how their "Triumphs" involved not military conquests, but rather "torments, racks, and gore." For theirs was a defensive war and a victory like that of the Cross: "They rul'd the Church, & held the shield / To conquer in a suff'ring Field."[7] This is the point the poet makes in *The Hind*, too, that the Church is ever engaged in a defensive war to maintain the legacy of her ancient faith, even at the cost of martyrdom.

Boldest of all, the Hind speaks of her traditions as an awe-inspiring army on the march. This image is from Canticles 6:2, where the Bridegroom declares that the Bride's beauty is as "terrible as the armie of a campe set in aray." The phrase "set in array" refers to an army marching under flying banners. Cardinal Hugo's comment on this verse is that the Bride awes the heretics, thanks to her learned clergy—by the "number and valour of her warriors, their long training in arms, their loyalty, zeal, and unanimity in battle: and because Christ is in the foremost line with the Apostles, followed by martyrs and confessors" (RFL, 273). Dryden, however, develops this image by depicting the Hind's traditions, rather than her personnel, as warriors on the march.

It seems that the Panther has hired some of the Hind's traditions like foreign mercenaries to subdue "domestick foes of *Hierarchy*." She has engaged them to defend the authority of English bishops but will not let them defend the antiquity of the Catholic belief in Purgatory: "For *purging* fires traditions must not fight; / But they must prove Episcopacy's right" (2:286–87). But now that the Hind suddenly enjoys freedom of the press after more than a century, the Panther finds herself deserted by her

7. *Hymns Attributed to John Dryden*, ed. George Rapall Noyes and George Reuben Potter (Berkeley and Los Angeles: University of California Press, 1937), 174. *Latin Hymns*, 114.

hired traditions. For seeing "their countrey-men at hand, / marching against 'em under church-command," these traditions disband and take their rightful place in the Catholic army of patristic lore (2:286–89). Considering what a panic Titus Oates had caused a decade earlier by pretending that a foreign Catholic army was poised to invade England, the poet takes a risk in having the Hind speak of her "traditions" as an army that leaves the Panther defenseless. But the "soldiers" marching in from Europe here are the writings of the Church fathers supporting the Catholic Church's teaching on the Real Presence.

Near the end of Canticles the Bridegroom speaks of "a vineyard" that he delivered to "keepers" but still watches over: "My vineyard is before me" (8:11–12). A note in the 1615 Douay version states that this is Christ's promise to give continuous assistance to the guides of his Church: having once established the Apostles and their successors as "keepers" of his Bride, "Christ sheweth that together with the pastors, himself especialy hath care of his Church, always assisting the visible governers therof with his invisible grace." Dryden professes his belief in that special Providence for the chief pastors or guides: "all the promises are to the guides" (2:103). For him, too, as for St. Augustine in Epistle 165, one splendid sign that the promises of Christ have been fulfilled is that there has been an uninterrupted succession of Church-guides ever since the Apostles: from the time "faith was planted first, / Succeeding flocks succeeding Pastours nurs'd" (2:309–10).

The poet prays for grace to take that Church "alone for my Directour" whom "thou hast promis'd never to forsake" (1:71). Since he believes the Bridegroom and the Bride are one mystical body, the poet desires to enter the Bride as one enters a "vessel." He finds blessed assurance by being incorporated within the Bride of Christ, who is herself sustained by the Bridegroom in the hidden sanctuary of the marriage bed, the Cross.

It is surely no coincidence, then, that so many of the attributes of the Bride of Canticles—as delineated in the allegorical commentaries—can also be found in Dryden's Hind: she is a shepherdess, a queen, a doubly unspotted spouse, a spring gushing from Christ's side and growing into a reliable stream to water all gardens, an enclosed garden, a deathless plant, a tower of defense, and an army in array. In addition to these marks, she leaves onlookers "amazed" by her three ascents from persecution to peace and opens her door to one whose hair is covered with the dewdrops of the night. There might be still another echo of the Lady of Canticles in Dryden's Hind. Cardinal Hugo thought there were four "chambers" into which the Bridegroom wooed the Bride in Canticles: the historical, with coarse food; the tropological, with oil, wine, balms, and spices; the allegorical, with the arms of the warriors; and the anagogical, with the pure gold and precious stones of eternal life (RFL, 19). Speaking for her Bridegroom, the Hind woos the Panther in all four of these chambers, though not in the same order: she offers her a "course dyet" of literal poverty (2:672); she offers "Anodynes" to soothe her troubled soul (3:82); she shows the Panther the proper arms of the Church Militant for spiritual combat (2:364–66, 533–37); and she reveals her unity with Christ by being "one solid shining Diamond" of a faith (2:527).

CHAPTER 9

Spirit and Fire: The Zeal of the Wolf

If the true Church is a bride and mother, it follows that the Wolf, that aggressively masculine church in *The Hind and the Panther*, is wrong-gendered. The Wolf cannot make the spousal surrender to the Beloved, cannot patiently submit to the hand of Providence. Dryden condemns the Puritan Wolf's idea that armed rebellion against constituted authority, if successful, can be justified by Providence. In *The Medall* (1682) he observes wryly that when Puritans win by violence or fraud, they claim that God was on their side: "Successful Crimes alone are justify'd" (208). On the contrary, the poet argues, the sign of God's blessing is that some people succeed by long-suffering patience, as in the case of the early Christians: they never rebelled against the Roman state during ten great persecutions, yet their religion became the established one by the fourth century (*Religio Laici*, 156–67).

The poet agrees that the Puritans were instruments of Divine Providence in the civil wars, but not as they imagine. In *Annus Mirabilis* (1667) he depicts the Plague and the Great Fire of London as temporal judgments sent by Providence in requital for English disobedience (849–57, 1065–66). In his view, the Wolf's rebellion in the 1640s was another such temporal judgment, a permitted evil within a larger providential plan for England. The Puritans were unwitting ministers of divine wrath, like the ancient Assyrians invading an Israel fallen into disobedience. The Wolf produced no "fruit" in the Interregnum, but simply ravaged the grain, pasture, and soil of England with a fire "quickn'd" from below. The land was ruined for the cultivation of the arts: "As where the lightning runs along the ground, / No husbandry can heal the blasting wound" (1:223–24). Dryden calls this fire "zeal," the zeal that leaves desolation and famine in place of plentiful harvests: "Such warrs, such waste, such fiery tracks of dearth / Their zeal has left, and such a teemless earth" (1:227–28).

In Canticles 8:6 we read of a jealousy or zeal in religion that is "hard as hell." In the English Protestant Bible versions, from as far back as Myles Coverdale's 1535 translation, this zeal was said to burn like "coals of fire" and a "vehement flame" or "flame of the Lord." Dryden's image of Puritan zeal in the Interregnum as a strange fire that devours seems to be derived from the Protestant translation and interpretation of this particular verse in Canticles, especially as Puritans enlarged on it by association with other passages from Scripture. Also, when he compares Puritan zeal to lightning running along the ground and to fairy dances, Dryden seems to be taking a clue from commentaries on the Septuagint version of this verse, where the zeal burns like "wingings round" (RFL, 361). Seventeenth-century Puritans gladly applied Canticles 8:6 to their zeal, but they said the fire came from above, not below. Thomas Wilcox, who died in 1608, said the "coales of fire" in Canticles 8:6 represented a godly zeal that would "consume and purge" the "cursed corruptions" in religion. Alluding to 1 Corinthians 3:12, he called this zeal a "*flame from the Lord*" that would lick up merely human works like "straw or stubble before it."[1] Likewise, in his notes on chapter 8 of Canticles, Ainsworth said that the "fiery coales" of this verse were a zeal that "flieth and burneth" like a "devouring lightning" and a "consuming flame." He linked this zeal to Hebrews 12:29, where God himself is such a "consuming fire." It is worth noting that Ainsworth uses the exact combination of images Dryden employs later to describe the zeal of the Wolf in the 1640s: flying, flashing, burning, consuming.

Dryden insists that Puritan zeal is a fire "from below," as in Daniel 7:10, a permitted evil. In antiquity some commentators regarded the flaming

---

1. Wilcox, *The Works*, 79. Thomas Brightman and the Puritan Francis Quarles also interpret the zeal in Canticles 8:6 as a purifying, testing, devouring fire from God, not from hell. The Puritan interpretation seems close to Origen, as cited in *Origen, Spirit and Fire*, 325–29.

jealousy of Canticles 8:6 as hostility toward the true Church, either the hostility of unbelievers toward the Jewish faith, or the hostility of the Jewish Church toward early Christianity (RFL, 362). In *The Hind*, we find these two forms of zeal combined against the Hind in Britain: the jealous Church of the Law inflames the "*Goths* and *Vandals* to demolish *Rome*" (3:1214).

The sly partner of the Wolf's rampage against the Anglican establishment in the 1640s was the opportunistic Fox. When Dryden first mentions the Fox in *The Hind and the Panther,* he alludes to Canticles 2:15, a verse about the Bridegroom's vineyard having to be protected from "little foxes," lest they spoil the flowering vines. In allegorical commentaries, these foxes stood for false teachers who re-interpreted the divine mysteries according to natural reason. Not only Catholics, but also Puritans like Thomas Wilcox said that the foxes in Canticles were heretics who were hinderers of the "church's growth."[2] The keepers of the vineyard were supposed to be vigilant and prevent these foxes from getting in, or else catch and eject them if they were already inside.

Using the terms "spoil" and "*Reynard*" to glance at Canticles 2:15, Dryden writes "False *Reynard* fed on consecrated spoil" (1:53). The "graceless" Fox has already entered England's garden to feed on sacred mysteries. The poet mourns that the Fox, that is, the Socinian clergyman, peers at Christ with carnal eyes, "And natures King through natures opticks view'd" (1:57), not discerning the eternal Word in the Child of Bethlehem: "Nor in an Infant could a God descry" (1:58–59). In *Physiologus* the Fox simulates death to deceive foolish birds, and according to Origen, Cardinal Hugo, Denys le Chartreux, and others, this means that he is a hypocrite who makes "a special show of sanctity and deadness to the world, in order to deceive the unwary" (RFL, 101). During the Interregnum, "graceless" Reynard traveled with the Wolf, the "beast of Grace," that is, he shared his zeal against idolatry in order to make natural reason the measure of all religious truth. Dryden thinks that "all" the "swarming" sects will arrive at this Fox-like rationalism: "here they all will end" (1:61).

Early in his poem Dryden contrasts the Fox to the Boar, alluding to Psalm 79:14 (80:13), where the Boar uproots the vineyard as another beast quietly feeds there: "The boare of the wood hath destroyed it: and

2. Wilcox, *The Works,* 18.

the singular wilde beast hath eaten it." Glancing at the takeover of Munster in the sixteenth century, Dryden depicts the Anabaptist Boar as desecrating the sanctuary with "fat pollutions" to purge it of alleged idolatry. The Boar imagines himself as John the Baptist "leveling mountains" (Lk 3:5) for the coming of Christ: "And mountains levell'd in his furious race" (1:46). Unlike the Boar, the Fox avoids overt sacrilege, using "greater guile" to undermine the mysteries from within. He is the "singular wilde beast" sly enough to feed securely while he secretly destroys.

Dryden depicts Puritan zeal as producing famine. The fiery Wolf and the hypocritical Fox in the 1640s together "freed" the English Church from its Laudian guides: they entered England's cultivated bower and burned the "bearded corn" and "bladed grass," symbols of the Eucharist (1:225–28). In this way, they left the English Sheep deprived of pastor and pasture. In one account Dryden gives of the Wolf's conception, Zwingli and Calvin were both present when the hungry Wolf was conceived, when a doglike creature "lin'd" his "consort" in a "nuptial bed" near Lake Leman. Thus the two Swiss Protestants who denounced the Catholic Mass as idolatry were both present. The poet says that "fi'ry *Zuynglius*"—"fi'ry" probably because he was filled with such zeal against the Real Presence—bred the affection, and that "meagre *Calvin*"—"meagre" in all likelihood because he had reduced the Real Presence to a moment in the worthy receiver's soul at communion—blessed the bed where the Wolf was made (1:180–81). The Wolf was born "famish'd" and came to Britain inflamed with zeal against the eucharistic food of the Sheep. There seems to be a hint here of Aesop's dog in the manger, who envies that others should enjoy the food he cannot eat. He fell in with the rationalist Fox, and together they destroyed the pasture, the grain, and even the soil itself. The poet compares their zeal in the 1640s to "Poisons of the deadliest kind" and "magick plants" which are luckily confined, however, to a Puritan commonwealth (1:229–33). Later in the 1690s, Dryden again shows famine to be the result of zeal-inspired revolution. In *Eleonora* (1692), *Cleomenes* (1692), and *Love Triumphant* (1693), hunger is his major theme. On the other side, he associates a "double Harvest" of food and arts with a government and church shaped from afar by Divine Providence (*Threnodia*, 356–61).

Besides losing the communicating food, the Wolf, the Fox, and the other sects lost the communicating word. Having chosen a jarring individualism in religion, they began to bark, snarl, and howl at one another; they were unable to make intelligible sounds. They had a voice but no speech. Indeed, their sounds were twice as "confused" as those heard in the Tower of "*Babel*" (2:470). Along with the rest of the famished "herd" attending the Panther in 1687, the Wolf and Fox are "mutes," yet they make noisy sounds (1:159, 535). The chief reason for their lack of intelligibility is that they turn the Bible, their rule of faith, into a "dumb rule" and a "mute" text (2:203, 359). For none of them agrees with any other about the meaning of the signs on its pages. They insist that the "words" are clear, yet "*sound* and *sound* a diff'rent sense explains" (2:379–80, 442) and, in the end, "'tis onely clear / What vowels and what consonants are there" (2:385–86). For Dryden, the Fox's "private reason" and the Wolf's "private spirit" are at the opposite extreme from the Holy Spirit. Whereas they have become mute or unintelligible in spiritual matters, the Holy Spirit at Pentecost made foreigners understand the language of St. Peter when he spoke for the universal Church (Acts 2:4). The poet hints that the private way in religion is fatal self-deception: "Thus, with full sails, they ran upon the shelf; / Who cou'd suspect a couzenage from himself?" (2:257–58).

Dryden leaves a loophole for the return of the Wolf and Fox into the fold by characterizing them as stray dogs. He hints that the Wolf and Fox may someday lie down with the Hind again in the millenial peace of the garden. Aesop has a fable about a wolf debating whether or not to become a dog, but this fable only confirms that it is the wolf's nature to remain wild and wear no collar. The animal symbolism of the Bible is not so fatalistic. The idea of the wild and the garden in *The Hind and the Panther* can be illuminated by Cardinal Hugo's gloss for Canticles 2:2, where the Bride is called a lily among thorns. The cardinal says that the Bride was "lurking like a wild beast" among the reprobates, when the hound of heaven found her: "The Lord acted like a hunting dog, which pursuing wild game, thrusts its head amongst the prickles of thorns, fearing no wounds so that it may take its prey" (RFL, 62). Because of her sin, the Bride drawn from the Gentiles was at first a savage animal, but in time she was sweetly tamed. Similarly, in Dryden's poem, the Panther can stop being "salvage" if she responds to the summons of the Bridegroom calling her from within the all-inclusive Bride.

In his notes on Canticles drawn from St. Ambrose, Guillaume de Saint-Thierry uses the same sort of animal symbolism to show how one loses "form" through sin: he says that first it is like falling down from the sky to a halfway point, but then, if one persists, one sinks into an abyss of unlikeness: "We fell through our sin from God into ourselves, and fell from ourselves beneath ourselves into such an abyss of unlikeness that no hope was left." Saint-Thierry notes that a dove may turn into a vulture by being thus cut off from grace.[3] This very idea seems to underlie the Hind's tale, that the English Church is in danger of losing every vestige of the form of the Dove. When the story opens, the English Church has lost the unity of the Dove and has dwindled to a flock of jealous "Pigeons." As the story progresses, the Pigeons are so eager to take a Buzzard as their head that they resolve to abandon their "Forms": "Give up our Forms, and we shall soon be friends" (3:1127). The word "forms" refers both to high-church ceremonies and to the remains of the Dove-form within them, the part that still dimly mirrors the Bridegroom, because in Canticles the Bridegroom is also a dove. At the end of the tale, the form of the Pigeons is literally dissolving away (3:1272). In other words, they are being replaced in their church livings by Buzzards who make a feast of their incomes. The Hind tells this story to warn the Panther that her secret mating with the Wolf will cause the high church to be transformed into a low church with no remnant of Catholic sacraments and liturgies; and then the Panther will lose her very form.

Dryden points out in one of the genealogies of the Puritans that both the Wolf and the Fox may have had an ancestor in Noah's Ark: the Dog. Like the panther, the roebuck, and the dove, the dog is a hieroglyph of Christ. Cardinal Hugo depicts both Christ and the zealous soul as a "gallant hound" (RFL 17, 62). Learned clergymen were traditionally imaged as good barking watchdogs guarding the sheepfold of the Church. The Wolf and Fox had been such gallant dogs till they became "wild currs" by running away from their bishops or pastors and starting a rebel race (1:192–96). The poet hints that granting nonconformists their native rights in Britain might well summon the Wolf and Fox sweetly back to docility.

The poet sees this moment as auspicious for James II to include Catholics in a royal grant of freedom of worship. The formerly hostile sects are weak, ashamed, or without organization: the Independent Bear

---

3. Saint-Thierry, *Exposition on The Song,* 58.

is "Unlick'd to form" (1:36), the Quaker Hare is "timorous," and the Anabaptist Boar still lurks unseen, concealing his "shame" for what happened in Munster (1:52). Even the Presbyterian Wolf skulks around in embarrassment because of his role in the Rye House assassination plot of 1683: "His ragged tail betwixt his leggs he wears / Close clap'd for shame" (1:163–64). Together, they are like the chorus of the Daughters of Jerusalem in Canticles, ignoring the Church of the Law and admiring the new Bride drawn from the Gentiles, the infant Church. They ignore the Panther because they resent the way she executed all the laws against them in 1683–1685, during the so-called Tory revenge: "None of her sylvan subjects made their court; / Levees and couchees pass'd without resort" (1: 515–16).

This extraordinary friendliness of the sects toward the Hind, however, stirs up the Panther's jealousy. Now everything depends on the Panther. If she remains docile, the Wolf will too. Only she can inflame the Wolf's zeal against the Catholics again. Only she can make his iconoclasm formidable, can summon "*Goths* and *Vandals*" against "*Rome*" (3:1214). And this is why the Panther's "wandring" heart, her jealousy of the Hind, her contemplating renewed adultery with the Wolf, is such an important matter in this poem.

CHAPTER 10

The Wooing of the Panther
and Her Refusal

In ancient Christian commentaries, Canticles was believed to have a poignant plot: the Sulamitess, the Jewish "mother" of the Bride, had rejected the Bridegroom under the Cross, but now, in Canticles 6, she was summoned four times to "return" to a New Jerusalem grown worldwide since her refusal (RFL, 299). Dryden adapts this plot for *The Hind and the Panther* so that he has not just a dialogue but a little drama about a wooing in the night that fails in one sense but may succeed in another. True, the estranged Panther refuses to come into the universal marriage, but just as the Bride has a "little sister" in Canticles 8, interpreted in a number of commentaries as a "newly planted" church not yet old enough to produce offspring or give the milk of good doctrine, so the Panther has a daughter called "Lavinia" in Dryden's poem (3:776), a Bride-to-be who is immature, unable to speak for herself, but destined—the name tells us—to marry the returned prince Aeneas. The masculine name "Aeneas," like "Pan," operates as a codename for the Bridegroom hidden within the renascent Catholic Church in England.

It may seem strange that the Hind takes the Panther into her home to woo her for the Bridegroom, but since the Hind is an inclusive *figura* comprised of all the nations of the world, she may indeed woo a separated

national church to return into the nuptial mystery. That the Beloved himself is really the one wooing the Panther through the voice of the Hind
becomes clear when the dialogue is nearly over. Dryden interrupts his
narrative to say that the motherly Hind has failed in her commission:
"The *Matron* woo'd her Kindness to the last, / But cou'd not win; her
hour of Grace was past" (3:892–93). The phrase "hour of Grace" implies
that this was a night of divine visitation for the Panther. This wooing is
one of the main events of the poem, and its failure causes a change of
tone, a mood of "weeping over Jerusalem" in its last part. As we will see,
the Hind evokes Luke 13:34 when she shows the Anglican Pigeons persecuting the Catholic Hens, the very ones who would, in time of danger,
have gathered the young Pigeons under their wings.

While the Hind and the Panther have been walking and conversing in
part 2, the atmosphere has grown dark and threatening. So the Hind invites the stranger Dame to enter her leafy home and share her food and
couch for fear that "travelling so late / Some evil minded beasts might lye
in wait" (2:688–89). Similarly, in Canticles 4:8, the Bridegroom invites
the Bride with a triple "Veni" to "come" to him and leave behind the dangerous beasts. To imitate this triple "Veni," Dryden uses the word "welcome" three times in the extended, ardent invitation the Hind gives to
the Panther, summoning her to leave behind the predators of the night
and come within the ever-verdant shelter (2:676, 700, 704).

The Hind also speaks of "dews unwholsome" and "vapours" as another reason why the Panther should enter her "shed." She points to the
"dew drops" on the Panther's "silken hide" and argues that a "tender constitution" like hers cannot bear such "rough inclemencies of raw nocturnal air" (2:664, 684–87). It does not seem, however, that the Hind herself
is cold with dew, perhaps another indication of the ever-present care of
Providence. In Canticles 5:2 the Bridegroom's head is "ful of dew," and
his hair is covered in "the drops of the night" when he knocks on the
door, asking the Bride to open to him; and when she opens to him after a
delay, he is gone. St. Augustine writes on this verse that "*night* denotes iniquity, and its *dew* and *drops* are they who grow cold and fall, and chill the
Head of Christ, that is, cause that God, Who is Christ's head, should not
be loved. And these are carried in the *locks*, that is, they are admitted to
outer Sacraments, but they do not reach the inward meaning." Augustine
and Philo of Carpasia regard the knock of the dew-chilled Christ as a

summons to the Bride to exert herself in active missionary work. Other commentators observe that the Bride's act of unlocking the door to her afflicted Bridegroom represents liberality to the poor and a frank rebuke of sinners. Although the Bridegroom is not visible when the Bride opens her door, Richard of St. Victor believes that Christ is there all the same, though she does not perceive his presence (RFL, 209–26).

In Dryden's poem the dewdrops on the Panther's hair may signify that the English Church is still a branch of the Universal Church, though separated, and that her estrangement from the Bride afflicts Christ. The Hind responds with charity to the needs of the Panther: she tries first to embrace her in friendship, then to heal her from the wounds of jealousy, and finally to reclaim her by sharp yet charitable rebukes. Thus, the Hind sees the dewdrops on the Panther as a knock on her door, a plea for her to exert herself even more urgently in her dealings with the English Church. Yet, just as the Bridegroom cannot be seen when the Bride opens the door in Canticles, so in Dryden's poem the Panther becomes utterly void of grace once she has entered the Hind's "shed." Even so, the Hind continues to call to her: she "woo'd her Kindness to the last" (3:892).

The Hind's "Veni" also parallels Evander's invitation to Aeneas to enter his humble home. Although Evander could not know it, he was living where the glorious center of Rome would one day stand and be ruled by the descendants of his Trojan guest. This is Evander's welcome as it appears in Dryden's translation of Virgil's *Aeneis* (1697):

Mean as it is, this Palace, and this Door,
Receiv'd *Alcides*, then a Conquerour.
Dare to be poor: accept our homely Food
Which feasted him; and emulate a God.
(8:477–80)[1]

It is important to note that in framing her parallel invitation to the Panther, the Hind humbly casts herself in the role of Evander, the Greek who sacrificed his only son in the service of Aeneas and who therefore had no descendants to perpetuate his line in Rome:

Nor yet despise it, for this poor aboad
Has oft receiv'd, and yet receives a god; . . .

1. *Poems: The Works of Virgil in English, 1697*, ed. William Frost and Vinton A. Dearing, in *The Works of John Dryden* (1987), 6:623.

Be emulous of him, and pomp disdain,
And dare not to debase your soul to gain.
                    (2:707–8, 712–13)

By giving the role of Aeneas to the Panther and keeping the lesser role of Evander for herself, the Hind hints that the glorious destiny might be the Panther's. All she has to do is imitate Evander's former guests—the exiled Trojan prince and Hercules, a figure for Christ —in their humility and poverty. Thus the Hind knowingly receives without envy a guest she knows could surpass her; moreover, she is willing to serve her and be absorbed into the foundations of this future Rome, this universal empire of the last age.

After she enters into the Hind's "shed," however, the Panther changes from a guest into a hostile owner. She refuses to regard herself as the stranger who has been welcomed and instead begins to disdain the Hind as the stranger who has come without invitation onto her own property. She begins to imagine that she is not at all like Aeneas and that the Hind is not a bit like Evander. In her rhetoric the Panther shows that she indeed hears a would-be Bridegroom speaking to her from within the Hind-Bride, but now, casting herself in the role of Virgil's mad Latin queen, the doomed Amata, she declares that she will not let such a beggarly foreigner marry her daughter Lavinia (the next generation of the high-church Anglicans) and take her land from her. Even though she plainly hears the masculine wooer speaking through the Hind, she no longer regards herself as the one being wooed by the Bridegroom. Crazed with jealousy, she threatens to take strong action against the "intended wrong":

Methinks such terms of proferr'd peace you bring
As once *Aeneas* to th' *Italian* King:
By long possession all the land is mine,
You strangers come with your intruding line,
To share my sceptre, which you call to join.
You plead like him an ancient Pedigree,
And claim a peacefull seat by fates decree.
In ready pomp your Sacrificer stands,
T' unite the *Trojan* and the *Latin* bands,
And that the League more firmly may be ty'd,
Demand the fair *Lavinia* for your bride.
Thus plausibly you veil th' intended wrong. . . .
                    (3:766–72)

The Panther's words make it clear that she does not know Virgil very well. In the *Aeneis* the Trojan prince never makes a "Demand" for Lavinia, as the Panther claims here. Rather, King Latinus offers the bride to the Trojan because of the wondrous signs and auguries he has received, portents indicating that the descendants of this match will raise his people to the stars. But by having the Panther impose the role of Aeneas on the Hind and that of Amata on herself, Dryden shows her as unwittingly disinheriting herself and passing the worldwide destiny to one who was too humble to claim it.

Like Aeneas, the Hind desires nothing more than a foothold of land and a chance to grow in peace, but like Amata, the Panther rouses the barbarians against her civilized guest by telling them that this foreigner wants to rule them. Her wild anger will not, however, stop the course of providential history. Dryden expects his readers to know that Lavinia married Aeneas after Amata's suicide, in accordance with the signs and her father's promise. The Panther's remark to the Hind, "You plead like him an ancient Pedigree," hints that she is as jealous of the Hind's ancestry as Amata was of Aeneas's lineage. She fears that the Hind might have a better title to be the national church. As Dryden pointed out earlier in the poem, the Panther's church is the "noblest" in England, but only after, or "next the Hind" (1:327), and her line does not go back very far: her house is "not ancient, whatsoe'er pretence / Her clergy Heraulds make" (1:347–48). By paralleling her with Amata, who was driven to madness by a Fury from below, Dryden glances once more at Canticles 8:6, "Dura sicut infernus aemulatio," or "jealousie is hard as hel," a verse that he associates elsewhere with the Puritan Wolf (1:200–234). In Queen Amata and the Panther an infernal zeal works to destroy the gracious and the civilized: the Latin queen offers her daughter to the barbarous Turnus in exchange for his promise to drive the gentle Trojan out of Latium; likewise, the Panther offers the next generation to the rough Wolf in exchange for his offer to drive the gentle Hind from Britain. In the Hind's tale, too, the Anglican Pigeons offer the next generation of Pigeons to the wild Buzzard in exchange for his act of driving the Catholic "Domestick Birds" from the Farm.

In her welcome to the "shed," therefore, the Hind invites the Panther to heed the signs and see that her descendants might be the ones to attain spiritual royalty, give laws to others, and close the gates of war. Indeed, in some medieval interpretations of Canticles, there were to be four Brides in succession for the four ages of humanity, the last one "sub Antichristo" to be the Bride of the North.[2] Dryden seems to be glancing at some such great plan of Providence, some high destiny awaiting the British Church as the center of Christianity in the eschatological events that will usher in the climax of sacred history. He alludes to Virgil's thousand-year plan of Rome's rise and growth to suggest that no one will foil the designs of Providence.

The Hind tells the Panther in still another way that she will lose her glorious destiny by her jealous zeal. She applies to her the ancient prophecy that the dying Jacob left to Judah in Genesis 49:8–10, even quoting the line in the Protestant way: "Shiloh comes the scepter to remove" (3:1258). The Catholic version of this line is "till he come that is to be sent." The Hind warns that just as Judah or the Synagogue retained the scepter until his descendant Christ (Shiloh) came to confirm or remove it, so the Panther has retained her scepter in matters of faith until this day of her visitation. But now the Bridegroom has come to her in the person of his Bride to confirm or remove it. In her tale, the Hind warns that if the English Church refuses him, "Here ends the reign of this pretended *Dove*." From now on, she will lack all claim to spiritual authority and be no more than a state-supported sect: "Reduc'd from Her Imperial High Abode, / Like *Dionysius* to a private Rod" (3:1258–60).

Dryden implies that spiritual authority is like the palanquin of Canticles, the movable bed/throne of the Bridegroom. The Jesuit Lapide says that the palanquin shows that sovereignty in divine matters can move from place to place, as when it went from the East to the West in the early Middle Ages, Christ turning aside "from the Arian East to His faithful in Gaul" (RFL, 265). The poet hints that this is the moment when the Panther might seize her destiny, but if she refuses, that destiny will devolve upon another, not to another geographical area but to another historical period, in the persons of the descendants of Aeneas and Lavinia. The poet trusts that religious liberty will prevail from now on and that, like the Trojans in Latium to whom the Panther compares them (3:767), English Catholics will eventually melt in, because they will henceforth be educated in England, rather than in Europe. Unable to take university de-

2. E. Ann Matter, *The Voice of My Beloved: The Song of Songs in Western Medieval Christianity* (Philadelphia: University of Pennsylvania Press, 1990), 63.

grees without abjuring their religion, upper-class English Catholics had to go abroad for their education in the seventeenth century and therefore seemed somewhat foreign and suspect to their countrymen when they returned from their European studies. James II hoped to change all that and to have at least one college at Oxford where Catholics might take degrees with impunity. In pursuance of that short-lived policy, Dryden allowed his own son, who had been studying unofficially under the Catholic convert Obadiah Walker at University College, to become an "intruded" Catholic fellow at Magdalen College, Oxford, in 1688, after the Protestant fellows there were ejected by the king's visitors for their contumacy.[3] Thus, by insisting that the Hind is really Aeneas, the Panther augurs unintentionally that Catholics will eventually blend into the native culture and transform it from within, as Aeneas's descendants did, losing their Trojan name and language to appease Juno's wrath. That is, Catholics will lose their names of "Romish" and "Popish," as well as their European breeding, but while being absorbed they will lift their countrymen out of their insularity into a worldwide prominence in matters of faith.

If the renascent Catholic Church in England is Aeneas after all, then it follows that "seek your ancient mother" in Dryden's epigraph from Virgil—"Antiquam exquirite matrem"—applies especially to her. Just as Aeneas came looking for his "ancient mother" in an Italy occupied by barbarous tribes and found only war and a postponed marriage, so the Hind comes looking for her "ancient mother" in England and finds the same inauspicious beginnings for the restoration of the old faith. In the Hind's tale, the ancient mother is called the Dove for whom the English dovehouse was built long ago (3:956).

The use of the word "mother" in Dryden's allegory is twofold: first, it can apply spatially to the Universal Bride in relation to its parts, and second, it can apply historically to a particular church in relation to one that comes later. The Puritan William Guild observed that in Hebrew first the whole Church may be called the "mother" and the parts thereof "daughters" and "sisters," and second the true Church of one era may be called

3. The Repealers' view of the events at Magdalen College in the years 1687 to 1688 can be found in Nathaniel Johnston's *The King's Visitatorial Power Asserted* (London: Henry Hills, 1688). The contempt with which the fellows of Magdalen College, "led by the Populacy" (p. 111), treated the king's visitors was part of the public backlash against James II for his trying to repeal the Test Acts.

the "daughter" of the true Church of former times.[4] According to the first idea of motherhood, the Hind as Universal Bride would be the mother whom the English, as a national church, must seek. But according to the second idea, the immemorial British Church would be the ancient mother whom the Hind, as the infant Church in Britain, would have to seek out so as to seem no longer a foreign intruder to the English. According to legend, Joseph of Arimathea planted this ancient Church in Glastonbury in the apostolic age and endowed it with the Holy Grail, the communion cup used at the Last Supper. However, the Protestant historian Thomas Fuller, in his mid-seventeenth century ecclesiastical history, heaps scorn on this "monkish" fable.[5]

The Hind speaks of "friendship" at the very center of the action, just after the Panther has entered her "shed" (3:47, 86). Likewise, in Canticles 5:16, at the center of the epithalamium, the Bridegroom calls the Bride "Friend." It is the "*Lyon*'s peace" newly "proclam'd" that lets the Hind couch "securely" side by side with the Panther during that night and invite her to be her friend (2:676, 722, 3:20–22). The poet alludes to Isaiah's vision of the last times, when the wolf and the lamb, the leopard and the kid will lie down and feed side by side securely (Is 11:6, 65:25). While she is trying to "express her plain simplicity of love," the Hind discovers that the Panther is deeply wounded with "envy" and "jealousy" (3:31, 70–75). Undeterred, she uses "Anodynes t' asswage the smart" (3:82) and later employs the sharper medicine of rebukes to heal the Panther. By dawn, however, it is clear that the Panther is resolved to wage outright war against the Hind's "intruding line" (3:769).

---

4. William Guild, *Loves Entercours between the Lamb and His Bride, Christ and His Church; or, A Clear Explication and Application of The Song of Solomon* (London: Ralph Smith, 1658), 43, 273.

5. Thomas Fuller, *The Church History of Britain* (London: John Williams, 1655), 6. Fuller calls this legend the "leaven of Monkery."

CHAPTER II

The Panther's Soft Dismission
from the Sky

While defending the Hind as doubly "unspotted," Dryden several times reminds the reader that the Panther's beauty is doubly spotted, within and without, by inborn and outward stains (1:328, 572; 3:357). Since the Hind's close union with her Bridegroom keeps her pure, it follows that the Panther's estrangement from him—both in her original separation and in her daily continuance—makes her twice discolored. Alluding to the Vulgate reading of Canticles 8:5—"Under the apple-tree I raysed thee up: there thy mother was corrupted, there she was defloured"—the poet traces the Panther's "inborn stains" to her beginning, when Henry VIII "compressed" her mother in a "shade." Dryden's choice of the word "compressed" implies not only that King Henry violated the ancient religion of England, but also that he made her smaller, more insular, more dependent (1:349–52). She became the present-day Panther, who is figuratively called her "daughter." Now the Panther is being called to undo her mother's action by entering the Hind's shed and remaining there. Surely the "shade" in which the Panther's mother sinned and the "shed" where the Panther could return are the same place. This is the shade of the Tree of Life, or the Bridegroom's presence. Henry VIII deflowered the Panther's mother by usurping her Spouse's rights, that is, by claiming to be her head and protector in the place of Christ. The English Church was to rest in his mortal shade from now on. When the Hind invites the Panther to embrace voluntary poverty at the end of part 2, she hints that the Panther will have to divorce herself from royal supremacy and accept Christ as her only head and shade.

On the historical level, Dryden's allegory seems drawn from the most important Catholic account of the English Reformation, Nicholas Sander's *The Rise of the Anglican Schism*.[1] Sander depicts King Henry as intimidating the English clergy with the threat of criminal indictments under the fourteenth-century praemunire law. In 1529 the terrified clergy surrendered to him the title of supreme head of the church in England in exchange for his verbal promise not to claim by that title any more authority in spiritual matters than his royal predecessors had. In short order, however, the king, with parliamentary approval, became the ultimate court of appeals in matters of faith in England, and even appointed Thomas Cromwell, a layman, as his "vicar." Thus, from being part of the Universal Bride, the English Church from 1529 to 1534 was "compressed" to a national church.

The poet says that Henry VIII's "left-hand marr'age" veiled his sin and legitimized the birth of the Panther, that is, the "schism." This phrase about a "left-hand" wedding refers to the parliamentary law passed in 1534 that confirmed the king as the "supreme head" of the state church. This marriage was illicit because the Church was already married to Christ. It is in this allegorical sense, then, that Henry covered "adult'ry with a specious name" (1:354). Alluding to Christ's words, "you shall know them by their fruits" (Mt 7:16), Dryden shows that "the fruit" of Henry's church revealed "the plant": souls were "starv'd," while senses were "gratify'd" (1:61–70). Soon the Panther was "match'd" with "sacrilege" (the term "sacrilege" refers to the dissolution of the monasteries, as recounted in Sander and Spelman[2]) and begot "graceless heresie" in the reign of Edward VI. The epithet "graceless" reminds the reader of the "graceless" and hypocritical Fox (1:54, 354–56). Thus Dryden traces the origin and progress

1. Nicholas Sander, *The Rise and Growth of the Anglican Schism*, trans. and ed. David Lewis (Rockford, Ill., TAN, 1988). This is a reprint of an edition first published in 1877. The original Latin edition appeared in 1585 and shaped the European view of the English Reformation.

2. Henry Spelman, *The History and Fate of Sacrilege* (London: John Hartley, 1698), 187–287. Written in 1632, the 1663 printing of this work was stopped by the authorities.

of the Panther-Church in allegorical form, just as he allegorically derives the Wolf from such former churches as the Lollards, the Zwinglians, and the Calvinists. In this plot drawn from Canticles and its commentaries, churches are mothers, sisters, or daughters; they are universal or national; and they are civilized or wild.

It is notable that in his account of the "down-hill Reformation" (1:372) Dryden equates the Panther with the schism in Henry's reign, not with the "graceless heresie" in Edward VI's reign. In short, the poet identifies the Panther with the high church of Henry VIII and William Laud. She is that part of the national church that seems "nurst" in "Popery" to other English Protestants because of her Catholic forms and ceremonies. On the "main question" of the Real Presence, however, she has remained "dumb," that is, ambiguous since the time of Elizabeth, at least until she inserted the communion rubric against the Real Presence in the *Book of Common Prayer* at the start of the Restoration (2:25–34). Indeed, this is a very Anglo-Catholic Panther.

In the century of the Stuart kings, the Panther has been "the mistress of a monarch's bed" (1:393); the words "mistress" and "bed" here hint at concubinage, or at least a relationship something less than the divine matrimony her mother had enjoyed before Henry VIII. In 1649, the poet says, she acted like a pagan or "*Indian* wife" committing suttee on the grave of "murdr'd Monarchy" (1:442), but in 1661 she preferred to lose the "meat" of her Eucharist rather than suffer "martyrdome" to defend the "real presence in the sacrament" (2:30–59). For over a century the Panther has been a vine clinging to the royal poplar tree in England (1:439–40), while the Hind has remained joined in a "deathless plant" with her Bridegroom and has accepted martyrdom as the cost of her fidelity (1:24). Of course, the Panther's idea of divine right, her adherence to the hereditary line of kings, has been premised on the belief that Divine Providence directs the royal lines and thereby shapes Britain's history.

Despite her long intimacy with royalty, the Panther now leans toward the archenemy of kings, the one who says that Providence shapes history by the inspired revolutionary's sword, not by tradition, custom, or hereditary lines: "The *Wolfe* begins to share her wandring heart" (1:338). The word "wander" does not occur in the King James Bible but it is found in the Douay version of Canticles, where the Bride asks to be guided lest she wander ("vagari" in the Vulgate) after other flocks: "Shew me, o thou, whom my soule loveth, where thou feedest, where thou lyest in the midday, lest I begin to wander after the flocks of thy companions" (1:7). R. F. Littledale observes that the majority of Christian commentators had interpreted the phrase "the flocks of thy companions" to mean heretics. Likewise, Jewish exegetes had seen pagan nations in that phrase. In the allegory, the Bride of Canticles worries that if she wanders after other flocks, she will be unfaithful to the Bridegroom (RFL, 29–30). Besides using the phrase "wandering heart," Dryden also applies the phrase "stranger dame" to the Panther (2:671), alluding to Proverbs 5:3 and 5:20, where we read of a "strange woman" whose lips drop honey but whose end is as bitter as wormwood and as sharp as a sword.

Dryden seems disappointed by the Panther's refusal to accept friendship with the Hind and the Catholic king. He finds several ways of saying that the Panther is really only half-fallen: she is the "fairest creature of the spotted kind"; she "dropt half way down"; and "she's the fairest of the fallen crew" (1:328, 344, 450–51). Whereas the other animals are wholly of the "spotted kind," the Panther's spots somehow seem localized, for she is the "Lady of the spotted-muff" (1:572). While the Panther has "in-born stains" as the consequence of her parent's sin, she could easily be purified by the Bridegroom (1:329–30), just as sinful Israel could soon be washed clean by Yahweh in Isaiah 4:2–4, so that her "branch" might bear "fruit" again. Dryden thinks it would take only a little turn for the severed English branch to graft itself onto the "deathless plant," and for the Panther to become as milky and spotless as the Hind once again.

In the Hind's tale the Panther is pictured as "a sort of *Doves*" acting so contrary to the nature of the Dove that they are given the pejorative name of "Pigeons." But for all that, the mention of the name "Dove" is significant. It means that the role awaiting the Panther or her daughter's descendants is unique, for in Canticles 6:9 the Bridegroom declares that his "dove" is but "one." Some ancient expositors thought the name "dove" denoted the Jewish-Christian Church as "Mother of us all" (RFL, 283). Dryden may thus be giving the strongest clue here that the original English Church, hidden within the spotted Panther, dates from Jewish times. He images the return of this Panther to the Universal Bride as the return of the Synagogue, found again at the eleventh hour and now assuming that scepter that once was hers for the last great battle against Antichrist.

Thus, for Dryden, the English Church's re-entering the worldwide marriage is poetically a culmination and transformation of sacred history.

Even though the Hind says, in her tale, that the English dovehouse "Was built, long since, God knows, for better Birds" (3:956), she does not depict the Catholics in the story as the Doves who have returned to reclaim the dovehouse. On the contrary, she portrays the Catholic mission in England as a group of "Hens" led by Chanticleer the White. The Hind observes that this "miter'd" rooster is the very one that called St. Peter to repentance after his denial of Christ: "The Bird that warn'd St. *Peter* of his Fall" (3:1006). Chaunticleer has come, then, to summon the Pigeons to return, return to the single Dove they once were, to the holiness they practiced before they imagined they knew better than "to Fast and Pray" (3:1017–18). In the imagery of this fable can be found the Hind's reply to the Panther's false fears: there is no possibility that the Poultry will supplant the Pigeons in the dovehouse.

When the Hind depicts the Catholics as "Hens," she evokes still another hieroglyph for Christ. For when Jesus wept over Jerusalem because the city had failed to know the hour of her visitation, he said that he had tried to protect the city just as a hen hides her chicks under her wings to protect them from birds of prey. The Rheims version of 1582 reads: "how often would I gather together thy children as the henne doth gather together her chickens under her winges, and thou wouldest not?" (Mt 23:37). And the marginal note that accompanies this verse indicates that it means that the Jews "lost their preeminence, by their owne free will" (Lk 13:34). The Hind glances at this text and its note when she ends her tale by saying that the Pigeons will lose their "Scepter" (3:1258–59) now and become vulnerable themselves to the Buzzard, the bird of prey they introduced into their midst so that he could persecute the Catholic Hens. By so doing, they lost the friendship of the Catholic Hens, who, as modern embodiments of those divine wings sheltering Jerusalem, would likewise have covered the young Doves at the first sign of a Buzzard.

The choice of the name "Dove" for the Panther is especially poignant because it is the endearment that the Bridegroom uses for the Bride in Canticles when he summons her in the night: "Open to me, my sister, my beloved, / my dove, my perfect one" (5:2). In ancient animal symbolism, the dove is like the panther in having the gift of eloquence. For just as the panther had a perfumed breath, an irresistible speech capable of drawing all wild animals, so the dove represented the Holy Spirit, whose presence was revealed by the gift of tongues, a speech able to draw all foreigners together at Pentecost. In the Hind's tale, the "sort of Doves" abuse their gift of speech and turn all the animals in the farmyard against the Poultry by false zeal or canting (3:1208). Besides being eloquent, the dove was also supposed to be faithful, simple, tender, and free of gall. In his commentary on the dove in Canticles 1:10, Bede said that a soul that loves Christ is like a dove and therefore "not fired, like hawks, with greed for things without, nor plans evil against any living things." St. Anselm of Laon wrote that this bird "nourishes young ones not her own," "wounds not with her beak," and has "no gall" or "unreasonable anger" (RFL, 49–50). In the Hind's tale, however, the "sort of Doves" are "Voracious Birds" who "abound with Gall" (3:947–50). Far from being tender to the young of the Hens, they attack them all they can: "But with their Quills, did all the hurt they cou'd, / And cuff'd the tender *Chickens* from their food" (3:1223–24).

In a sermon on Canticles devoted entirely to the dove, Richard Sibbes characterizes the bird in yet another way that sheds light on the Hind's tale. Sibbes declares that while there is a simplicity in the dove that is admirable, there is also a dovelike silliness that is sinful. This is the "*fatal* simplicity" that goes "before destruction when we hate those that defend us, and account them enemies, and relie more upon them that are enemies indeed then upon friends." He explains that in Hosea 7:11 Ephraim (the Northern Kingdom of Israel) becomes simple "as a dove that is decoyed" by trusting Egypt and Assyria more than God and the Prophets.[3] Likewise, in the Hind's tale, the "sort of Doves" out of pure envy make a silly, suicidal alliance with the anti-Catholic Buzzard: "And fondly clos'd with former Enemies; / For Fools are double Fools endeav'ring to be wise" (3:1106–7). By inviting the Buzzard (as Ephraim did the Assyrians) to come and fight for them against the chosen tribe, the Pigeons created an instrument of vengeance against themselves. They elected for themselves a Prince "more proper to revenge, than save; / A King, whom in his wrath, th' Almighty gave" (3:1197–98).

---

3. Sibbes, *Bowels*, 168–69.

CHAPTER 12

"*Boreas* got the skyes": The Panther's Tale

In Canticles 1:6 the Bride asks the Bridegroom where he feeds his flock at "midday." St. Bernard of Clairvaux interprets this word "midday" to mean the "true noonday" of the divine presence, a fullness of light that causes the yearly cycle to be henceforth without the darkness and cold of winter. Since God's face is the noon of that "perennial solstice," winter is either a time of "rest and festival" or it is simply "over and gone" (RFL, 28).

In the Panther's tale the Catholic Swallows have this mystical vision of Canticles: they say that God is "abroad and walking" in England and that his "foot-steps" are reforming the year (3:554–55). The Panther, however, believes in the inevitable return of winter. Her tale is a warning to English Catholics that they must expect the onslaught of "persecuting cold" as soon as James II can no longer give them protection (3:430). In the abrupt outbreak of the winter she envisions, they will suffer by their own fault, because they were too foolish to arrange a timely flight across the Channel. The Panther mocks the Catholic Swallows for their "gaudy" hopes (the same word she used for the Catholic butterfly in 3:66). She finds it ridiculous that they should anticipate a miraculous "holy day of spring" after the autumn season.

Like so much of the Panther's discourse, her tale is extremely revealing, but not at all in the way she imagines. On a first reading, the tale is superficially witty, but a second, more careful reading reveals that it lacks internal coherence. For the Panther treats "winter" as part of an expected natural cycle in northern climes and, at the same time, she makes it represent a period of "persecuting cold" in England's religious history. But the twenty-four Penal Laws against nonconformists were enforced irregularly, not at all with the regularity of the natural seasons. Also, many of these statutes had been in existence for no more than three generations; they certainly did not resemble the immemorial, natural order of things in Britain. Thus, the Panther confuses man-made statutes with the natural order.

There is another curious side to this tale. Boreas, the north wind, is parallel to the Buzzard in the Hind's tale and to the Wolf in the overall poem. Boreas is the one who will spearhead the punishment of the Catholics for their "gaudy" hopes. In the overall poem, the Panther is going to summon the Wolf, and in the Hind's tale the "sort of Doves" will summon the Buzzard to execute the harsh laws. In the Panther's tale, this role of awakening the avenging force is given to the "infant moon." This may be appropriate since Dryden compares the Panther to the moon in the first part of the poem. But why an "infant" moon? This image evokes the crescent moon, the symbol of the Ottoman Empire, identified by English Catholics at the time as the Antichrist.[1] Dryden has the Panther predict gleefully that the infant moon will cause a total eclipse just when the Catholics think "the virgin balance shou'd remount" (3:600), that is, when they imagine that Astraea, ancient justice, has returned to the world. The Panther takes the "virgin balance" in a naturalistic or astrological sense and declares that when this sign mounts into the sky, winter cannot be far behind. Dryden has the Panther reveal her lack of internal coherence here. Just as she confuses sign and substance in her liturgy (1:410–29), so, he implies, she is blind to the deeper spiritual meaning of the symbols in her tale.

The "infant moon" of the Panther's tale represents an iconoclastic clergy, which is called an "infant" because it is, by implication, the small beginning of the future Anglican Church. This church party is imaged as a crescent to suggest that it serves as the false prophet of the "Beast," that is, the Antichrist (Rev 19:20). As will be shown later, some iconoclasts in the clergy were eclipsing the king's light in 1685–1688 by a flood of defam-

1. See my essay, "Islam as Antichrist in the Writings of Abraham Woodhead, Spokesman for Restoration Catholics," in *Restoration* 15 (1991): 89–98.

atory sermons against his supposed "idolatry." The "infant-moon" thus prepares the scene for the north wind called Boreas, who will enter and pelt Catholics with snow and hail, that is, enforce the statutes against them. The avenger's initial letter "B" (Boreas and Buzzard) in both the Panther's tale and the Hind's tale could point to Batavia (i.e., Holland), but, since the assembled forces of Antichrist are implied here, the initial may well point to the "Beast" of St. John's Revelation summoned into Britain by the false prophet.

In Canticles 2:11–12, when the Bridegroom comes as a roe to visit the Bride, he calls to her to join him outside because "winter is past." In the old allegorical commentaries, this verse was applied to linear church history, not to the cycles of nature. The end of winter was the coming of the Gospel, and so the Bride was invited to rise and come forth to see the flowers in the springtime of the Bridegroom's restored garden. Applying this verse to his own times, Luther said that it represents a "hope" to which God calls his people and "encourages them to embrace," that there will be "tranquillity in church and state."[2] These glosses illuminate what Dryden might mean by a "holy day of spring" in this poem. The end of winter would be an era of religious peace followed by the fruit of prosperity after a century of religious strife. In *Britannia Rediviva* Dryden exclaims: "Betwixt two Seasons comes th' Auspicious Heir, / This Age to blossom, and the next to bear" (17–18). The Panther refuses this hope and in her tale blames the victims for not fleeing a "persecuting cold" that she sees as England's inevitable future.

Throughout Dryden's poem the Panther has a wintry quality, for she speaks "coldly" (3:56), has a "faint embrace" (3:78), wears a muff (1:572), and seems "dim, and doted" from age (3:152). According to Guillaume de Saint-Thierry, the "discolored" Bride of Canticles is likewise cold and darkened, as if she were a planet or moon not fully warmed by the sun: "the Sun of Justice" has withdrawn "the light of grace" from her, without which "colors cannot exist and all warm things turn cold."[3] In her tale, the Panther rejoices in the coming of the avenger from the North, that is, the cruel Assyrian foe of the Chosen People. The Hind warns her that if she continues doing what she has done in the past, she will look like the remains of winter once the springtime of religious freedom arrives: "Like

2. Luther, "Lectures on The Song," 219.
3. Saint-Thierry, *Exposition on The Song*, 40.

Snows in warmth that mildly pass away, / Dissolving in the Silence of Decay" (3:1271–72).

In Canticles 4:16 there is a summons to the "north wind" to "awake" and to the "south wind" to "come" and blow in the garden. In ancient commentaries this verse was thought to denote the coming of great but temporary persecutions against the Church (RFL, 195). It is noted that two opposite winds are invoked: the north wind, representing Antichrist, is summoned to wreak permitted havoc, while the warm south wind, representing the Holy Spirit, is called in to do battle against the north wind in the skies. The two winds fight an apocalyptic battle for possession of the garden, the Church-Bride. The Panther's tale has just this very feature of Canticles 4:16: there is a battle between the cold north wind Boreas and his warm antagonist, and these two powers engage each other in a strangely eclipsed sky. The Panther first speaks of "*Equinoxes*," or gales, when the Swallows misread the signs in the sky and fail to fly away from the impending "persecuting cold." She again mentions two opposed winds on the day when the snow begins. On that day in late afternoon, after the sun is suddenly "eclips'd" by an "infant moon," a horrid night-in-day is succeeded by a totally dark night:

And fear increas'd the horrour of the night.
Night came, but unattended with repose,
Alone she came, no sleep their eyes to close,
Alone, and black she came, no friendly star arose.

(3:606–9)

The phrase "the horrour of the night" echoes the line "propter timores nocturnos" in Canticles 3:8, about the evil beasts of the night beyond the enclosure of the true Church. The Swallows are indeed far from their home and are caught in the horror of winter, reminding us of Matthew 24:20 about the days of Antichrist: "But pray that your flight be not in the winter." They had come to "conduct" their young on the way, their little missionaries going to "plant abroad." The total eclipse of sun, moon, and stars evokes a text which, according to the 1582 Rheims New Testament, depicts the arrival of Antichrist: "the sonne shal be darkened and the moone shal not give her light, and the starres shal fal from heaven, and the powers of heaven shall be moved" (Mt 24:29).

In the Panther's tale the two winds begin to fight for possession of the dark skies, and Boreas wins mastery for a short time, sending missiles upon the Swallows who are fixed on the "bare" ground in "Panick fright":

> T' augment their woes, the winds began to move
> Debate in air, for empty fields above,
> Till *Boreas* got the skyes, and powr'd amain
> His ratling hail-stones mix'd with snow and rain.
>
> (3:618–21)

Now since this total eclipse and the attack from the north are well-known scriptural signs, the Panther's tale unwittingly celebrates the temporary triumph of the enemies of true religion. Similarly, she seems totally unaware of the implications when she casts herself in the role of Queen Amata summoning the barbaric Turnus to fight her prospective son-in-law Aeneas, the gentle inaugurator from afar of Roman civilization. Dryden carefully puts these implied comparisons in the mouth of the Panther herself, to hint that the Anglicans opposing James II *know not what they do*. He also gives hope to the English Catholics that no matter how bad the coming persecution may be, it cannot prevail for long in the artistic design of Providence.

When the Hind tells her own tale in response, she represents the Panther as a foolish Dove making a fatal alliance with her natural enemy the Buzzard, a symbol of dullness and ignorance. She assumes that the Panther is so blind with envy that she is unaware of the implications of her tale, and so the Hind will make these plain in her own tale. She reminds the Panther that it is suicidal for her to unleash hatred of "popery" by summoning ignorant iconoclasts to attack the renascent Catholic Church in England, because in their sight the Panther is no better than the Hind.

Perhaps because she sees winter as her ally and spurns the renewing powers of spring, the Panther seems to be growing old, surrounded by "pretended sons" who cheerfully measure her mental deterioration by her "crazy temper." This characterization of her evokes an elderly Laudian, high-church remnant surviving at the head of a far different clergy. The Hind warns that the Panther is too "dim" of sight now to realize that many of her supposed "sons" are no kin to her at all and have simply foisted themselves on her line: "how many sons have you / who call you mother, whom you never knew!" Like the Synagogue in Jeremiah 5:21, this Church of the Law has "eyes" but cannot "see." They will rejoice when the Panther dies and they can squander what she has saved of the old faith: "once possess'd of what with care you save, / The wanton boyes wou'd piss upon your grave" (3:144–70). In her tale the Hind foresees that the Pigeons will themselves provide a "falling feast" for the multiplying Buzzards; they will be manna from heaven (3:1272) for those iconoclasts who will inherit the livings of high churchmen.

The Panther's sterility, her slow decline into eccentric old age, her suicidal alliance with low churchmen who despise her forms, her identification with the forces of winter—all this reveals that she is a branch cut off from the "deathless plant" and beginning to wither. Earlier in the poem, the Hind explained that error has a rise, a progress, and a decay (2:611), and in her tale she predicts that the implacable Pigeons will end "in the Silence of Decay" (3:1288).

CHAPTER 13

The Embrace Offered to the Stranger

In Canticles 2:5 the Bride asks to be propped up with flowers and surrounded with apples, because, she explains, "quia amore langueo." The Douay version translates this phrase as "I languish with love." Origen said that the Bride here is the Church wounded with love of Christ and longing for the flowers and fruits of catechumens. St. Augustine adds that anyone who is not so wounded with divine love cannot attain true health (RFL, 76). We find this "quia amore langueo" of Canticles as a theme in Dryden's poem, too. He mentions a series of yearning gestures or proffered embraces that reveal the same wound of love in the Hind and others like her, that same eagerness to cross the distance between the self and the stranger. Unfallen Adam offers to embrace the wild animals he has just met; Joseph yearns to hug the brothers who long ago sold him into slavery and no longer recognize him; the Hind opens her arms to receive as "owner" of her tabernacle the Panther who has persecuted her in the past; the "pious Pastor" Innocent XI protects non-Catholics; and James II welcomes Huguenot refugees. Each one of these extends love unilaterally and comes forward to embrace another who is a stranger. But there is no guarantee in any of these cases that the embrace will be returned.

These rapturous offers of love in Dryden's poem lead into the very heart of his theme, that the Church is Christ's love made manifest to all. The poet urges the reader to recognize the Universal Bride by her yearning for catechumens, by the warmth and breadth of the embrace she extends to those who are estranged. For example, in the following passage the Hind stands ready to embrace the Panther "with open arms." In rich double-stopped chords, the poet compares her love for the Panther to the Father's yearning toward his returning Prodigal Son and to Joseph's longing to rush forward, hug, and feed the brothers who once sold him into slavery:

> See how his church adorn'd with ev'ry grace
> With open arms, a kind forgiving face,
> Stands ready to prevent her long lost sons embrace.
> Not more did *Joseph* o'er his brethren weep,
> Nor less himself cou'd from discovery keep,
> When in the croud of suppliants they were seen,
> And in their crew his best beloved *Benjamin*.
> That pious *Joseph* in the church behold,
> To feed your famine, and refuse your gold;
> The *Joseph* you exil'd, the *Joseph* whom you sold.
> (2:639–48)

The line "to prevent her long lost sons embrace" alludes to Luke 15:21, where the Father of the Prodigal is impelled by his longing to "prevent" or to run ahead and meet halfway the starving son who once so ungraciously forsook him. This Father is eager to provide a homecoming feast, a feast that Catholic commentators agreed was a figure of the Eucharist. Dryden fuses this image of the loving Father with that of the equally loving Joseph, who sees himself as having been prepared from afar to be an instrument of special Providence for his hungry brothers. He even regards their betrayal of him as having worked into this larger plan of salvation. In the Douay version of Genesis 41:45, the Egyptian name that Pharaoh gives to Joseph is "Saviour of the world." St. Jerome comments that Joseph deserves the name because he "delivered the world from the imminent ruine of famine" and is a fitting type of Christ, "the true Saviour of the world." The Hind resembles both the Father feeding the Prodigal and Joseph feeding his brothers and the rest of the world. She forgives the injuries of the past and longs to feed the English in their spiritual "famine." Her "noble nature" strives to "express her plain simplicity of love" to her guest (3:30–31). She welcomes the Panther into her house and way of life, not wishing to supplant her but only to leave her the "owner" of this gracious, newly integrated family of Christ in England.

In Dryden's account of the Creation story, it is a loving embrace that makes Adam appear godlike to the animals. Adam himself was born and nurtured in a divine embrace, for while God "Struck out the mute creation" on nature's anvil, he opened "the sacred treasures of his breast" for Adam and kneaded him up with divine milk. This is an allusion to Isaiah 66:12–13, where God speaks of giving his milk to his chosen. Because he had received such nurturing, Adam before the Fall could extend a unilateral embrace to his fellow creatures when they were still strangers (1:261–62). Rather than wait for the beasts to come and pay him homage as their new king, he ran forward to greet them with an open-armed gesture of love: "With open hands, and with extended space / Of arms, to satisfie a large embrace" (1:272–73). This trusting offer of love made the animals gentle: "He charm'd their eyes, and for they lov'd, they fear'd" (1:265).

In the poet's account of the Fall, Adam cuts himself off from the divine source of love by misapplying knowledge and growing proud of empire. Once the Creator's milk in Adam's veins is "sour'd" by sin, a loveless religion ensues. Launching the first persecution, Cain kills Abel "For dif-f'ring worship of the Deity" (1:281). Thus, persecution replaces open-armed welcome of the other. After Cain, religious intolerance spreads till "farther space / Produc'd the mighty hunter of his race," that is, Nimrod, the figure of Antichrist. Finally, "blessed *Pan*" the Bridegroom arrives and restores his garden, a place where the divine milk becomes accessible again. He opens his arms to protect and feed his sheep as pastor and pasture, "Content to fold 'em from the famish'd beast" (1:285). Pan thus creates a bower filled with divine food and safety in the wilderness and ensures that his sheep will not feel the hunger and insecurity that drive the Wolf and the Panther to persecute. Alluding to Luke 9:54, where Christ rebukes the Apostles for wanting to call down fire from heaven on unbelievers, Dryden says that Pan leaves behind mild laws about how to treat nonbelievers, so that his true "Sheep and harmless Hind" are "never of the persecuting kind," but are instead protectors of "their foes" (1:286–90).

The idea at the heart of the poem is that the embrace of love offered to a foe is the ultimate sign of the true Bride. This theme is reflected in the second epigraph of the poem, "Et vera, incessu, patuit Dea," from Virgil's *Aeneid* 1:405, meaning that the true goddess will be revealed by her grace-filled motion. This is why there are a series of identical motions in the poem, a series of wide-armed embraces offered to those who are wild and estranged. Dryden portrays unfallen Adam, blessed Pan, James II, Innocent XI, and the Hind all offering the same embrace, to indicate by this grace-filled motion that there is divine milk in their veins. The gesture they all repeat is that of the corpus on the Cross, the dying Savior opening his arms wide to embrace the human race estranged from him by sin. On the Cross, too, the offer is unilateral and does not guarantee a response. In every case the one offering the embrace comes with firm faith and trust that there is a Divine Providence sustaining this risky offering of love.

As in the allegory of Canticles, the design of Dryden's poem forms a complete circle, going from fallen-earth time, to eschatological time, then back again to earth time. Canticles was thought to end as it began, with the Bride still visibly separated from her Spouse on earth. She may be in temporal distress, yet she is joined to him in a hidden, mutual indwelling and repose. Dryden's poem opens with the spotless Hind "doom'd to death, though fated not to dy" (1:8), that is, condemned by British law but guaranteed by Christ's promise to endure until the end of the ages. Later, in a moment of realized eschatology, she couches herself side by side with the Panther in the night, in the faith that "she cannot dye / Till rolling time is lost in round eternity" (3:18–19). At the end, after the Panther has spurned her love, the Hind retires to her mystical repose. In his commentary on Canticles, Origen speaks of the Church as being at one level so thoroughly united with Christ the Sun of righteousness that she "can no longer be seen or understood by human viewers."[1] Thus, even though she seems outwardly to be in a state of worldly insecurity in Britain, the Hind can rest invisibly in the bosom of the divine Bridegroom, who maintains her by special Providence. She keeps vigil in her spirit, like the Bride in Canticles 5:2: "Ego dormio et cor meum vigilat." For now, Dryden says, "Ten thousand angels," that is, the Bridegroom's attendants, "waite" on her to comfort her with visions of the great design of sacred history—"With glorious Visions of her future state" (3:1297–

1. Balthasar, *Origen, Spirit and Fire*, 356.

98). Again, Origen speaks of the Bride of Canticles as "having made such progress that she is now something more than the kingdom of Jerusalem. For the Apostle says that there is a 'heavenly Jerusalem'" (Heb 12:18–24). The Bride at this level has followed Christ and "passed through all the heavens."[2]

2. Balthasar, *Origen, Spirit and Fire*, 359.

CHAPTER 14

Dryden's Conversion and "Averte Oculos Tuos"

From antiquity to the seventeenth century Canticles was also read on a level of allegorical exegesis called the tropological: it was interpreted as a song about the road to personal surrender to Christ. Each soul was conceived as having a receptive principle that could yield as *sponsa particularis* to the love of the eternal Bridegroom. This principle had the appropriately feminine name of *anima*. The motif of soul surrender in Canticles is an important one in the design of *The Hind and the Panther*. It enables the poet to tell us indirectly or poetically about his own conversion. Dryden tells us that his road to Catholicism consisted of a series of steps paralleling those of the Bride in Canticles. At first, he searched for Christ the Bridegroom but did not find him. Instead, it was he who was found, who yielded to the divine summons and enjoyed the divine embrace and the resulting repose. He declares that in this yielding he found release from prior soul-suffering: "Rest then, my soul, from endless anguish freed" (1:146). He ends his private quest for assurance by turning to the public faith of the Church, where he finds peace: "my doubts are done" (1:78).

Conceiving of the sacred mysteries as partly revealed and partly concealed, Dryden prays that he may be content hereafter to go no further than the Church's teachings about them: "O teach me to believe Thee thus conceal'd, / And search no farther than thy self reveal'd" (1:68–69). In this couplet he alludes to Christ's remark to the doubting St. Thomas the Apostle, "Blessed are they that have not seen and have believed" (Jn 20:29). Like the Spouse in Canticles 2:9, he is content to listen in the darkness of mortal life to the voice of the invisible Beloved, "vox dilecti mei."

In Canticles the Bridegroom says "Averte oculos tuos a me," which the Douay version translates as "Turne away thine eies from me, because they have made me flye away" (6:4). Commenting on this passage in the fifth century, Theodoret wrote that the Bridegroom here warns the soul to "gaze not steadfastly on Me beyond measure, lest thou shouldst suffer some harm thence" (RFL, 275). In part 1 of his poem, Dryden resolves from this time forward to lower his eyes with reverence before the Church's mysteries. He abjures the way of the rationalist Fox, who uses "natures opticks" to peer impiously at the Incarnation and then proceeds to deny Christ's divinity. The poet tells his soul to believe in the Incarnation and the Real Presence in the sacrament without using science or sensory perception to seek out proofs: "Nor sciences thy guide, nor sense thy creed" (1:147). He prays that his soul will be content henceforth to worship Christ as really there, *sub umbra et figura*.

During the Restoration most English Protestants assented to the divinity of Christ, but they dismissed as idolatry the Catholic belief in the Real Presence of Christ under the forms of bread and wine after consecration. Dryden himself may have shared this view before his conversion. In *Absalom and Achitophel* (1681) the speaker ridicules the Real Presence in the Sacrament of the Altar, even though he is otherwise sympathetic to the persecuted "Jebusites," or Catholics:

> Th' *Egyptian* Rites the *Jebusites* imbrac'd;
> Where Gods were recommended by their Tast.
> Such savory Deities must needs be good,
> As serv'd at once for Worship and for Food.
>
> (118–21)

The phrases "*Egyptian* Rites" and "savory Deities" belong to a common type of raillery against Catholic worship. Latitudinarians like Edward Stillingfleet represented many in the Restoration clergy when they charged that Catholic adoration of Christ in the sacrament was worse than the ancient Egyptian idolatry of the leek.[1] In *The Hind and the Panther*, six years after he wrote those lines, the poet now realizes that the charge of idolatry against Catholics for adoring Christ in the Eucharist is a dangerous slander. He has the Hind tell how the jealous Pigeons mount a freak show to make the other farm animals believe that the Catholic birds are hideous idolaters who worship "Garden-Gods, and barking Deities" (3:1046). After a century of religious strife in England, everyone knew that ancient Scriptures called for idolaters to be destroyed and their idols broken (Ex 23:24). In his essay *Of True Religion* (1673), Milton argued that English Catholics, because of this supposed "idolatry," did not even have a right to worship in secret; he urged that their hidden masses be stopped and their "idols" of bread and wine forcibly taken from them.[2]

In *The Hind and the Panther* Dryden reflects deeply on this charge that Catholics are idolaters of the sacrament. He uses the images of concealment, disguise, and veiling in part 1 to suggest that the forms of bread and wine on the altar are sacramental veils surrounding the divine presence which alone is adored. In the Eucharist as in the Incarnation, he believes Christ is hidden from our eyes but revealed to our ears and minds (1:68–69), so that one's "opticks" cannot be guides to the hidden presence of the godhead. The Hind observes that the Real Presence is really the "main question" (2:28) in that era, the chief subject of religious controversy between Protestants and Catholics during the Restoration. Perhaps more than anything else, the Real Presence is a key to Dryden's conversion, for he describes his conversion to Catholicism as a surrender to Christ in the sacrament.

The first thing he wrestles with is the public side of the sacred mysteries. The Fox has put his private reason in the scale against the public testimony of the Church, the "weight of ancient witness," by deciding that Christ's miracles are impossible, that those "wonders wrought by pow'r divine" never happened, never asserted "the god-head of th'eternal Son" (1:117). The poet prays that he will not use his carnal reason this way to

1. Stillingfleet, *Discourse*, 62.
2. See my essay "Milton's Parody of Catholic Hymns in Eve's Temptation and Fall," *Studies in Philology* 91 (1994): 216–31. Dryden believed in a natural right to liberty of conscience, while Milton believed only in a scriptural right that excluded idolaters, a group that in his view and that of most iconoclasts included Catholics.

devour scriptural testimony as prey, but rather that he will be directed by
the Church to lower his eyes with reverence:

> But, gratious God, how well dost thou provide
> For erring judgments an unerring Guide?
> Thy throne is darkness in th' abyss of light,
> A blaze of glory that forbids the sight;
> O teach me to believe Thee thus conceal'd,
> And search no farther than thy self reveal'd;
> But her alone for my Directour take
> Whom thou hast promis'd never to forsake!
>
> (1:64–71)

The person Dryden addresses as "Thou" in this prayer is Christ, because
in the last line he alludes to the promise Christ gave before the Ascension
to abide with his Church till the end of time (Mt 28:20). When he says
"Thy Throne is darkness," he implies that the risen, glorified Christ is enthroned with the Father and concealed from view by the dark cloud of
our mortality. Through this cloud he gives us glimpses of an "abyss of
light," of a fire so blinding that it may not be looked at: "A blaze of glory
that forbids the sight" (1:68). At the time when he showed his divine
glory, Yahweh covered the eyes of Moses with a protective hand and
warned, "there shall no man see me, and live" (Ex 33:20). Dryden reflects
that Christ also puts a protective hand over our mortal eyes by concealing
from them and natural reason the "abyss of light" within the Sacrament
of the Altar. In the imageless dark of contemplation, the soul may surrender to the divine Guest.

Dryden's rhetoric in this passage echoes commentaries on Canticles
2:9, the verse where the Bridegroom stands near the Bride but she cannot
see him because of the wall between them. St. Gregory the Great writes
that Christ's divinity lay hid behind a wall of flesh in the Incarnation: "because human weakness could not endure His infinity, were He to disclose
it, He interposed the barrier of flesh, and whatever great work He
wrought among men, He did as though hiding behind a wall." The Jesuit
Lapide says that Christ interposes a second wall in the Sacrament of the
Altar: he "looks out steadfastly on faithful souls from behind the wall of
the species of Bread and Wine in the Holy Eucharist, showing Himself in
part to them even there" (RFL, 90).

Looking back at his spiritual journey of fifty-six years, Dryden sees himself as having long pursued increasingly evanescent lights:

> My thoughtless youth was wing'd with vain desires,
> My manhood, long misled by wandring fires,
> Follow'd false lights; and when their glimps
>   was gone,
> My pride struck out new sparkles of her own.
>
> (1:72–75)

In this passage he resembles the Bride in Canticles 3 who for a time seeks her Beloved in the night along the streets of the city. Her refrain is "I have sought him, and have not found." Suddenly, though, it turns out that the Bridegroom has been very near. St. Augustine followed this vain quest, too: "I went very far to seek Thee, and thou wast very near." On Canticles 3:1–4, St. Gregory Nyssen wrote: "she sought Him by reasonings and meditations, but He is beyond them all, evading the grasp of the mind" (RFL, 109). This is what the poet means by his mind's flying toward the sky in youth, pursuing will-o'-the-wisps in young manhood, and striking out sparks on his flinty pride in maturity. His quest was "endless anguish" because he found less light instead of more. Darkness began to surround him when all that remained were momentary sparks "struck out" in the night. Theodoret explains how darkness might be the result of a too-bold pursuit of light in his comment on Canticles 6:5. This ancient Father speaks in the voice of the Bridegroom and commands the soul to turn away from the blaze of divine light: "For I am past searching out, and incomprehensible, not only by men, but by angels; and if thou shouldst pass the bounds, and vainly occupy thyself with matters above thy powers, not only wilt thou fail in thy search, but thou wilt make thine eye dimmer and feebler. For such is the nature of light, that just as it illuminates the eye, so it punishes with hurt its insatiability" (RFL, 275–76). In his poem, then, Dryden confesses that he searched too boldly for the light and found only increasing darkness; now he is content to lower the eyes of his carnal reason before the abyss of light veiled in sacred mysteries: "my doubts are done." He is still the same man by nature, but Christ has bent down to help him: "Such was I, such by nature still I am, / Be thine the glory, and be mine the shame" (1:76–77).

In the first part of *The Hind and the Panther*, Dryden shifts abruptly to a time just before his conversion and lets us witness the final steps that brought him to surrender to the mystery of the Real Presence. The poet asks whether he can believe that God, by his omnipotence, *disguised* himself in the flesh of a child. And then, since he does believe this, he asks himself what prevents his believing that God could, by the same omnipotence, *disguise* himself in the sacrament:

> Can I believe eternal God could lye
> Disguis'd in mortal mold and infancy?
> That the great maker of the world could dye?
> And after that, trust my imperfect sense
> Which calls in question his omnipotence?
>
> (1:80–83)

The phrase "imperfect sense" in this passage echoes "sensuum defectui," found in St. Thomas Aquinas's well-known hymn to the Real Presence, "Pange Lingua gloriosi Corporis," which concludes with the better known stanza beginning "Tantum ergo sacramentum." The poet alludes to the last part of that stanza: "praestet fides supplementum / sensuum defectui." And this is how he later translated the "Tantum ergo":

> To this mysterious Table now
> Our Knees, our Hearts and Sense we bow;
> Let Ancient Rites resign their Place
> To nobler Elements of Grace;
> And Faith for all Defects supply,
> Whilst Sence is lost in Mystery.[3]

In his adaptation of this hymn for English Catholics, he puts even more emphasis than Aquinas does on the ineffability of the sacrament, using both the words "mysterious" and "mystery." Likewise, in *The Hind and the Panther*, he emphasizes the ineffability of the Real Presence of Christ in the sacrament, rather than emphasizing the *modus* of the Real Presence, that is, transubstantiation, for he hopes to find common ground with the high-church Anglicans.

We find the words "disguised" and "concealed" used in medieval hymns in exactly the way Dryden uses them to speak of the Real Presence and the Incarnation. In another eucharistic hymn attributed to Aquinas, "Adoro te devote," the speaker addresses Christ as the hidden Truth of God who lies concealed under the appearance of the sacrament: "Adoro

---

3. *Latin Hymns*, 84; *Hymns Attributed to Dryden*, 151.

te devote, latens deitas, / que sub his figuris vere latitas." In the third
stanza, he says that Christ's divinity was hidden by his suffering humanity
on the Cross, but now his humanity also lies hidden within the appearance of the sacrament: "In cruce latebat sola deitas, / ad hic latet simul et
humanitas."[4] Richard Crashaw's version of this hymn, which Dryden
may well have known, expresses beautifully the idea that the Eucharist is a
double hiddenness, the appearance of the sacrament being a veil over
Christ's humanity, which in turn is a veil over his divinity:

> Though hidd as GOD, wounds writt thee man,
> Thomas might touch; None but might see
> At least the suffring side of thee;
> And that too was thy self which thee did cover,
> But here ev'n That's hid too which hides the
>   other.
>
> (22–26)[5]

In the following lines about the "veil," Dryden makes the same point,
that the hiddenness of the Incarnation is a single covering over the divinity of the Word, while the hiddenness of the sacrament is, as it were, a
double covering:

> Could He his god-head veil with flesh and bloud
> And not veil these again to be our food?
> His grace in both is equal in extent,
> The first affords us life, the second nourishment
>
> (1:134–37)

When he says "veil these," the poet suggests that the forms of the sacrament are a second veil over the first veil of "flesh and bloud." This is what
Crashaw meant when he wrote "That's hid too which hides the other." In
the adaptation of "Pange lingua" attributed to him, Dryden also makes
the same point in these lines:

> How Christ, the Gentiles King, bestow'd
> His Flesh conceal'd in human Food;
> And left Mankind the Blood, that paid
> The Ransom of the Souls he made.

---

4. *Latin Hymns*, 76.
5. *The Complete Poetry of Richard Crashaw*, ed. George Walton Williams (New
York: Norton, 1970), 175.

Here in a kind of mysteriously layered hiddenness, Christ is at once Creator, Redeemer, and Food.

So now Dryden asks himself this question: If Christ had the power to *veil* his divinity with his humanity to redeem us, why should he not have the power to *veil* both his divinity and humanity with the sacramental forms to nourish us? He thinks that the grace he receives from the Cross and that he receives from the Lord's Supper are "equal in extent." The word "veil" which Dryden uses can also be found at the end of the hymn "Adoro te devote," in a poignant line where the speaker asks Jesus to show himself unveiled in eternity: "Iesum quem velatum nunc aspicio." Crashaw translates this line with ardor: "for thy veil give me thy FACE." In *The Hind and the Panther* 1:80–145, Dryden writes as if he were engaged in his final moments of wrestling with the mystery of the Real Presence before his conversion. He observes that "sight, and touch, and taste" perceive no change in the sacrament (1:84–86), here virtually translating a line from "Adoro te devote," "Visus, tactus, gustus in te fallitur." But since "we" make our "Superiour faculties" submit to the mysteries of the Trinity and the Incarnation, he wonders, why let "subservient organs" such as sight, touch, and taste tell us what is present on the altar? If these bodily senses could "perceive" the Real Presence, he reflects, Christ would not have had to reveal it at the Last Supper: "For what my senses can themselves perceive / I need no revelation to believe" (1:91–92).

The chief question regarding the Lord's Supper that troubled English Protestants during the Restoration was whether Christ had the *power* to be really present both at the right hand of the Father and in the Lord's Supper simultaneously, even within the soul of the worthy receiver. In his poem Dryden uses the verbs "could" and "can" to phrase two climactic questions about Christ's power: "Could he" hide himself in the Incarnation and not be able to do the same in the sacrament? "If he can," then there is no need to make all this effort to deny the literal meaning of his words, "This is My Body":

> And if he can, why all this frantick pain
> To construe what his clearest words contain,
> And make a riddle what He made so plain?
>
> (1:138–40)

He urges the clarity and plainness of "This is My Body" as an argument for a literal reading of the text when he writes "his clearest words" and

"He made so plain." He makes belief in the Real Presence a matter of taking the Divine Word at his word.

Since the body of Christ concealed in the sacrament would be the same body the Apostles saw and touched after the Resurrection, the poet asks those who say that Christ has no power to be really there in the communion "Host" to explain how he came to have the power to pass through a closed door and join his disciples in John 20:19. He thinks that this Gospel text sheds light on Christ's ability to be bodily present with his Church:

> Can they who say the Host should be descry'd
> By sense, define a body glorify'd?
> Impassible, and penetrating parts?
> Let them declare by what mysterious arts
> He shot that body through th' opposing might
> Of bolts and barrs impervious to the light,
> And stood before his train confess'd in open sight.
>
> (1:92–99)

When Christ's risen body went through that door, the poet argues, "two bodies" occupied a "single place" at one time. So now, the same omnipotence that made him able to transcend physical laws on this occasion can also let him be present as "one body" in many "places" in the Eucharist: "And sure the same omnipotence as well / Can make one body in more places dwell" (1:102–3). Dryden confesses that Christ has the power to make his "one body" dwell in heaven and on earth, and also in every "Host" that is received, remaining "one body" in all places, completely present to each communicant.

Those who called the Real Presence an idol said that the miracles of Christ in the Gospel had been perceived by the eyes and hands of the witnesses; therefore the Real Presence should be perceived by the eyes and touch, too, not just the ears. Dryden dismisses this objection as "chaff that flies before the wind" (1:113), that is, something worthless, but he still responds, saying that during his ministry Christ worked miracles before eyewitnesses to assert his divinity. After his Resurrection, however, as St. Thomas the Apostle learned, he expected his followers to believe without seeing (Jn 20:29). Dryden is not denying that miracles have continued to occur, but he does deny that they must be visible to attest to the truth of the Christian mysteries. After the apostolic age, it became necessary for Christians to rely for the "mysterious things of faith" on "the Proponent, heav'n's authority" (1:121). The word "Proponent" here echoes the Scholastic term for the Church's authority in matters of faith: "Regula proponens." The poet explains that bodily senses are "scaffolding" that may be removed when the "building" gains a stronger foundation: "As when the building gains a surer stay, / We take th' unusefull scaffolding away" (1:124–25). This image of a "building" having attained a sure foundation in the Apostles' testimony evokes the image of the Church as a temple rising out of living stones and founded on "rock" (Eph. 2:20). In Canticles 4:4 and 8:10 the Bride is likewise a strong building with battlements, an image commentators applied both to the Church and the saintly soul.

We seem to witness the verge of Dryden's conversion when he invites us to join him and enter the "vessel" where Christ is "Pilot," that is, the Church where he is truly present to guide:

> Why chuse we then like *Bilanders* to creep
> Along the coast, and land in view to keep,
> When safely we may launch into the deep?
> In the same vessel which our Saviour bore
> Himself the Pilot, let us leave the shoar,
> And with a better guide a better world explore.
>
>   (1:128–33)

Earlier he had used the pronoun "I" when he asked if he could really believe in the Sacrament of the Altar. Now, standing on the gangplank of the vessel, he uses the pronoun "we," urging his readers to accompany him into the great ark of the Church. He explains that as a Protestant he navigated in a "Bilander," a small boat hugging the familiar English coastline. The phrase "land in view to keep" hints that fear of superstition or idolatry prevented him from launching into the "deep" of sacramental life. Indeed, in his earlier poem *Religio Laici* (1682), an apologia for his Protestant faith, he had completely ignored the mystery of the Lord's Supper, along with the other sacraments, even though he had earnestly acknowledged Christ as his redeemer and spoken highly of the ancient Fathers as guides in biblical exegesis. His idea of faith in that poem was very intellectual; it amounted to his working out the scriptural content of a saving faith under the auspices of his "mother," the national church. For him at that stage, Christ was not the intimate Bridegroom, but the Judge who would return to reward and punish him at the end of time. In *The Hind and the Panther,* however, Christ offers a loving embrace to the Church and the Soul, a mystical repose within the holy mysteries.

Looking back at the spiritual "anguish" of his former life, Dryden is relieved to find passage on an ocean-going vessel where Christ is the "Pilot." This image of the seaworthy ship links up with other images in the poem about the Bride's ocean domain reaching "all shoars" (2:551). Even the Panther concedes grudgingly that the Hind is mistress of the circling ocean, saying that the Penal Laws and Test Acts are necessary banks to stop the Hind's encroaching tides, that is, to repel missionaries sent to bring the sacraments to English Catholics (3:831). Although she claims the mastery of the seas for worldly trade, Dryden points out, England is confined to one coast in matters of faith: "To foreign lands no sound of Her is come" (1:404), and again, "Religion is the least of all our trade" (2:567). Since Christ commanded his Church to bring the good news to all nations, the poet rejoices that he is entering now a vessel with a global commerce, one that diffuses the Gospel "from Pole to Pole" (2:552).

Dryden's language is full of rich chords when he ponders the mystery of the "vessel" where Christ is "Pilot." The word "vessel" means at the same time a cup, a body, and a ship. For instance, in 2 Corinthians 4:7, St Paul calls bodies "vessels": "we have this treasure in earthen vessels." Thus, the *vessel* in Dryden's line, "in the same vessel which our Saviour bore" (1:131) is three things at once: first, it is the Holy Grail Christ lifted at the Last Supper, brought to England by Joseph of Arimathea; second, it is the Body of Christ that he bore as a veil to cloak his divinity; and third, it is the great seagoing ship of the Church that has carried Christ as its pilot throughout Christian history, the ship into which Dryden enters by taking communion. By using the word "vessel," then, Dryden can suggest that when he receives, he is received: when he eats Christ's body, he is taken into the Mystical Body of Christ, the vessel of the Church, and the old religion of England. Commenting on this motif in Canticles, Hugo of St. Victor writes, "God will enter in unto thee that thou mayest enter in unto Him," and Gilbert of Hoyland declares, "it makes but little difference whether thou enter into Him, or He to thee" (RFL, 122, 226).

Harking back to his last struggle before his conversion, Dryden recalls

reaching the decision point when he realized that his refusal to acknowledge the Real Presence on the altar amounted to refusing to take Christ at
his word: "To take up half on trust, and half to try, / Name it not faith,
but bungling bigottry" (1:141–42). He feared that if he persisted, he
would lose his faith in the other mysteries as well. Since he already acknowledged the Trinity and the Incarnation, he was like a merchant who
would pay out great sums to his creditors and then declare bankruptcy
for a tiny debt: "For who wou'd break with heav'n, and wou'd not break
for all?" (1:143–45). The word "break" here means "to separate from," but
it also connotes "to go bankrupt." He would plunge his soul into ruin for
a small debt if he balked at taking Christ at his word, that the Bread of the
Altar is his very flesh.

In the end, the poet decides that the literal meaning of "This is My
Body" is the safest assurance of eternal life: "Faith is the best ensurer of
thy bliss; / The Bank above must fail before the venture miss" (1:148–49).
Unless heaven should go bankrupt, the reward of eternal life is promised
to those who eat Christ's body and drink his blood (Jn 6). Thus he has all
to gain and nothing to lose by taking literally what Christ said plainly
about the bread of life. In making his choice, he seems to glance at two
lines in "Adoro te devote":

Credo quidquid dixit Dei filius:
Nil hoc verbo veritatis verius.

Either the Word speaks truly, or there is nothing true.

After revealing the last steps of his conversion, Dryden later returns to
this subject in a very poignant, clearly autobiographical passage (3:290–
305) and describes what seems to be his first communion. He tells the
story indirectly but the intense emotion breaks through. In these lines,
the Hind dramatizes how she brings one of her "sons" (i.e., Dryden himself) to conversion and to the embrace of Christ by a process of self-emptying. She tells this "son" who has suffered "from ill tongues" and who
"flounders at the cross" that he must now place his good name, his "darling fame" on the altar of sacrifice:

That fame, that darling fame, make that thy sacrifice.
'Tis nothing thou hast giv'n, then add thy tears
For a long race of unrepenting years:
'Tis nothing yet; yet all thou hast to give,

Then add those *may-be* years thou hast to live.
Yet nothing still: then poor, and naked come,
Thy father will receive his unthrift home,
And thy blest Saviour's bloud discharge the
   mighty sum.

(3:290–97)

In the first lines of this passage, as in peripheral vision, we see the offertory of the Mass begin. Though the bread and wine of human sufferings have no intrinsic value for atonement, they are placed on the altar. The Hind tells her "son" that his suffering from defamation, however painful to him, amounts to "nothing" as an offering to God. Yet she does not tell him to remove his "darling fame" from the altar of sacrifice. Rather, she urges him to add on top of it his tears for all his "unrepenting years." But this, too, is "nothing." Neither his suffering nor his repentance is a sufficient price to ransom his soul and merit divine love. So then she urges him to pile on top of his offering those "*may-be* years" he has to live as a penitent. Even so, the heaped-up offering of all his life and soul is "nothing yet," though all he has to give. Like the Prodigal Son, he stands before his Father empty-handed now. He has "nothing" more to give, nothing worthy of the divine love he lost by worldliness and sin, a love he cannot regain by any human works.

In Canticles 8:7 a parallel use of the word "nothing" occurs. We read in the 1615 Douay version that "if a man shal give al the substance of his house for love, as nothing he shal despise it." Dryden seems to have had an eye on this text in Canticles because the commentaries on the verse illuminate his lines beautifully. For example, Cassiodorus remarks that "the Saints gave up all for the love of Christ, and yet they seemed to themselves to give up nothing." And Hugo of St. Victor addresses Love in these moving words: "it may be that thou exceedest my narrow means, and thy price is not in my power. Yet I will give that I have, and all that I have, and will barter all my house for thee, and when I have given all, I will count it as nothing" (RFL, 365).

At this point in Dryden's poem, when the Hind's son feels he has "nothing" to offer in exchange for love, a miracle occurs. The self-emptying of humility has prepared him to be filled with love at communion. He has passed through *exinanition,* the psychological equivalent of the emptying of the substance of bread and wine in the consecration.

Like those sacramental forms, he looks the same, but he is now a vessel ready to receive Christ. The Hind-Bride urges her "son" to come forward as he is, "poor and naked," and let his "blest Saviour" receive and redeem him: "Thy father will receive his unthrift home, / And thy blest Saviour's bloud discharge the mighty sum." With the words "thy father" and "his unthrift" Dryden alludes a second time in his poem to the Parable of the Prodigal Son. Earlier he had focused on the Father and had used the parable to highlight the Hind's forgiving the Panther for past persecutions. But now he focuses on the Prodigal Son. He uses the story as an example of the trustful surrender of *anima*, the soul coming forth from the wilderness of sin into the gracious embrace of Christ.

The return of the Prodigal evokes, of course, the great welcoming feast that his Father gives. On Luke 15:23, the Douay version has a note drawn from St. Augustine pointing out that the feast celebrating the Prodigal Son's return is a figure of the blessed Sacrament of the Altar. Dryden likewise speaks of "thy blest Saviour's blood" as the explicit atonement and the implicit sacramental food awaiting the Hind's "son." This blood is the embrace of love which the Father gives. Moreover, the human offering that was worth "nothing" until now has been transformed by being united with the sufferings of Christ and those of the saints in the Mystical Body. And so, when the new convert's "darling fame" is assailed henceforth, he feels he is not alone. He can acknowledge meekly that "suff'ring from ill tongues he bears no more / Than what his Sovereign bears, and what his Saviour bore" (3:304–5). Dryden thus parallels the Prodigal's homecoming with the convert's partaking of the Eucharist. The parallel holds as the Prodigal and the Hind's "son" both receive and are received. The Prodigal receives the feast, and is received into the bosom of his Father, while the convert receives the redeeming Blood and is received into the bosom of the Bride, the Mystical Body of Christ.

Thus the poet has borrowed from the allegory of Canticles the story of the bridal Soul's surrender to Christ and her rapturous repose in his embrace. This was long regarded as the tropological sense of Canticles. From the third century to the seventeenth, the story of the soul as the Bride of Canticles—searching, not finding, being found, embracing, and resting—was held in very high esteem among Christian mystics like St. John of the Cross and St. Teresa of Avila. By borrowing this paradigm from Canticles, Dryden has been able to link the motif of his private conversion firmly to the larger design of *The Hind and the Panther*, the design of the three "ascents" of the Universal Bride from the desert of persecution to the light of freedom in England, and of the wooing of the English Church to return, return to the Universal Bride and be restored to the sweet-breathed melodious authority she once had, the power of "Pan-thera" to gather irresistibly into one family and one garden all the denizens of the wilderness.

Modern Freedom

CHAPTER I

The Repeal Campaign, 1685–1688

In Canticles, the Bride declares, "I am blacke but beautiful" and complains that "the sonnes of my mother have fought against me" (1:5–6). A number of ancient Fathers and medieval Doctors interpreted her first statement to mean that the Church on earth is "black with suffering and persecution, and nevertheless comely in holiness and reward." They interpreted her second statement to mean that the Jewish Church had tried to crush "the infant Church" of Christ at its birth, but became instead the involuntary means of its worldwide expansion (RFL, 21, 24).

This double aspect of the Bride of Canticles is reflected in the two halves of Dryden's poem: in the first half the Hind is the universal Bride, revealed in the full daylight of her doctrine, while in the second half she is the harmless infant Church in England, overshadowed with persecution by the Church of the Law but intended by Divine Providence to inaugurate from afar the worldwide kingdom of peace. Dryden's use of the Aeneas myth in the second half of the poem reinforces the idea of a small, vulnerable start to the greatest of destinies. Dryden figures the Catholic party in England as pious Aeneas, restored to his ancient mother country but threatened by Queen Amata, who incites the rude populace with false fears to make war against the tiny, harmless Trojan camp.

The Lady of Canticles laments that the keepers of the walls have "strucke me, and wounded me" and taken away "my cloke," or outer veil

(5:7). In ancient times some expositors said that this was the Bride of Christ persecuted by pagans; other expositors said that this was the Jewish Church wounded to the heart by the rebukes of the Bride of Christ and stripped of her cloak of the Law (RFL, 230–33). Both Church-Brides are wounded in the second half of Dryden's poem. On the one hand, the Hind is hurt when she offers friendship, for the Panther responds with threats of imminent persecution. On the other hand, the Panther is sharply wounded by the Hind's rebukes and stripped of her cloak of justice: first, she is "gauled" and tries to hide that she is "shrewdly pain'd" by the Hind's words about her Wolflike behavior (3:131–33); second, she is stripped bare of her pretenses when she admits that "interest," not "conscience," makes her hostile to the Hind (3:825–30) and that the Test Acts she supports against Catholics are "laws unjust" (3:836).

For its length, part 3 constitutes the second half of the poem. In this part, the Hind is one particular church within the universal Bride; she is the English Catholic Church of the 1680s. When the poet portrays the Hind as both universal and particular, plural and singular, age-old and modern, he follows a common practice among Catholics; for example, Serenus Cressy observes that Stillingfleet's attack cannot pierce the "Rock" of the universal Church but can indeed "pierce into the very bowells of the Persons, fortunes and conditions of English Catholicks, whose destruction he seems to design"; John Gother also speaks of the "Mother teeming Church" as bringing forth "particular Churches" that are "integrally composed" by subordination and have a "central radical unity" different from state-imposed "uniformity."[1]

A sudden change of mood, a declaration of hostility on the part of the Panther, occurs at the start of part 3. In part 2, when the Hind revealed her identity in the great "I am she" (2:398), the Panther fell down awestruck, became drenched with dewdrops, and agreed to be the guest of the Hind; but in part 3 the Panther turns against the Hind with jealous rage and insists that the Test Acts should exclude Catholics from any share in public employment. In part 2 the debate was set against the backdrop of Monmouth's Rebellion (2:655), hostilities which at first brought

---

1. [Serenus Cressy], "To the Reader," *Fanaticism Fanatically Imputed* ([Douay?], 1672) ; [John Gother], *An Agreement between the Church of England and Church of Rome, Evinced from the Concertation of Some of Her Sons with Their Brethren the Dissenters* (London: Henry Hills, 1687), 63–68.

Anglicans and Catholics together against the insurrectionists; but in part 3 the conversation is set on or after 7 June 1685, when the House of Commons passed a unanimous resolution asking James II to proclaim the enforcement of all the laws against Catholics and other nonconformists. At this point the Panther turned against the Hind by insisting that the least yielding on the Penal Laws and Test Acts would re-establish Catholicism, that is, allow the old religion to regain its first rights. According to the French ambassador Barrillon, the king blamed the Anglican bishops for this resolution which made him look ridiculous and put him in danger.[2]

Complaining bitterly about Catholics in public employments, the Panther accuses the king of having "cast" her "away," while letting the Hind bask, like a butterfly, in the sunlight of his patronage: "You, like the gawdy fly, your wings display, / And sip the sweets, and bask in your Great Patron's day" (3:66–67). She repeats several times that the Hind will have only one "day" of "flaunting fortune in the *Lyon*'s court" (3:136–38) and that James will not rule long: "The Sun (already from the scales declin'd) / Gave little hopes of better days behind" (3:505–6). Indeed, this is the theme of her tale, in which the Catholic Swallows "feather'd well" their "nest" by taking public employments and foolishly hoped "that heav'n some miracle might show, / And, for their sakes, the sun shou'd backward go" (3:436, 533–34), that is, they hoped the king would live fifteen more years, as in Isaiah 38.7. The Panther's eagerness for the end of the present reign makes the Hind rebuke her: "The sun-shine that offends the purblind sight, / Had some their wishes, it wou'd soon be night" (3:659–60).

The Panther's image of a sun that creates light and warmth out of season can also be found in Canticles. When the Bride asks the Divine Shepherd, "Shew me o thou, whom my soule loveth, where thou feedest, where thou lyest in the midday" (1:7), St. Bernard sees a reference to the "perennial solstice" caused by God's shining face in heaven, where "winter alone is over and gone" (RFL, 28–30). Thus, the Panther uses imagery that undercuts her: first she shows James II as that constant sunlight evocative of divine love in Canticles, and second she depicts the Catholic party as basking in that light in the manner of a butterfly, that is, an

---

2. Letter from Barrillon to Louis XIV, cited in French in Charles James Fox, *Appendix to a History of the Early Part of the Reign of James the Second* (London: William Miller, 1808), lxxxi and xci.

embodiment of Psyche or the soul. Elsewhere, when she wants to show Catholics as dangerous, she likewise undercuts herself by comparing the Hind to Swallows and to gentle Aeneas. By this means, Dryden shows the reader that the Panther is truly "dim, and doted" (3:152), lacking internal coherence in her speech.

At first, the Hind tries to pacify the Panther and repeats mildly that there is no cause for alarm, because only a small number of Catholics have been excused from the Test Acts, and their employments take nothing away from the Panther: "But much more just your jealousie would show, / If others good were injury to you" (3:88–89); the Catholics "glean the fallings of the loaded wain," so their "mite" cannot decrease the Panther's harvest (3:103, 113). In the word "glean," the Hind glances at the biblical Ruth, who, like Aeneas and the Bride of Canticles, is at first a vulnerable and afflicted guest in the land of promise; yet since Ruth is the ancestor of David and Christ, she inaugurates from afar the messianic kingdom. The Hind's meekness only inflames the Panther, who refuses to recognize "*Shiloh*" when he "comes" to her in the person of his Bride (3:1258) and instead summons her natural enemy to her assistance, without realizing that she herself will be the prey. Thus part 3 evokes Christ's prophecy to the Jewish Church, when she calls in the Roman Eagle to prey on him: "thy enemies shall cast a trench about thee, and compass thee round . . . because thou hast not known the time of thy visitation" (Lk 19:43–44).

The declaration of war in part 3 obliges the Hind to utter a series of sharp rebukes against the Panther for her support of the Test Acts, the political ground of the new hostilities. In her tale, the Hind justifies the alliance between Catholic and Protestant nonconformists for mutual defense, an alliance which, in Dryden's design, parallels the one that Aeneas forged with his former enemies the Greeks, when Queen Amata had inflamed the barbarians to war against the tiny Trojan camp. This alliance of former enemies is what produced the rich and varied anti-Test literature of 1685–1688, the literature that establishes the political context of *The Hind and the Panther*.

First, however, the campaign to repeal the Test Acts must be distinguished from the older, more popular campaign for toleration. The campaign to "take off the Test" was from the beginning about eligibility for government employment, military commissions, and university degrees, regardless of religion. On the other hand, the campaign for toleration was about securing permission for nonconformists to worship privately while the laws against them remained unenforced, but unrepealed. Those in the repeal campaign warned that mere toleration would leave nonconformists without full citizenship, and they were right. For when Parliament passed the Toleration Act of 1689 that gave most Protestant dissenters freedom of worship in England, it still left them as criminals under the law. We see evidence of this in Blackstone's *Commentaries* (1770), where we read "that the penal laws against Dissenters had only been suspended by the Toleration Act and that the fundamental illegality of Nonconformity had not changed in the succeeding eighty years."[3] In one history of the Test Acts, we learn that judges before 1789 held that "the Toleration Act only exempted from penalties, but did not remove the crime."[4]

In Dryden's poem the Hind asserts without being contradicted that the anti-royalist "sects" wooed James II when he first came to the throne and offered him treasure "to espouse their part," but he chose to lean on the Panther's party, which soon proved a "broken reed" (3:796–98). After the hostile resolution in Commons in June 1685, James tried to win the Panther over until 1686, and then he began looking for allies among the Protestant nonconformists. In her tale, the Hind evokes ancient biblical prophecy when she depicts this amazing alliance. She portrays the king as "a Plain good Man" obliged by his word and by law to maintain the Anglican Pigeons: "bound by Promise, he supports their Cause, / As Corporations priviledg'd by Laws" (3:953–54). However, he has his own tame Poultry behind the House, who receive from his hands a "Modicum" of daily grain, that is, of public employments by his prerogative. Although these Catholics Birds are few and "barely for his use," the Pigeons say there is a "Sheaf in ev'ry single Grain" they get (3:1002), their jealousy thus creating an imaginary multiplication of loaves. As a result of their

3. William Blackstone, *Commentaries on the Laws of England* (1770), 5 vols., ed. W. D. Lewis (Philadelphia, 1898), 4:1463–64; cited in Thomas W. Davis's "Introduction" to *Committees for Repeal of the Test and Corporation Acts: Minutes 1786 and 1827–8* (London: London Record Society, 1978), viii. The latter work will be cited hereafter as *Repeal Committee Minutes.*

4. [Samuel Heywood], *The Right of Protestant Dissenters to a Compleat Toleration Asserted; Containing an Historical Account of the Test Laws, and Shewing the Injustice, Inexpediency, and Folly of the Sacramental Test, as Now Imposed, with Respect to Protestant Dissenters,* 2d ed. (London: J. Johnson, 1789), 35–36. Heywood was a judge and a leader of the Protestant repeal committee in the 1780s.

self-torment, the Pigeons beat the young Chickens, insist on their eating a poisonous weed (the Test), and employ slanders to incite the other animals to use violence against them. The Farmer now reflects that if his tame Birds suffer so much from the Pigeons, then the wild Birds on his farm must have suffered, too. He deems "that Proof a Measure to the rest" and concludes that his wild Protestant Fowl "too unjustly were opprest." And so he "makes all Birds of ev'ry Sect / Free of his Farm" and promises to protect them equally, leaving the Pigeons their "Wealth and State," but not their "licence to oppress" (3:1233–46).

In the prophetic vision that ends the Hind's tale, the wild "Republick Birds" are joined in "common Int'rest" with weak "Domestick Birds" and live side by side under the protection of "th' Imperial owner" (3:1250–55). This imagery and rhetoric derives from Ezekiel 17:23, where the prophet declares that in messianic times "all fowl of every wing" shall dwell together in the shade of a "great cedar." Earlier in part 3 the Hind had called James the "imperial Cedar" (3:704). The joining of wild and tame fowl, then, is a sign to the English that the reign of James is a harbinger of the messianic peace that is to culminate sacred history. The political context of this imagery in the Hind's tale is that James, in 1685, had stopped the persecution of those whose families had served his father in the Civil Wars, which was a way of giving relief to "His own Domestick Birds" the Catholics, but on purely political grounds. Meanwhile, the laws continued to be enforced against the dissenting "Republick Birds." In 1686, however, as the anti-Catholic rhetoric of the Anglican Panther's party kept growing, James began to extenuate the former conduct of sectarians, his "Fowl of Nature," saying that they, too, must have been "unjustly" oppressed.

Foremost among the "Fowl of Nature" in the repeal campaign of 1685–1688 were William Penn, Henry Care, and Giles Shute, all of whom attacked the Test Acts in plain, vigorous, battle-hymn rhetoric. Penn took the front rank in the struggle, partly out of friendship for a king who had released over a thousand Quakers from prison. A new note was struck when Protestant dissenters made common cause with the Catholics for a limited political goal, even while each side held tight to its condemnation of the religious view of the other. William Penn expressed the driving principle behind the coalition in these words: "the Question is not who is in the right in Opinion, but whether he is not in Practice in the wrong,

that for such an Opinion deprives his Neighbour of his common Right?"[5]
Penn's idea is that a citizen has a "common Right" to public employment
regardless of his religious tenets. By contrast, John Locke wanted most
nonconformists to have freedom of worship, but not access to public employment. This is not surprising, since Locke was the personal secretary
of Anthony Ashley Cooper, earl of Shaftesbury, at the time when the latter spearheaded the campaign for the enactment of the Test Acts of 1673
and 1678.

The new note heard in Penn can also be heard in part 1 of *The Hind
and the Panther*, where Dryden gives no theological quarter to Puritans
and minces no words about their misdoings in the Interregnum, yet he
pleads, even so, that they should be entitled to again enjoy their "native
walks" in peace after the rigorous enforcement of the laws against them in
1683–1685. He indicates his belief that they should be punished only for
criminal conduct, not for their religious tenets:

> Of all the tyrannies on humane kind
> The worst is that which persecutes the mind.
> Let us but weigh at what offence we strike,
> 'Tis but because we cannot think alike.
> In punishing of this, we overthrow
> The laws of nations and of nature too.
>   (1:239–44)

The poet calls the English parliament tyrannical here for penalizing nonconformists for no other "crime" than their beliefs. Similarly, in *Britannia Rediviva*, he writes against the Test Acts: "No force the Free-born
Spirit can constrain, / But Charity, and great Examples gain" (301–2). Religion, he implies, should not be maintained by coercive civil statutes, but
by fervent teaching, acts of compassion, and saintly example.

Within the small, choice band of those fighting to repeal the Test Acts
there were a few high-church Anglicans, among them Nathaniel Johnston, James Paston, and two bishops—Samuel Parker and Thomas
Cartwright. Dryden takes note of these episcopal friends in his preface to
The Hind and the Panther, when he says that "there are some of the
Church by Law Establish'd, who envy not Liberty of Conscience to Dissenters; as being well satisfied that, according to their own Principles,

---

5. [William Penn], *Good Advice to the Church of England . . . to Abolish the Penal
Laws and Tests* (London, Andrew Sowle, 1687), 58.

they ought not to persecute them. Yet these, by reason of their fewness, I could not distinguish from the Numbers of the rest with whom they are Embodied in one common Name." At this time, the campaigners for repeal were using the phrase "liberty of conscience," as Dryden does here, to mean "taking off the Test." Their risky strategy was to refuse to distinguish the Test Acts from the fearsome Elizabethan and Jacobean statutes against nonconformity. They insisted that the Test Acts were an intrinsic part of former persecution and had to fall with it.

The idea behind the repeal campaign was that a civil test, rather than a religious test, should be sufficient for citizenship. This appears to be what Dryden proposes here: "Themselves unharmfull, let them live unharm'd; / Their jaws disabl'd, and their claws disarm'd" (1:299–300). By his use of the words "disabled" and "disarmed," he implies that so long as subjects pledge not to overthrow the established government by force or conspiracy, they should be left in peace about their religious ideas. On this common ground of a civil test, citizens of the most widely divergent tenets could meet. However, the defenders of the Test Acts used the terms "civil" and "religious" indistinguishably at that time. For example, one of them called the oath of supremacy, by which the king was accepted as supreme head of the Church, a good "Civil Test," while another called the sacramental test for public office one of those "Religious Laws" to keep the pope and slavery out of England.[6]

The repeal campaign of 1685–1688 based one of its main arguments on the ancient British constitution, challenging the modern Test Acts as unconstitutional. Article 6 of the U.S. Constitution simply makes explicit what the repealers said was already in the unwritten, ancient law of Britain. In 1787 the American Founders declared in Article 6 that "no religious test shall ever be required as a qualification to any office or public trust under the United States." So important was this article that it was placed not among the amendments but among the first articles of the Constitution. Thus, the Congress of the United States was forbidden to imitate the parliament of Charles II and give a single church party a monopoly over public employments and the military. Article 6 is the kind of constitutional guarantee that the repealers wanted to see enacted in the

---

6. [Henry Maurice], *The Project for Repealing the Penal Laws and Tests* [London, 1688], 30; [Samuel Johnson], *Letter from a Freeholder*, 2–3. Maurice's book was written in 1685.

parliament of 1689. It was for this reason that they tried to persuade the electorate, up to the eve of the 1688 revolution, to send to parliament only those who would "take off the Test."

A modern historian acknowledges that the Toleration Act of 1689 "specifically reinforced" the Test Acts and confirmed Protestant nonconformists in their second-class citizenship.[7] A 1689 commemorative medal highlights the central importance of the Test Acts in the revolution: on the obverse side is a bust of William III, and on the reverse an image of Liberty holding a paper in her hand with the word "*TEST*" upon it, the legend stating that the Test was what preserved Britain from slavery.[8] The idea of the Test as the liberty for which the revolution of 1688 was fought is premised, of course, on the supposed threat of "popery and slavery" if the Test Acts were repealed. Students of the Restoration are well advised to entertain some skepticism about the alleged danger of "popery." The philosopher David Hume, no friend of Catholicism, gave this shrewd warning: "the violent animosity, which had been excited against the Catholics in general, made the public swallow the grossest absurdities when they accompanied an accusation of those religionists." Concerning the panic of 1678–1682 over an imaginary Popish Plot, he adds: "in all history, it will be difficult to find such another instance of popular frenzy and bigoted delusion." Ten years later, he sees the same bigotry making the populace swallow the "incredible" story that James II had made a commoner's bastard his royal heir so that the child might "after his death support the Catholic religion in his dominions." It was surely a "singular" thing, Hume observes, that "the same calumny" proven false in 1682 should be "renewed with such success" in 1688.[9] Indeed, it was the major reason for inviting William of Orange into England, that Princess Mary had been disinherited by a "suppositious child" brought into the queen's bed inside a warming-pan, while about forty witnessess stood in the room. At first, William of Orange promised a full investigation, but then he was careful not to carry it out. Thus did the 1688 revolution save the Test from being repealed and preserve English liberty—but not for all.

7. W. A. Speck, *Reluctant Revolutionaries* (Oxford: Oxford University Press, 1988), 187.

8. Paul Rapin de Thoyras, *The Metallick History of the Reigns of King William III and Queen Mary* (London: John and Paul Knapton, 1747), 6, Medal #9.

9. David Hume, *The History of England* (London: Baynes, Priestley, 1822), 8:67, 79, 263. This slander was first mentioned in the *Observator,* a weekly, August 23, 1682.

CHAPTER 2

Three Test Acts and Seven Grounds for Repeal

It was the Cavalier parliament, suspicious of the Catholic tone of Charles II's court, that passed the three test statutes as a security for the newly settled church and state. The Corporation Act, the first Test Act (13 Charles II, c. 1, sect. 12), was passed in December 1661 and excluded nonconformists from public employment at the local level. From this time forward, mayors, aldermen, recorders, common-councilmen, bailiffs, and town clerks were to abjure the Covenant and kneel to receive the eucharistic sacrament before taking office. Next, the Test Act of 1673 (25 Charles II, c. 2) excluded nonconformists from public office at the national level, that is, from civil or military employment under the Crown. Now sheriffs, stewards, justices, officers of the mint, officers of the navy, deputies, treasury officials, public notaries, heralds, messengers at arms, collectors of customs and excise, and schoolmasters were required to take the Test. A soldier serving at land had to take the oaths before his first muster and then kneel for the sacrament before his second muster. Some inferior civil officers were exempted, but theirs were places of burden rather than of profit or honor, such as being an overseer of the poor. Finally, the third Test Act of 1678 (30 Charles II. Stat. 2) drove the last remaining Catholic

122

peers from the House of Lords by requiring them to swear, among other things, that the Mass was superstitious and idolatrous.[1]

Few people realize that the Test for public office required two entirely different actions: the first was an oath abjuring the belief in transubstantiation, a term which in that age (as we will show) had come to mean the same thing as the Real Presence; the second was kneeling before witnesses to receive the sacrament of the national church. The first action excluded Catholics, while the second one excluded some Presbyterians and most Independents. Regarding the second action, it should be noted that *kneeling* for communion was a posture that Puritans had condemned as idolatry for more than a century. For them it signified adoration of the Real Presence of Christ, whereas Anglicans argued that this posture was only intended to signify humble thanks.

The Test was thus an instrument designed to cut off from public employment the nonconformists at both ends of the religious spectrum. It gave a monopoly over political power and patronage to a central coalition of high-church Anglicans, conformist Presbyterians, and Hobbists who would go along with any religion imposed by parliament. The 1673 Test stipulated that a candidate for employment under the Crown had to "receive the sacrament of the Lord's supper, according to the usage of the church of *England*," which meant kneeling. Two witnesses had to certify that the candidate had taken the Test in the year prior to his assuming public employment, under penalty of forfeiture of office and the payment of a fine of five hundred pounds (an enormous sum), and being "disabled from thenceforth to sue or use any action, bill, plaint, or information in course of law, or to prosecute any suit in any court of equity, or to be guardian of any child, or executor or administrator of any person, or capable of any legacy or deed of gift, or to bear any office." It is hard to know which of the two penalties inspired more horror, the prospect of being barred from any recourse to law or that of having to face a five-hundred-pound fine.

Under the 1673 Test Act, the candidate, besides taking the oaths of supremacy and allegiance and kneeling to receive the communion of the established church, had to abjure solemnly this specifically Catholic belief:

1. *The Statutes at Large, from the Twelfth Year of King Charles II.* [1660] *to the Last Year of King James II. Inclusive,* ed. Danby Pickering (Cambridge and London: Charles Bathurst, 1763), 8:389–95, 427–32.

I, A. B., do declare, That I do believe that there is not any transubstantiation in the sacrament of the Lord's supper, or in the elements of bread and wine, at or after the consecration thereof by any person whatsoever.

The Test of 1678 went even further, for now the candidate had to swear that Catholicism was idolatry. This third Test required each member of Parliament to take the following oath before a "full house" of peers or members of Commons at the start of each succeeding parliament:

I, A. B., do solemnly and sincerely in the presence of God profess, testify and declare, That I do believe that in the sacrament of the Lord's supper there is not any transubstantiation of the elements of bread and wine into the body and blood of Christ at or after the consecration thereof by any *person* whatsoever: (2) And that the invocation or adoration of the virgin Mary or any other saint, and the sacrifice of the mass, as they are now used in the church of Rome, are superstitious and idolatrous. (3) And I do solemnly in the presence of God profess, testify and declare, That I do make this declaration, and every part thereof, in the plain and ordinary sense of the words read unto me, as they are commonly understood by English protestants, without any evasion, equivocation or mental reservation whatsoever, and without any dispensation already granted me for this purpose by the pope, or any other authority or person whatsoever, or without any hope of any such dispensation from any person or authority whatsoever, or without thinking that I am or can be acquitted before God or man, or absolved of this declaration or any part thereof, although the pope, or any other person or persons, or power whatsoever, should dispense with or annul the same, or declare that it was null or void from the beginning.[2]

The insinuation in the second half of the oath is that Catholics have dispensations to perjure themselves. One spokesman for Catholics later asks "[B]ut where are these papal dispensations?" and replies: "[T]hey are to be found in the libraries of *British Controvertists,* in monthly mag[azine]s, in weekly journals, and in the mouths of public orators." He laments that a "prejudice" which European Protestants had long ago discarded still prevails in eighteenth-century Britain in "its full and obnoxious force."[3] It was surely to overturn this prejudice that James II proceeded so urgently to give Englishmen an experience of Catholics in office. In Dryden's poem,

2. Heywood, *The Right of Protestant Dissenters,* 14; *The Statutes at Large,* 8:392, 428.
3. Nicholas Lord Viscount Taaffe, *Observations on Affairs in Ireland from the Settlement in 1691* (London: W. Griffin, 1766), 22.

when the Lion commands the Hind to take a "sober draught" of royal patronage at the watering place in 1685, the English sects are "amaz'd" to discover that a Catholic in public office is no ten-horned "monster" (1:537).

A contemporary of Dryden tells us that during the reign of James II the Test Acts became the "Table-talk" of England. They were "almost a National Text for all People to Comment and Preach upon."[4] All the chief arguments raised against the Test in 1685–1688 — the same ones that resurfaced in the repeal campaigns of 1786–1790 and 1827 — are to be found in *The Hind and the Panther*. They are located briefly in part 1, when Dryden pleads for mercy for Protestant nonconformists, despite what happened in the Interregnum (1:235–300), and in part 3 when the Hind launches into a veritable battery of arguments and tells the tale of the Pigeons to illustrate the injustice of the Test. When her words are examined in the context of the literature for repeal of the Test, it is clear that the Hind in part 3 is the Catholic party engaged in the struggle for repeal.

The Hind deploys six major arguments also found in the other literature of the 1685–1688 repeal campaign. Her seventh argument is based on Catholic pamphlets that criticized the revision of the communion service in the 1662 edition of the Book of Common Prayer. These are her six arguments: first, an appeal to compassion, because the Test incapacitates nonconformists from public employment for no crime at all; second, an appeal to native rights, because the Test takes away an Englishman's immemorial birthright to serve his country and prevents the king from choosing him as the best qualified person for an office; third, an appeal to the property rights of peers, because the statute of 1678 robs Catholic noblemen of their seats in the House of Lords which had been inherited from time immemorial with their titles and their estates; fourth, an appeal to the European context, because the English Test is harsher than the Dutch one, and because nonconformists are as badly off in England under the penal statutes and Test Acts as the Huguenots are after the Revocation of the Edict of Nantes; fifth, an appeal to royalism, because the Test was designed to put the king and his friends in danger by branding Catholics as idolaters; and sixth, an appeal to piety, because the Test contains an

---

4. Giles Shute, *A New Naked Truth; or, The Sandy Foundation of the Sacramental Test Shaken, by a Warning-Piece Discharged from Heaven against All Sorts of Persecutors* (London: George Larkin, 1688), 3–4.

oath against the Real Presence devised by secular men, and because it is a sacrilege to offer communion merely as a test for secular employment. This final argument about sacrilege resurfaced in 1827 and persuaded the Anglican bishops to vote unanimously for repeal, even though ultra-Tories were still defending the Test exactly as they had in Dryden's day, calling it the bulwark of the establishment and warning that its repeal was revolutionary.[5]

The above-listed arguments are almost all found in the following memorandum that James Bertie, earl of Abingdon, made of his interview with James II on 18 November 1687, a few months after *The Hind and the Panther* appeared. When the earl of Abingdon told the king that he was not "prejudiced" in favor of the Test, James II asked him if he would "hear reason and be convinced." Abingdon welcomed such an opportunity,

and then his Majesty said, these tests were against his prerogative, for they debarred him of the use of his subjects. Instancing that some Church of England men had pretended those tests, to excuse themselves from serving him etc. Secondly they were against the peers, by excluding some from their votes in Parliament, and thirdly against the people, by debarring them the choice of representatives. And lastly, they declared him an Idolater. . . . He then fell upon his declaration, and the sincerity of his desires, that all persons might live lovingly and quietly. Declaring how much he abhorred persecution, and said the Church of England had always been a persecuting Church. . . . He said he had delivered twelve hundred Quakers out of prison. . . . [W]as it not as bad for us to send men to prison, and take away their goods for conscience, as for him [Louis XIV] to quarter six dragoons upon them? . . . I told his Majesty he would find great difficulties in this matter, because that he knew his neighbour on the other side the water [Louis XIV] had broke through all laws and promises, so that nobody knew what to trust to. The King said he knew that, but could not tell how to help it. As for his own opinion, it had been always otherwise.[6]

In this scene, the king appeals to compassion and to the property rights of peers; he mentions how the slander of idolatry embedded in the 1678 Test, as well as in the earlier parliamentary discussions related to the 1673

5. Raymond Gibson Cowherd, *Protestant Dissenters in English Politics* (Philadelphia: University of Pennsylvania Press, 1942), 41.

6. "James [Bertie] Earl of Abingdon's Discourse with King James the Second, Nov. 18th, 1687, from His Own Memorandum of It," in *H. M. C. Lindsey*, ed. C. G. O. Bridgeman and J. C. Walker (London: Historical Manuscript Commission, 1942), 270–72.

Test, undermines his kingship; and he alludes to the European context by contrasting his own treatment of nonconformists with Louis XIV's persecution of the Huguenots. The argument about sacrilege is not mentioned here but it is fully developed in the king's memoirs. In reply to the king's plea, the earl of Abingdon defends the Test exactly as Dryden's Panther does, insisting that his "conscience" and his "interest" are both concerned in it. Like others in the church party, Abingdon calls the Test and the penal laws against nonconformity "the bulwarks of our religion."

Besides using these six arguments, Dryden also provides the Hind with a unique seventh argument, about which he might (as historiographer royal) have had privy information. He has the Hind suggest, at the start of part 2, that the origin of the Test was a secret quid pro quo between the government and the Savoy Convocation of the clergy at the start of the Restoration. In December 1661 the Anglican clergy consented to restore to the Book of Common Prayer a Puritan rubric from the days of Edward VI. After this rubric denying the Real Presence was inserted, many Presbyterians were suddenly willing to take the sacrament in the newly settled Church of England. At the same time, parliament passed the Corporation Act, which required kneeling for the sacrament as a test for local office. The Hind speaks of these mutual concessions as the secret adultery of Panther and Wolf, of high-church Anglicans and conformist Presbyterians. As we will show, the Panther admits that she mated with the Wolf when she inserted that rubric, but she pleads that she did not consent, but instead was forced to take this action.

One may well ask why Dryden puts all these arguments against the Test in the mouth of the Hind. Could he not make these points in his own poetic voice, just as he narrates the history of the Reformation in part 1? Evidently, he wanted these arguments to have spiritual authority, so he has the Hind make them, she who embodies ancient faith in modern times. Throughout *The Hind and the Panther* it is apparent that Dryden thinks that political victory, in the form of repeal of the Test Acts, may be one or more generations away. Nevertheless, he sees clearly that a spiritual victory is within easy reach. Even if the Test remains statutory law for a time, he wants to prove by argument that it is a grave injustice. Indeed, he has the Hind present the Test as something far worse than a man-made prohibition; it is *malum in se*, evil in itself, and therefore the king in all justice is obliged to dispense from it.

Dryden has the Hind use the word "repeal" in such a way that she vindicates the justice of the repeal campaign of 1685–1688. She tells the Panther not to blame the "first Reformers" for all those "bloudy" Penal Laws, because she now has a choice whether "to keep" or repeal them: "'Tis plain, that not repealing you allow" (3:695–97). She also says that the Panther clings to the unrighteous Test Acts only to wreak an unchristian revenge: "Who would not now repeal would persecute" (3:854). In her tale, too, the Hind depicts the Pigeons as crying aloud "to Persecute" by refusing to allow any "rigour of the Laws to be releas'd" (3:1216).

In part 3 the Hind wins a series of spiritual victories in the debate over the Test. The first victory, which plainly shows the justice of the repeal campaign, occurs when the Hind strips the cloak off the Church of the Law and gets her to admit frankly that the Test Acts are "laws unjust":

> Think not my judgment leads me to comply
> With laws unjust, but hard necessity:
> Imperious need which cannot be withstood
> Makes ill authentick, for a greater good.
>   (3:835–38)

In these lines, the Panther says that her "Imperious need" for security requires her to use "laws unjust" as means to that end. In her response, the Hind reminds the Panther about keeping faith in Divine Providence and tells her she has no need, as a Church, to find security in "unrighteous Laws" if there is "justice" in her "Cause," for Christ promised there would be a special Providence for his Church-Bride: he pledged to remain with her always and assured her that the gates of hell would not prevail against her (Mt 16:18, 28:20). Hence, the Panther's finding shelter behind the admittedly sinful Test means that she doubts she is Christ's Church:

> T' intrench in what you grant unrighteous Laws,
> Is to distrust the justice of your Cause;
> And argues that the true Religion lyes
> In those weak Adversaries you despise.
>   (3:866–67)

Earlier in the poem, the Hind said that the Panther detested Christ's "promises" to assist his Church because she feared those promises were not meant for her (2:493–96). Returning to this point in part 3, the Hind reproaches the Panther for pursuing worldly "Int'rest" instead of leaning on divine promises: "But Int'rest will not trust, tho God should plight his Word" (3:1066). She then links the Panther's distrust of James's word to her distrust of God's word: since kings are "Heav'ns Trustees," it follows that when James II says he wants only to "repeal" her "*Test*" and the Panther insists that he must mean something more (i.e., he intends to disestablish her), the Panther's distrust strikes at heaven itself. In this passage the Hind wounds the Panther, for the latter "did not much rejoyce" to have her unreasonable distrust of royal and divine promises exposed (3:882–91).

The Hind's idea of faith as trust in promises was a distinctive mark of Catholics in that century, as Bishop Mountagu noted in 1625: "amongst the *Papists*, many learned make *Faith* not only an *intellectuall*, but a *fiduciall* Assent unto the Promises of GOD in the *Gospel*."[7] Because of his great emphasis on Providence, Dryden had centered his faith on divine promises even when he was a Protestant: in *Religio Laici* (1682) he alludes to the promise of Isaiah 35:8, that God will open a path in which even fools will not go astray, and affirms that the "unletter'd Christian" who takes Scripture as his guide will not fall into sinful misbelief (322); however, he adds, if someone insists on using Scripture for controversy, then the safest thing is to follow "*all the Church before*" (438). The implication is that Divine Providence guided the "*Church before*." After his conversion, the poet declares that "all the promises are to the guides" (2:103), that is, that the Church's infallibility in matters of faith is the corollary of Christ's promise not to let the gates of hell prevail against her.

In Canticles 3:4 the Bride says she will hold on to the Bridegroom "til I bring him into my mothers house, and into the chamber of her that bare me." The note in the Douay version interprets this verse to mean "til the Jewes shal at last also find him." At this point in the poem, the Hind has returned from hiding and exile, and she is in her "mothers house" in Britain, which is figuratively Israel. However, she is no longer welcome. The one who will be reconciled to the Hind is clearly not this English Panther, whose "hour" is past, but the infant Panther of a future age.

---

7. Richard Mountagu, *Appello Caesarem* (1625), in facsimile (Amsterdam: Theatrum Orbis Terrarum/New York: Da Capo, 1972), 213.

CHAPTER 3

English Catholics in the Restoration

When she sees her guest mortally grieved that the king has given Catholics public employments, the Hind at first tries to placate the Panther by saying "I am but few" (3:114). She argues that Catholics are such a tiny minority in England that they cannot reasonably be feared. Alluding to the familiar fable in Aesop, the Hind says the Panther's accusations cloak her real intentions:

> When at the fountains head, as merit ought
> To claim the place, you take a swilling draught,
> How easy 'tis an envious eye to throw,
> And tax the sheep for troubling streams below,
> Or call her, (when no farther cause you find,)
> And enemy profess'd of all your kind.
> But then, perhaps, the wicked World wou'd think
> The *Wolf* design'd to eat as well as drink.
>
> (3:123–30)

In Aesop's fable, the Wolf first makes an absurd accusation against the Lamb, and then, while the victim is denying the accusation, seizes and devours it. The Hind insists that the Panther is raising "False Fears" against Catholics (3:1205) for the same purpose and that her only real "fear" is that the "encreasing race of *Chanticleer*," that is, the Catholic clergy, will prevail by "Holy Deeds" and "awfull Grace" over her sons' "Arts" and "alluring

Baits," thereby causing a flood of conversions to Rome (3:1112, 1038–41).

According to the Compton Census of 1676, Catholics during the Restoration period made up a mere 1 percent of the population of England, about 50,000. At this point in English history they were so small a party that William Penn referred to them as "a Spirit without a Body," and to James II as a "General without an Army."[1] When the Anglican Roger L'Estrange was reviled as a "papist" for writing in defense of the Catholics in 1679, he explained that he had done so for the same motive he used to give out pennies, when walking through London, to rescue birds and other small creatures from "the cruelty of Boys in the Streets."[2] In L'Estrange's image we see the fragility of the Catholic party and the casual cruelty of those empowered to hurt them.

English Catholics were watched and numbered with jealousy because they were preponderantly upper class and close to the court. Over the past century they had become, by necessity, courtiers and defenders of the royal prerogative. William Penn explained that hostile parliaments had forced Catholics to find shelter behind the throne and had made them friends of the king's prerogative.[3] Those same parliaments had then branded Catholics as the enemies of liberty. At the time of the Gunpowder Plot, English Catholics were collectively reviled as traitors to kings, but in the reign of Charles I they were collectively reviled as champions of the prerogative. During the Restoration, they were regarded with jealousy because they were able to cast a number of votes on the king's side in the House of Lords, perhaps as many as one-fifth of the total. At least they were able to do so until 1678, when Titus Oates falsely accused the Catholic lords of treason. Parliament then enacted the third and final Test Act of 1678 to eject Catholic peers from parliament. The Hind passionately condemns this last Test as a quid pro quo, like Judas's thirty pieces of silver, which the Panther's party took in exchange for giving countenance to the perjuries of Titus Oates.

    1. Speck, *Reluctant Revolutionaries*, 170; Henry Compton, bishop of London, *The Compton Census of 1676: A Critical Edition*, ed. A. Whiteman (Oxford: Oxford University Press, 1986); Penn, *Good Advice*, 49. See also "How Many Catholics?," in John Bossy, *The English Catholic Community, 1570–1850* (New York: Oxford University Press, 1976), 182–94.
    2. Roger L'Estrange, *A Further Discovery of the Plot* (London, 1680), 2. *Discovery upon Discovery* (London, 1680), 27.
    3. [William Penn], *A Perswasive to Moderation to Church Dissenters* ([London]: [Andrew Sowle, 1686]), 29.

One historian reflects that behind the low Catholic numbers in the Compton Census lay "a large but indeterminate number of people who habitually sat on the fence, ready to come over" when they thought it safe.[4] Perhaps so, but Dryden observes that the more Catholics declined in visible numbers, the more they were scapegoated. In *Absalom and Achitophel* (1681) they are compared to Jebusites, the ancient inhabitants of Jerusalem whom the Jews reprobated more and more as they got weaker and weaker: "And every loss the men of *Jebus* bore, / They still were thought God's enemies the more" (90–91).

At the accession of James II there was a small increase in the number of Catholics due to conversions. In Dryden's poem the Panther boasts that her "sons" have "sharply tax'd" those converts as irreligious men "al-lur'd with gain" who became Catholic only "for miracles of bread" (3:195–97). The Hind retorts that anyone with a profit motive would not convert at the present juncture:

> Judge not by hear-say, but observe at least,
> If since their change, their loaves have been increast.
> The *Lyon* buyes no Converts, if he did,
> Beasts wou'd be sold as fast as he cou'd bid.
> Tax those of int'rest who conform for gain,
> Or stay the market of another reign.
>
> (3:223–28)

A self-interested person, she says, would wait for the Protestant "market" of William and Mary, the rulers next in line, rather than be reconciled to Rome under a king so advanced in years (and whose ill health contributed to the belief that he was not destined to live much longer). To become a Catholic in 1686–1687 was to have the prospect of only a short "respite" from certain "punishment" (3:382–83).

The new accessibility of books about Catholic doctrine in 1686 surely helped to spark conversions. After a year of complaining to the Anglican bishops about the virulent anti-Catholic propaganda pouring out of pulpit and press, the king gave permission, on 25 March 1686, for Catholic works to be published. For the first time in more than a century, books defending Catholicism could be published (many at the king's expense by his printer, the convert Henry Hills) and sold openly. One historian notes

4. Malcolm V. Hay, *The Enigma of James II* (London and Glasgow: Sands, 1938), 69.

that "a new controversial situation was thereby created. Hitherto the use of publicity had been confined to the Protestants, who had employed the privilege of press without restriction of competition. They had been able for generations to criticize their opponents without risk of retaliation." So now the Catholics promulgated their doctrine freely, while the Anglicans continued to issue "books denouncing popish plots, Jesuit intrigues, and the superstitions and idolatries of Rome."[5]

This battle of the books is depicted in parts 2 and 3 of Dryden's poem. In part 2 the Hind publishes her ancient doctrine to the "amaz'd" Panther, and in part 3 the Panther tries to stop her from gaining a foothold in England by raising public fears over the king's campaign to repeal the Test. The Hind observes that the Panther's sons "struck the foremost blow" against her (3:1061), her phrase echoing Canticles 5:7, "the keepers that goe about the citie found me: they struck me," which expositors said denoted the persecution of the infant Church by magistrates. In doing so, she says, they rashly attacked Providence itself: for when Stillingfleet "revil'd" Charles II and the Duchess of York for their conversions, he generated "clouds of smoke" and "thundring peals" aimed ostensibly at those converts of the royal family but actually at God's rule over his Church: "So to permitted ills the *Daemon* flyes: / His rage is aim'd at him who rules the skyes" (3:314–15). The Hind teaches each proselyte to endure such "publick shame" meekly, in the knowledge that "suff'ring from ill tongues he bears no more / Than what his Sovereign bears, and what his Saviour bore" (3:304–5). Indeed, any English convert would have known that James had been publicly reviled ever since his refusal to take the Test in 1673.

Because seventeenth-century English Catholics regarded suffering for religion's sake as an honor, their accounts concerning the severity of their afflictions can be misleading. For example, the lawyer Richard Langhorne, on the eve of his execution by hanging and quartering in 1679 (the result of Oates's perjuries), lists twelve ways that his gruesome death will be an *imitatio Christi*: he too will die on a tree, ignominiously, at the hand of the public executioner; he will be stripped naked; all his blood will be shed, as an enemy to the government; public officials will declare that his death is necessary for the people; the mob will shout for his

5. Richard E. Boyer, *English Declarations of Indulgence 1687 and 1688* (The Hague and Paris: Mouton, 1968), 37.

death, then rejoice at it; and all this will be occasioned by false witnesses, men induced by malice as well as rewards. He regards all this walking in Christ's footsteps as an unmerited honor.[6]

The usual penalty for being Catholic during the Restoration, however, was not bodily suffering but what the Hind calls "the Homicide of names" and "black detraction" (3:258–59). This point is made clearly when the Hind teaches her "son" to "welcom infamy and publick shame" and give "a long farwell to worldly fame" (3:283–84). Around the time of his own conversion in 1686, the poet wrote a *Defence* of the Duchess of York's conversion and summed up the psychological cost of being reconciled to the Catholic Church: one can expect "the loss of Friends, of worldly Honours, and Esteem, the Defamation of ill Tongues, and the Reproach of the Cross." The heroic meekness with which many English Catholics lived under this obloquy is captured in the following words of Abraham Woodhead, a learned and holy man who converted, like Dryden, in his fifties:

if yet further, by reason of the persecution of such a Religion, in the place where he lives, such a convert hath an occasion also offered him of leaving, Father, or Mother, Friends, or Fortunes, and, among the rest, not the least, his Reputation and good Name, in being esteemed a *Turncoat*, an *Apostate*, a *Seducer*, to imbrace again, in the Religion he turns to, nothing but Crosses and Fastings, Confessions and Penances, Resignation of Judgment, strict obedience to the Churches, as well as Gods, Laws, and many more hardships, set before him, if he purposeth to arrive at perfection; for a true enlightened Judgment, I say, will here consider: that this is one of the greatest Honours, that his Divine Majesty could do him upon earth; and a happiness next to Martyrdom.[7]

When Serenus Cressy was charged with inconstancy for having converted to Catholicism during the Interregnum, at a time when the Anglican Church was under the rod of Puritans, he made this moving reply, that he had chosen a church that was always under the rod in England: "it was persecution I fled to."[8]

6. *Richard Langhorn's Memoires, with Some Meditations and Devotions of His, During His Imprisonment* (N. pl.: N. pub., 1679), 16.

7. [Abraham Woodhead], *Considerations on the Council of Trent, Being the Fifth Discourse Concerning the Guide in Controversies* (N. pl.: N. pub., 1671], 248.

8. Serenus Cressy, *Exomologesis*, 2d ed. (Paris, 1653), 438, 455. The Restoration Catholics esteemed this book so highly that their enemies called it their "Golden Calf."

Of course, there were other converts who were far from meek. One of these was Roger Palmer, Lord Castlemaine, the one-man "antidefamation league" of the Restoration. He printed his books, he said, to clear both the English and the Irish Catholics from "all matter of Fact charg'd" against them "by their Enemies." His panache is demonstrated in *The Earl of Castlemain's Manifesto* (1681), when he demands his bail after being indicted "only for high treason," as he puts it, in the imaginary Popish Plot. He charmed the crowd at his trial and they cheered him when he was acquitted, partly because of his witty defense, in which he noted that it is incredible to think that Catholic aristocrats like himself would trust their deepest secrets to an ignorant, low-bred person like Titus Oates. A man who regarded himself as the descendant of the hot-blooded Percies of Northumberland was not one to sit back while he and his fellow converts were called "ignorant" and "desperate." Castlemaine retorted "that not only the *Catholics*, that have bin from their Infancy bred so, are of the chiefest Ranck in *England*, and inferior to none in all natural and artificial Endowments, but that our *Converts* were, and still are of Persons of Eminency both in their Parts and Quality . . . either for their Families or Accomplishments." Indifferent to the jealousy he might inspire, he insisted on the great contributions of Catholics to the Anglican king Charles I, giving detailed evidence of the disproportionately high number of them who died in battle for the royal cause in the Civil Wars. In every edition of his *Catholique Apology,* he reprinted the list of Catholic war heroes in red ink, along with the names of the battlefields they fell on, to suggest to parliament that the children of such men deserve at least to be as free to worship privately as they would be in the Ottoman Empire. More than any other publication in that era, the *Apology* was a work of pure antidefamation, sounding a modern note because it did not "meddle" (as the author put it) with theology, but instead simply exposed the lies, the stereotypes, and the false imputations of collective guilt on which the whole system of discrimination of the Test Acts was grounded. It is no surprise that the House of Commons ordered his work to be seized. Despite the government's efforts to suppress it, however, Castlemaine kept reprinting and expanding his book from

9. [Roger Palmer, Earl of Castlemaine], *The Catholique Apology with a Reply to the Answer Together with a Clear Refutation of the Seasonable Discourse, Its Reasonable Defence, & Dr. Du Moulins Answer to Philanax; As Also Dr. Stillingfleet's Last*

1666 to 1674.[9] By the reign of James II, according to the French ambassador Barrillon, he was one of the three acknowledged chiefs of the Catholic aristocracy and a member of the royal council.[10]

Castlemaine's testimony makes it plausible that seventeenth-century converts like Queen Anne of Denmark, Lady Falkland, Lord Baltimore, Walter Montague, the Duchess of York, James II, Charles II, the Duke of Berwick, Obadiah Walker, Serenus Cressy, Abraham Woodhead, and John Dryden were the typical ones. Whereas in Ireland Catholicism was the religion of the disenfranchised populace, in England it was the religion of a tiny elite close to the Stuart court, where Catholic queens regnant and dowager had chapels by treaty, and where their preachers, such as the Queen Mother's chaplain Basile de Soissons in the 1660s, expounded Catholic doctrine and converted many English courtiers. While keeping a low profile, this Catholic elite engaged in public life in spite of a milieu that was legally, religiously, and intellectually hostile to them. Denied freedom of the press, they still managed to publish, secretly or abroad, over a thousand explicitly Catholic books during the last sixty years of the century, according to *English Catholic Authors 1640–1700*, by Thomas Clancy, S.J. When we reflect on who these few Catholics were, it is no wonder that Dryden's Hind argues insistently in part 3 for the repeal of the Test for public office. Participation in public life would have seemed as natural as breathing for such as these. However, this Catholic party had a major flaw, in the view of the Anglican lawyer Roger North: they had not been clever enough to see the snares set before them and had "failed in their Politics . . . ever since the Reformation." North gives as proof of their being easily deceived that they made a "Practice" of "combining with Dissenters" to seek toleration.[11]

Gunpowder Treason Sermon, His Attaque about the Treaty of Munster, and All Matter of Fact Charg'd on the English Catholiques by Their Enemies, 3d ed. ([Antwerp?], 1674), 163–64. This extremely rare 600-page book, which starts with the first *Apology* of 1666 and then includes all defenses of this work from printed attacks, will be cited hereafter as *Apology.*

10. Charles James Fox, *Appendix*, cxxiii. Fox's *Appendix* contains the decipherings, in French, of Barrillon's letters in numerical code to Louis XIV in the year 1685. In November 1685 Barrillon wrote that Catholics had great confidence in Castlemaine and considered him a very able and zealous Catholic.

11. Sir Roger North, *Examen; or, An Enquiry into the Credit and Veracity of a Pretended Complete History; Shewing the Perverse and Wicked Design of It, and the Many Falsities and Abuses of Truth Contained in It. Together with Some Memoirs Occasionally*

Catholics in England were deeply divided on the policies of James II. Ambassador Barrillon reported to Louis XIV as early as 4 June 1685 that James intended to repeal the Test, and then, on November 12 of that year, he added that the richer sort of English Catholics, fearful of being ruined by this campaign, desired only toleration and were willing to continue under the Test. The party of the Prince of Orange encouraged these timid Catholics to abandon hope of civil or military employment.[12] Like William of Orange, Louis XIV disapproved of the repeal campaign; he saw the English as entitled to the same uniformity of worship that he was imposing on the French.

Dryden has long been misconceived by literary critics as being on the side of the rich Catholics and as mocking the bolder court Catholics through the Panther's tale. This is a misreading of that tale, in which the Panther unwittingly uses eschatological imagery that recoils on her own party. Even the character of the Martyn recoils on her, for the Hind says this church-begotten bird is much more typical of the Panther's clergy than her own: "Such *Martyns* build in yours, and more than mine" (3:654). Dryden was far from mocking those fellow converts who believed their countrymen could be persuaded by argument, just as they themselves had been, to yield up their hatred of Catholicism. The rhetoric Dryden puts in the mouth of the Hind in this poem and then takes up himself in *Britannia Rediviva* is virtually the same one used by Catholic repealers like James II, William Darrell, S.J., Lord Castlemaine, and the dramatist Henry Nevil Payne, whom Titus Oates dubbed Castlemaine's "true Second." In *The Hind and the Panther*, part 3, the poet expects to win the case against the Test Acts on the moral plane by the use of powerful biblical paradigms and arguments. After that, he knows the decision is up to the English nation to set the date for repeal, whether now or in some future generation.

Dryden plants many seeds of hope for English Catholics throughout his poem, giving them glimpses of a glorious, though distant future. In the part of his design which is classical, a part almost entirely adumbrated by the unwitting Panther herself, the Hind is Aeneas newly arrived in

---

Inserted. All Tending to Vindicate the Honour of the Late King Charles the Second, and His Happy Reign, from the Intended Aspersions of That Foul Pen (London: N. pub., 1740), 237.

12. Fox, *Appendix*, cxxxix, xc.

Latium, outnumbered in the struggle to retain a small encampment. Nevertheless, this supposedly "foreign" intruder is actually being restored by divine guidance to the "Ancient Mother" country and is the destined founder of future greatness for its people. For Aeneas and the Hind, however, much suffering and labor is to be expected in the near future. Worldwide glory is reserved for their descendants.

There are seeds of hope, too, in the design drawn from Scripture. In Canticles 8:8–10 we see a parallel to "Lavinia" in the Bride's "little sister," who has at first "no breasts" but soon declares: "I am a wal: and my breasts are as a towre." Richard Challoner's note to the eighteenth-century Douay version states that this "little sister" is the Church of the Law, the Jewish Church, converted toward the end of the world and finally built up into a great wall in the Church of Christ, the New Jerusalem. This note seems to sum up Dryden's idea of the inevitable embrace between the English Church and the Catholic Church in the last times. Like St. Paul who envisions the return of the Jewish Church after the fullness of the Gentiles has entered in (Rom 11:25–26), Dryden envisions a climactic return of the single-nation Bride, the Church of the Law, in apocalyptic times, after the Universal Bride has grown to the fullness of her worldwide expansion.

CHAPTER 4

The Appeal to Compassion

At first glance, the Test seems mild compared to those twenty-four Penal Laws for nonconformity that Henry Care lists in electrifying detail in his *Draconica* (1687). But the Penal Laws were only sporadically enforced, while the Test was a fixed barrier to public employment. The principle behind the Penal Laws was *inclusion*, to compel citizens to join in a uniform national worship, while the principle behind the Test was *exclusion*, to make nonconformists incapable of public employment.

Those who campaigned for repeal in 1685–1688 insisted that the Test was the same old persecution in modern guise, and so they refused to separate it from the Penal Laws in their writings. Henry Care called the Test "a main part of these very Penal Laws," explaining that if one is debarred of "Rights, Priviledges, or Advantages" merely for religious beliefs, this is to be a "sufferer for Conscience."[1] William Penn contended that the Test and the Penal Laws should all be repealed because the Test is just one more "Infringment of our Natural and Christian Liberty."[2] And John

---

1. H[enry] C[are], *Draconica; or, An Abstract of All the Penal Laws Touching Matters of Religion; and the Several Oaths and Tests Thereby Enjoyned* (London: George Larkin, 1687), 15. Care had been printing attacks on Catholics in the Popish Plot years and now joined them for the repeal campaign.

2. [William Penn], *Some Free Reflections upon Occasion of the Public Discourse about Liberty of Conscience* (London: Andrew Sowle, 1687), 10. This work will hereafter be cited as *Free Reflections*.

Wilson linked the Test and the penal statutes from his very title page, announcing that his book will treat of "the King's Supream Power in Dispensing with Penal Statutes: More particularly as it relates to the two Test-Acts of the Twenty-Fifth, and the Thirtieth of His late Majesty."[3] Samuel Johnson, a fervent defender of the Test and one whom Dryden had satirized as Ben-Jochanan in 1682, conceded that the 1673 Test put "new life into the Disabling Acts," that is, into the older Penal Laws against nonconformists.[4]

The Hind, too, speaks of the Penal Laws and Test Acts as all of a piece. She sees the Test as a "*Scorpion*" or hook added to the old, blunt "rod" or whip of persecution: "Curs'd be the wit which cruelty refines, / Or to his father's rod the *Scorpion* joins . . ." (3:689–90). In this couplet, she makes a subtle parallel between England and ancient Israel, alluding to the cause of division between southern and northern Israel, that is, conformist and nonconformist Jews. In 1 Kings 12:10–11 the northerners presented their grievances to King Rehoboam, but he followed his foolish counselors' advice and threatened them, saying that his finger would prove thicker than his father Solomon's loins and that he would add a hook to his father's whip. In the above couplet, too, the Hind implicitly blames Charles II for listening to foolish counsel and confirming his parliament's three Test Acts, when he ought to have kept the promise he gave to nonconformists before his Restoration and again in 1672 to grant them liberty of conscience.

Indeed, Charles II put the hook on his father's whip when he consented to enlarge the Jacobean statute on the reception of the sacrament. James I, known as the "British Solomon" by his supporters, was the first to enact a penal law obliging the English to take the sacrament. As Henry Care explains, under Statute 1 James I, cap. 4, nonreception of the sacrament was made punishable by a fine of twenty pounds the first year, forty the second, and sixty thereafter.[5] By means of the Test, Charles II made nonreception

---

3. John Wilson, *Jus Regium Coronae* (London: Henry Hills, 1688). He says he wrote this book defending the royal prerogative in 1686.

4. [Samuel Johnson], *A Letter from a Freeholder, to the Rest of the Freeholders of England* [London, 1689], in *A Seventh Collection of Papers Relating to Parliaments and the Penal Laws and Tests* (1689), 4. Johnson was known for *Julian the Apostate* (London, 1682), where he had paralleled James and his great-grandmother Mary Queen of Scots and justified killing a Catholic successor (xvii–xix).

5. Care, *Draconica*, 5.

of the sacrament punishable by an ongoing incapacity for public employment. This small extension of the old whip made it lethal. The Hind insists that the Test is actually more injurious to English nonconformists than Louis XIV's persecution of their French counterparts, the Huguenots: "Your finger is more gross than the great Monarch's loins" (3:691).

The Panther herself, in her tale of the Swallows, sees the Test and the earlier penal statutes as all of a piece when she describes the vengeance falling on the Catholic Swallows (3:625–38). She describes the secular Catholics becoming the "undefended prey" of "*Crows* and *Ravens,*" that is, being picked clean of worldly goods by informers collecting the penalties of the Penal Laws and Test. These Crows and Ravens are later identified by the Hind as the antiroyalist party or "Republick Birds" (3:1251). The priestly Martin, however, is killed by legal process: "For treas'nous crimes, because the laws provide / No *Martyn* there in winter shall abide" (3:633–34). This couplet alludes to the 1585 penal statute making it an act of high treason to administer Catholic sacraments in England. One hundred forty years after publication of *The Hind*, the Whig leader John Russell repeats the accusation that the Test is all of a piece with the earlier laws against nonconformists, calling it "the dregs of that persecuting spirit which caused the calamities of civil war." Dissenters are supposed to be grateful for the "supineness of laws," another M.P. exclaims in 1772, for the government's not being "rash enough to enforce" what it was "*unjust* enough to enact against them."[6] These words show that the Test Acts and the remnant of unrepealed Penal Laws were still viewed as a Damocles's Sword under which the nonconformists were obliged to sit.

The sacramental Test was the sort of persecution that left no scars. Perhaps its worst pain was a pain of absence. As Gray expressed it in "Elegy Written in a Country Churchyard" (1751), many a Cromwell, a Hampden, or a "mute, inglorious Milton" lay buried in private obscurity, rendered incapable of striving for liberty with a dauntless breast. The Hind appeals to the Panther's compassion (and to the reader's) when she observes that the Test buries her sons in obscurity and poverty. She makes a wry joke about how Catholics will at least not abuse the public trust as they starve at home in their Test-prescribed unemployment:

6. Cowherd, *Protestant Dissenters*, 34–36; *The Substance of a Speech Made by H-s L-she, Esq; In Debate on the Bill for Enabling Papists to Take Building Leases* (Dublin: N. pub., 1772), 19.

> The Papist onely has his Writ of ease.
> No gainfull office gives him the pretence
> To grind the Subject or defraud the Prince.
> Wrong conscience, or no conscience may deserve
> To Thrive, but ours alone is privileg'd to sterve.
>
> (3:745–49)

The word "privileg'd" implies that the chance to earn a living or make a mark in the public sector has been changed by parliament from a birthright to a privilege earned by taking the Test. The word "sterve" implies that this amounts to a death sentence by starvation for those public servants (like the poet himself) who in conscience cannot take the Test. In her tale, the Hind shows the Hens reduced to starvation by the Test: the Pigeons envy them their "little Food," drive them "from their food" with blows from their quills, and try to make them swallow deadly poison (by submitting to the Test) before being allowed to "peck on this forbidden Ground" (3:1003, 1070–79, 1224). Dryden portrays this same effect of the Test later in his tragedy *Cleomenes* (1692), where the hero is condemned by a hypocritical conformist to starve with his sons in a Tower of Hunger.

In "The Character of a Trimmer," George Savile Lord Halifax reveals that the Test was originally designed to create a different pain of absence. It was intended to exclude rich Catholics from "Publick Business" and to turn them into shameful drones or "Men of Pleasure" because they had dared to look on religion "as they do upon Escutcheons," undervaluing "Reformation as an Upstart." One of the foremost champions of the Test, Halifax gloats that it will make each Catholic aristocrat consider what it means

to have no share in Business, no opportunity of shewing his own Value to the World; to live at the best an useless, and by others to be thought a dangerous Member of the Nation where he is born, is a burthen to a generous Mind that cannot be taken off by all the Pleasure of a lazy unmanly life, or by the nauseous enjoyment of a dull Plenty, that produceth no food for the Mind, which will be considered in the first place by a Man that hath a Soul. . . . [7]

In these lines, the marquis anticipates that old Catholic families will be

---

7. *The Complete Works of George Savile, First Marquess of Halifax*, ed. Walter Raleigh (Oxford: Clarendon Press, 1912; rpt., New York: Augustus M. Kelley, 1970), 83–84. On the subject of the Test making nonconformists social outcasts, see John Spurr, *The Restoration Church of England, 1646–1689* (New Haven, Conn.: Yale University Press, 1991), 378.

humiliated but ignores the related fate of ordinary converts, like Dryden, who will also suffer by losing their public employment. Halifax's indifference to the fate of all Catholics can be gathered from his advice to Charles II in 1679, when nearly two thousand of them were imprisoned in the area of London, "that the Plot must be handled as if it were true, whether it were so or not."[8] When James II declared "that he would be served by none but those who would vote for the repeal of the tests," Halifax said he would never consent, gave up his office, and went home to write in defense of the Test Acts.[9]

In part 3, when the Hind presents several arguments about the injustice of the Test, the Panther looks on with smug disdain:

> But having gain'd a Verdict on her side,
> She wisely gave the loser leave to chide;
> Well satisfy'd to have the But and peace,
> And for the Plaintiff's cause she car'd the less,
> Because she su'd *in forma Pauperis.*
>
>   (3:757–61)

In these lines the Panther is pleased with her de facto right to the possession of the "But," which can mean both a barrel of wine and a boundary mark. Since she has the three statutes on her side, the Panther looks at the dispossessed beggar who pleads for a de jure right with "a yawning kind of pride" (3:765). Indeed, this smug disdain is often discerned in the writings of the defenders of the Test Acts and Penal Laws. In 1685, in an answer to the Duke of Buckingham's essay on liberty of conscience, one such defender dismissed Protestant nonconformists as "onely a Herd of Wolves and Foxes, Bears and Lions, and the most savage Animals in Protestant Skins."[10] Three of these animals are the same ones Dryden used two years later to represent the nonconformists of the 1640s: "The *Bear, the Fox*, the *Wolfe*, by turns prevail" (1:466). The dramatist Henry Nevil Payne answers this pamphlet (because Buckingham's essay, which appeared in May 1685, was a public letter to Payne) and says that in Holland a person may buy rosaries or crucifixes and "not one of those mighty

---

8. J. P. Kenyon, *The Popish Plot* (London: Heinemann, 1972), 166.
9. Boyer, *Declaration of Indulgence*, 43, citing Narcissus Luttrell, *A Brief Historical Relation of State Affairs*, 6 vols. (Oxford: Clarendon Press, 1857), 1:366–67.
10. Anon., *A Short Answer to His Grace the D. of Buckingham's Paper, Concerning Religion, Toleration and Liberty of Conscience* (London: For S. G., 1685), 16.

Herds of Wolves, Foxes, Bears, Lions, or other Savage Animals in Protestant Skins, will so much as grin at him." He means that the English Independents, at this point in time, will be just as peaceful in England as in Holland if they have liberty of conscience: they will "prove more True and Faithful Subjects to his Majesty for a bare Indulgence" than others for "Fat Livings."[11] In his pamphlet, Payne fires the opening salvo of the repeal campaign. Just when the Anglican party is beginning to call for a strict execution of the Penal Laws and Test Acts, Payne hints at the coming alliance between Protestant nonconformists and Catholics for the goal of repeal.

We again discern the Panther's "yawning kind of pride" in the words of James Harrington the Younger, writing from Oxford in 1688 about the huge fines that nonconformists should have to pay: "Penal Statutes are so many instances of our Charity to the poor, and only force the obnoxious to a compulsive liberality."[12] Also, when the Ulster Presbyterians complained of the Test as an "Odious Mark of Infamy" in 1715, William Tisdall told them roundly that those who cannot qualify by the Test are "but Partial Subjects," and though they may have a "Connivance" to free them from "Penal Sufferings," they can hardly expect to have rewards like those who obey laws "Fundamental to the Establishment of the whole Constitution."[13] Tisdall's word "connivance" for the toleration of Presbyterian worship shows how the Test Acts and Penal Laws were still linked: even after 1689 nonconformists were supposed to be grateful that they were spared the fines stipulated in the dormant, but unrepealed Penal Laws.

The Hind urges compassion when she says that the Test is like an exorcism to drive out nonconformists. In the Bible, the angel Raphael advises Tobias to "lay the liver of the fish on the fire, and the devil shall be driven

11. Henry Payne, *The Persecutor Expos'd: In Reflections, by Way of Reply, to an Ill-bred Answer to the Duke of Buckingham's Paper* (London: J. L. for the author), 22. George Villiers, duke of Buckingham, had published *A Short Discourse upon the Reasonableness of Men's Having a Religion or Worship of God*, in 1685, initially at the request of Payne, and had addressed it as a public letter to Payne. See Willard Thorp, "Henry Nevil Payne, Dramatist and Jacobite Conspirator," in *The Parrott Presentation Volume*, ed. Hardin Craig (Princeton, N.J.: Princeton University Press, 1935), 367.

12. [James Harrington, the Younger], "A Vindication of Protestant Charity," bound with his *Some Reflexions upon a Treatise Call'd Pietas Romanas and Parisiensis Lately Printed at Oxford* (Oxford: At the Theatre, 1688), 39.

13. William Tisdall, *The Case of the Sacramental Test Stated and Argu'd* (Dublin: Daniel Tompson, 1715), 2, 4, 10–11. He calls the leaders of the Ulster Presbyterians Mr. McBride and Mr. Boyse.

away" (Tb 6:19). The Test is likewise a smoke that expels the nonconformist from the public sphere as if he were a wicked "fiend":

> You toss your censing *Test*, and fume the room;
> As if 'twere *Toby's* rival to expell,
> And fright the fiend who could not bear the smell.
>
> (3:753–55)

By her use of the words "toss" and "censing," the Hind implies that the
Test is used around the public "room" to drive out those who might otherwise be invisible. The Test was called the law for the "discovery of Dissenters"[14] because it was used more aggressively than the words of the
statutes warranted during the Tory revenge of 1683–1685. For this reason,
the Hind compares it to a "*Shibboleth*" (3:1076), which in Judges 12:6 is a
password that forces Ephraim, the nonconformist Israelite, to betray himself and be killed; she also calls it an "Inquisition," or an active searching
out of nonconformists (3:1083). Parliament formalized such an expanded
application of the Test as *shibboleth* in the Statutes of the Realm, 1 William
and Mary c. 9 (1689). Under this act, a "suspected" Catholic in London
and four counties could be offered the long oath of the 1678 Test (declaring Catholic worship to be "idolatrous") whether or not he was elected or
appointed to office, and if he refused to take it, he was to "forfeit or suffer
as Popish Recusant Convict." The complaint of the Protestant Repeal
Committee a century later shows that nonconformists still feared to be noticed, even for meritorious acts: "[We] are made incapable of . . . receiving
from the king any reward for services done to the public without becoming liable to disabilities and penalties which would strip us of many of our
dearest rights and place us nearly in the situation of proscribed outlaws."[15]
Under the logic of the statutes, a nonconformist receiving a royal accolade
would need a pardon not to fall under the Test's enormous penalties.

There seems to have been another fear associated until 1767 with the
use of the Test as *shibboleth*. Heywood recounts that in places like London, where the inhabitants were obliged to serve if they were elected, it
was easy to expose and punish an "obnoxious" nonconformist by electing
him to an office that required him to take the Test: "for it was only to elect
him into a corporate office; which if he refused to serve, he might be

---

14. Penn, *Free Reflections*, 6.
15. *Repeal Committee Minutes*, 59.

prosecuted for the refusal; and if he served, he might be punished by virtue of the Corporation Act with loss of office, and of the Test Act (which extends to corporation offices) with the disabilities and penalties before mentioned." The Toleration Act of 1689 seems not to have curbed the use of this practice, which was rightly compared to "Procrustes' Bed," for in 1739 a "sumptuous palace" was built in London with the large fines that had been levied till then on nonconformists declining to be sheriff. In a speech given in 1767, in defense of one who had refused to be sheriff in London, Lord Mansfield exclaimed: "There was no occasion to revoke the edict of Nantes; the Jesuits needed only to have advised a plan similar to what is contended for in the present case; make a law to render them incapable of offices; make another to punish them (for it is admitted on all hands, that the defendant in the cause before your Lordships is prose-cutable for taking the office upon him): if they accept, punish them; if they refuse, punish them; . . . My Lords, this is a most exquisite dilemma."[16] After this appeal to their compassion, the Lords ruled that those who could not in conscience take the Test were to be excused with-out penalty when they were elected to local office. But long before this, Dryden's Hind had made a similar appeal to parliament's compassion: she had warned that the Test was a "Popular" but a "cruel Cause" (3:1091), that it was used as a *"Shibboleth"* and an "Inquisition" to dis-cover nonconformists (3:1076, 1083), and that it was a weapon against nonconformity more lethal than the older Penal Laws and more cutting than anything Louis XIV had done to the Huguenots (3:680–91).

The Test Acts and Penal Laws against nonconformity were all of a piece because they were meant chiefly to intimidate. Nonconformists complained that the statutes made them fear every stranger as a potential informer, no matter how peaceful the times, for the laws could be applied retroactively. Giles Shute explains that one could be ruined by "Free-Booters" who would swear falsely before a magistrate for a third of one's estate.[17] Likewise, Castlemaine, who prudently passed his estate to his brother in 1674 when he ended his travels and settled in England, tells how Catholics dreaded "the stranger," "the one who takes on hear say" and "zealously wounds."[18] In a semijocular vein, Henry Nevil Payne

16. Heywood, *The Right of Protestant Dissenters*, 35–36.
17. G[iles] S[hute], *A New Test in Lieu of the Old One* (London: Larkin, 1688), 25.
18. Castlemaine, *Apology*, 32.

points out that the conformist whose pamphlet he is answering had better get rid of the Latin book he cited because some "pious converts to Conformity, will for a sure reward swear they saw him say Mass: for which *Overt Act of Treason, Sedition, and Rebellion*, they will only Hang, Draw, and Quarter him."[19] This is only semijocular because, on the eve of the pretended Popish Plot, when Titus Oates wanted to create evidence against his former tutor, he asked him to write down some Latin verses on Christ and the Virgin Mary.[20]

Curiously, there was a corresponding fear on the side of the conformist, a fear of the nonconformist within himself. William Hubert, a Puritan who converted in the 1650s, wrote twenty years later that "many are afraid to have a better opinion of them [Catholics] than they are taught to have, though they even see they are much slandered, lest they should be convinced of the truth of their Religion, and then be obliged either to damn their souls if they would not embrace it, or loose their Estates and Preferments if they did embrace it."[21] Dryden mentions this "fear of future ill" in his list of worldly obstacles in the way of conversion (3:402).

In her appeal to compassion, the Hind draws a vivid picture of the Damocles's Sword under which Catholics sit in 1687. Although the king is there to protect them by royal prerogative, Catholics fear that the coming parliament will bring down the penalties of the Test Acts and Penal Laws on their heads. In his memoirs, James II explains that even though the ruling party "did not allways press a rigorous execution of these laws, yet they delighted to see Dissenters, and especially the Catholicks, in a continual tremble at the Iron rod which they took care should allways threaten them."[22] Cartwright, one of the Anglican bishops closest to James II, urged the repeal of both Penal Laws and Test Acts on this compassionate ground: that Catholics may "*lift up their Heads* above the danger of the Laws."[23] This goal of having a head lifted occurs frequently in

19. Payne, *Persecutor Expos'd*, 25;

20. William Smith, *The Mysteries and Intrigues of the Popish Plot Laid Open: With Depositions Sworn before the Secretary of State* (London: For C. W., 1685), 7.

21. [William Hubert], *The Puritan Convert* (n.p., 1676), 24.

22. *The Life of James the Second King of England Collected Out of Memoirs Writ of His Own Hand*, 2 vols., ed. Rev. J. S. Clarke (London: Longman et al., 1816), 2:114. This work will hereafter be cited as *Life*.

23. A. B. [Thomas Cartwright, Bishop of Chester], *An Answer of a Minister of the*

the anti-Test literature. On the other side, though, a defender of the Test finds Catholics too "Insolent" by far, even with "Halters about their own Necks."[24]

When the Panther congratulates herself that few are converting to Catholicism in 1687 and asserts smugly that those on her side follow "a nobler principle than gain," the Hind strips off that cloak of righteousness, as in Canticles 5:7 where "the keepers of the wals tooke away my cloke." She retorts that Anglicans abide in peace under James II and hope for no less in the future, while terrifying English laws still blaze like comets over the heads of Catholic "Proselytes":

> Your clergy sons their own in peace possess,
> Nor are their prospects in reversion less.
> My Proselytes are struck with awfull dread,
> Your bloudy Comet-laws hang blazing o're their head.
> The respite they enjoy but onely lent,
> The best they have to hope, protracted punishment.
> Be judge your self, if int'rest may prevail,
> Which motives, yours or mine will turn the scale.
>
> (3:378–85)

These comets resemble Damocles's Sword because they "hang" blazing over each convert's "head." An example of such an ominous law would be Statute 13 Eliz I., cap. 2, which made it high treason for someone to be reconciled to Rome, as Dryden and his three sons had been.[25] Obadiah Walker, the master of University College, Oxford, and several other prominent converts were indicted and imprisoned under this law shortly after the 1688 revolution. James II uses the same image that the Hind employs in his memoirs: "to talke of permiting Catholicks, either propertie, libertie, and life, while the penal Laws were in force against them, was like inviting them to Damocles his feast. . . ."[26]

The level of fear varied day by day: at the present moment the Hind need not "fear" because of the royal edict, but the Panther by her side is only marking time until her "furry sons" meet in parliament and she can "compleat" her "vengeance":

Church of England to a Seasonable and Important Question, Proposed to Him by a Loyal and Religious Member of the Present House of Commons (London: J. L., 1687), 30.

24. Johnson, *Letter from a Freeholder*, 7.   25. Care, *Draconica*, 4.
26. James II, *Life*, 2: 151.

Nor need she fear the *Panther*, though untam'd,
Because the *Lyon's* peace was now proclam'd,
The wary salvage would not give offence,
To forfeit the protection of her *Prince*;
But watch'd the time her vengeance to compleat,
When all her furry sons in frequent Senate met.

                            (3:20–25)

This is a candid picture of the bleak prospects for Catholics if a conformist parliament should be elected, and it goes a long way toward explaining why James II was trying to pack the next parliament with nonconformists pledged to vote for repeal of the Test. The Hind sees that the
Panther also awaits a new day of vengeance in the reign of William and
Mary: "To ripen green revenge your hopes attend, / Wishing that happier
Planet wou'd ascend" (3:855–56). Dryden's choice of the words "Comet-
laws" and "planet" for the Test Acts and for the reign of William and
Mary hints that persecution will have a brief and unilluminating ascen-
dance in the sky. For in 1681, after the judicial murders of some twenty
priests,[27] the poet had satirized Titus Oates as just such a comet: "yet
Comets rise / From Earthy Vapours ere they shine in Skies" (*Absalom*,
636). The perjuries of Titus Oates had indeed cast a weird, surrealistic
light on the nation, as when he accused the actor-playwright Matthew
Medbourne—who often *played* the roles of generals onstage and who
was playing Agamemnon when he was arrested—of being the *real* general of a pretended papal army poised to invade England.[28] The Anglican
lawyer Sir Roger North reflected later that the Popish Plot had been
"below Legend," and "below Idiots to credit," yet there had been a kind
of "Witchcraft" that "took away common Freedom of Speech," so that
"one might have denied *Christ* with less Contest than the Plot."[29] In the
next generation, Bolingbroke wished that, for the honor of his country,
the story of the "Popish Plot" could be razed from British history.[30] It is
telling, therefore, that the Hind links Oates, the "perjur'd murtherer"

---

27. John Kenyon, *The Popish Plot* , 47, 54; Henry Foley, *Records of the English
Province of the Society of Jesus*, 7 vols. in 8 (London: Burns and Oates, 1877–1883), 5:26n;
Bishop Richard Challoner, *Memoirs of Missionary Priests* (London, 1742), 2:376–474.
28. See my essay "Matthew Medbourne's *Tartuffe* (1670): A Satire on Land-
Acquisition during the Interregnum," *Restoration and Eighteenth-Century Theatre
Research* 9 (1994): 11–14.
29. North, *Examen*, 177, 187–93.
30. On Bolingbroke, see the anonymous *Considerations on the Penal Laws against*

who blazed briefly as a "Comet," to the current campaign of "black detraction" conducted by the Panther's Latitudinarian clergy in defense of those inseparable "Comet-laws" (3:256–57).

Henry Care observes that the men and women condemned to death in the past for their nonconformist beliefs had been valued as heroes and martyrs. The Test, he mourns, now creates an ignominious, unheroic Smithfield (once a place of execution for religion, near London). A person disabled by the Test is not honored, even though he is "as much a sufferer for conscience in Kind, tho not in Degree, as he that is actually put to Death for the same."[31] William Penn agreed:

And therefore it can in no wise be said to be of so different a Nature from that Liberty of Conscience we are speaking of. . . . I conceive not how any one can doubt it to be an infringement of that Liberty. For those Imployments being not hereditary, the way to them is by Nature open to every Man. . . . Now if a person otherwise duly qualified for such an Imployment, which might inable him and his Family to live in Ease and Comfort, shall by reason of some Opinion in religious Matters be excluded from that Imployment, and therby exposed to Penury and Hardship; this indeed is not a direct putting that Person to Death for that Opinion, but it is a taking away from him that Talent which Nature or Industry had given him as a Provision for the Comfort of his Life.[32]

When he says that it is not a "direct putting that Person to Death," Penn implies that making a person ineligible for employment because of religion may put him to death indirectly by "Penury and Hardship."

To such pleas for compassion, however, the defenders of the Test would reply that nonpossession of public employment is no persecution. Giles Shute sums up the Panther's smug response: "no Man is forc'd to come into the Government, and so no man is forc'd to receive the Sacrament on this Account." Shute strikes a truly modern note when he retorts that citizens have a God-given duty to engage in government, especially nonconformists, who need to have "their Proportion of Representatives in the Parliament-House, to defend and secure them" from "cruel oppressing Laws." As to their not being compelled to receive the sacrament,

Roman Catholics in England, and the New Acquired Colonies in America (London: R & J Dodsley, 1764), 33.

31. Care, *Draconica*, 15.
32. Penn, *Free Reflections*, 9–10.

he reminds his readers of the Jacobean statute that then loomed behind the Test and was its original foundation, the law "to force all Adult Persons to the Sacrament, once a year at least, at their Parish-Church." Shute claims to know people who have been put "in the *Exchequer*, for not paying it."[33] Making the same point as Giles Shute, the Hind quotes the Panther as saying:

> Still thank your selves you cry, your noble race
> We banish not, but they forsake the place.
> Our doors are open; true, but e'er they come,
> You toss your censing *Test*.
>
> (3:750–52)

Thus the Panther is revealed as blaming the nonconformists themselves for their suffering; she smugly insinuates that the nonconformists, by refusing to take the Test for religious reasons, have wilfully, capriciously incapacitated themselves from public employment.

33. Shute, *New Naked Truth*, 27, 31–32.

CHAPTER 5

The Appeal to Native Rights

The second argument against the Test in the campaign of 1685–1688 was that it deprived Englishmen of their "native rights." By protesting that despite their differences regarding worship they were indeed "Englishmen," nonconformists revealed that they felt their national identity impugned by the Test. Prejudged as untrustworthy and incapable of serving their country loyally either in civil office or in the military, they had been deprived of part of their English birthright for no real crime, but only for their religious opinions.

The appeal to native rights was based on the idea of an ancient British constitution, of a law almost as old as nature itself, and so beyond the power of modern parliaments to alter. Elsewhere Dryden claims that the British form of government is "Equal almost to Time in its extent" (*Threnodia*, 313–14), alluding to the belief that prevailed in his century that the earth was around six thousand years old, and thus that natural time and historical time were almost equal in length. J. G. A. Pocock explains that English common law was customary law, and that seventeenth-century lawyers, who defined "customary" to mean "of immemorial character," insisted that statutory law contained "no more than the wisdom of one man or one generation," while customary law, which they called "purely native," contained "the wisdom of many generations."[1]

---

1. J. G. A. Pocock, *The Ancient Constitution and the Feudal Law: A Study of Eng-*

It is clear from his writings that Dryden believed the foundation of English law to be the accumulated wisdom of many generations. He warns in *Absalom and Achitophel* that the voice of a single parliament is fallible: "the most may err as grosly as the few" (782), and notes that a given generation may be subject to "Lunacy" because infected with lies (788). Hence, the majority votes of any one parliament should not be allowed to shake a "Frame" of government that has been settled for many ages, one that is thriving under the care of Providence, for this would permit a single generation to decree in God's stead (758). What would be erected then would be "that Golden Calf, a State" (63–66), that is, a mere man-made idol of a government, as opposed to an "Ark," a government as a gift bestowed, developed, and protected for ages by Providence. Having seen the clamor of the House of Commons end up in a dictatorship in the time of Cromwell, the poet asserts that a pious care to conserve age-old constitutional guarantees is the best protection against an "unbounded Arbitrary Lord" (762).

Thus the poet sees a temporal as well as a spatial dimension to the English community, but the temporal aspect is what evokes his religious awe: the inherited constitution is the "Ark" or Holy of Holies to be kept from the unhallowed gaze and touch of modern parliaments (*Absalom*, 804–7, 1009). Dryden, alluding to Psalm 78, speaks of two kinds of "fathers" in English history: rebel fathers and obedient fathers (*Medall*, 112–30). The "Rebel-fathers" loathed the manna of inherited law, and got instead the poisonous quails of arbitrary rule; on the other hand, the obedient fathers were good growers: their human providence worked under Divine Providence to perfect a government that would thrive in an English climate, in the "wholesome Tempest" of the interplay between king and parliament (*Medall*, 246–55). It was easy for the poet to apply such principles to the three Test Acts: those statutes were enacted by one modern parliament transported with false, artificially generated fears over the "growth of popery." Meanwhile, the Test stripped away the inherited rights of Englishmen under the immemorial constitution.

The plea for native rights is recognizable in the campaign of 1685–1688 by the use of such recurring words as "native," "Englishman," and "birthright." For example, Penn declares that the Test makes an Englishman a

---

lish Historical Thought in the Seventeenth Century (Cambridge: Cambridge University Press, 1957), 31, 34.

foreigner in his own land only for his nonconformity, saying to him, "No Church-man, no English man," and likewise Bishop Cartwright reminds his readers that Catholic peers are "Englishmen" after all.[2] A Protestant Dissenter urges conformists to let "all other Free-born *English*-Men" enjoy their "Birth-rights" and to be satisfied with their "equal Proportion of the Government, in common with other Free-born *English*-Men, and fellow Subjects."[3] Following this line of argument, Dryden has the Hind reproach the ruling party for enslaving "their Fellow-Subjects" (3:1202); here the term "Fellow-subjects" implies that they were all born equal in their Englishness under the ancient constitution before the modern statutes made such a great division between them.

One way the Panther undercuts herself in this poem is that she keeps portraying Catholics as foreigners with no native rights and then contradicts herself by admitting that they have ancient roots in Britain. In her tale the Panther presents the Catholic Swallows as having no permanent home in Britain: if they refuse to fly across the Channel to Dorp when the "winter" penalties of snow and hail are about to fall on them from the northwind Boreas (i.e., a hostile parliament), then they are simply stupid and deserve all the punishment they will get. She even calls some of the Swallows who return to England during the unseasonable "summer" of James II's reign "foreign fowls." However, the Panther later forgets herself and unwittingly admits that the Swallows belong in England by inheritance after all: she says that they are going about to "repossess their patrimonial sky" and refurbish their "ancient houses, running to decay" (3:561–81). Her use of the words "repossess," "patrimonial," and "ancient" undercuts her other claim that they have no native rights in Britain.

In Canticles 2:10–12 there is an exquisite aubade in which the Beloved tells the Spouse "Arise, make hast my love, my dove, my beautiful one, and come. For winter is now past, the rayne is gone, and departed." The Church fathers interpreted the phrase "winter is now past" to mean the end of the rigors of Jewish Law, and the phrase "the rayne is gone" to mean the rising of Christ, the Sun of Righteousness (RFL, 93). In her tale, the foolish Panther is the Bride of the Law who prefers the rigorous winter and refuses to enjoy the summer sun, the love and liberty of religious

2. Penn, *A Perswasive to Moderation to Church Dissenters* ([London]: [Andrew Sowle, 1686]), 22; Cartwright, *An Answer of a Minister*, 47.
3. Shute, *New Naked Truth*, 39–40.

peace. She undercuts herself by her own rhetoric when she craves the eclipse of a just king who, in her own imagery, is as warm and benign as a summer sun, only because she is too insecure to trust him: "I believe him just, / And yet—" (3:884–85). The Panther likewise undercuts herself when she compares the Hind's sons to the Trojans in Italy: first, she says they are "strangers" who claim an "ancient Pedigree" but are actually "intruding" on her property; then she admits that she has no ancient claim herself, but only a long possession after intrusion: "By long possession all the land is mine" (3:766–80). This is typical of the Panther's lack of internal coherence. By her parallel from Virgil she proves unwittingly that the Hind has an immemorial origin in the land, a divine mandate for returning, and a native right to a foothold and a chance to grow in the land.

In her tale, the Hind creates a mirror image of the self-contradictory Panther: one minute the Pigeons admit that the Catholic Hens have an ancient lineage in Britain and that their "Forefathers" were "Expell'd" for excessive fasting and praying, as well as "for their Lands"; then, the next minute, the Pigeons speak of the Poultry as foreign "intruding" guests who are bringing in "Unnatural Fasts, and Foreign Forms of Pray'r" into England (3:1023–28). The Pigeons feel insecure because they are themselves intruders and have only a long de facto possession: their "House" was "built, long since, God knows, for better Birds," and so they "lodge in Habitations not their own." The Hind calls the Pigeons "Corporations priviledg'd by Laws" (3:954) to suggest that the de facto possession of Anglicans comes from modern written law, not from ancient inheritance. Nevertheless, it was the English Catholics who, despite their ancient roots, would continue to be treated like foreigners in Britain, as can be seen when, in 1764, a spokesman for them pleads that their "utmost wish" is to have parliament treat them like Jews and Moravians.[4]

Whereas the Hind, in part 3, appeals for the native rights of Catholics, Dryden appeals, in part 1, mainly for the native rights of Protestant nonconformists. The poet uses the key word "native" when he hints that the Puritans in Britain have a "native claim of just inheritance":

Oh happy Regions, *Italy* and *Spain*,
Which never did those monsters entertain!
The *Wolfe*, the *Bear*, the *Boar*, can there advance

---

4. Anon., *Considerations on the Penal Laws*, 59, 67.

No native claim of just inheritance.
And self-preserving laws, severe in show,
May guard their fences from th' invading foe.
(1:291–96)

The poet admits by indirection here that Dissenters have a right to freedom of worship in Britain because they have dwelt there from time immemorial. His view is exactly that of Castlemaine, who wrote that there
were two grounds for giving liberty of conscience to nonconformists in a
nation. The first was their numbers: "nor can any one justly blame us, if
we strive to keep new opinions (which have been so fatal to Christendom) out of Places wholy Obedient to the *Church*," such as Italy and
Spain, he says, but when sects grow numerous, then we may use only
"prayers, preaching, and Books" against them. This right to freedom of
worship because of numbers had been recognized in 1598, in the Edict of
Nantes. The second ground of freedom of worship was a long, uninterrupted continuance in a nation. Castlemaine asks, "[W]ho is it, that says
the Swedes are inhumane, because none except Lutherans shall live
among them?" He feels that the long absence of Catholics from Sweden
means that their laws are more severe in show than in practice. But he
thinks that in England, where not everyone "fell from Popery" and where
Catholics have continued to live since the Reformation, "there is not the
same just motive for punishment."[5]

In seventeenth-century Europe the ideal was still "one nation, one
church," but the reality was that England had been divided since the
time of Wycliffe. By tracing the Wolf's origin in England to fourteenth-
century Lollards in the first part of *The Hind*, the poet hints that Puritans
have been there from time immemorial. As much as he dislikes their
tenets, he insists on their right to enjoy their "just inheritance" in peace:
"Where birth has plac'd 'em let 'em safely share / The common benefit of
vital air" (1:297–98). The strategy Dryden uses here was still being employed a century later, when the unitarian Joseph Priestley included
Catholics in the Dissenting doctrine of religious liberty, and when the
Whigs worked for Catholic emancipation in the face of strong opposition

---

5. Castlemaine, *Apology*, 551–52. Charles Weiss says that Barrillon regarded Castlemaine as one of the three "chefs de l'aristocratie catholique" in whom James had complete trust, "la confiance la plus illimiteé"; see *Histoire des réfugiés protestants de France*
(Paris: Charpentier/London: Jeffs, 1853), 283.

from the same church party Dryden had tried in vain to persuade in 1687.[6] It is useful to place the repeal campaign of 1685–1688 in the larger context of the struggle against the Test from 1685 to 1827 in order to see that the strategies used in Dryden's day—particularly the alliance of Catholics with nonconformist Protestants for the limited political goal of repealing the Test Acts—were indeed successful in the end.

To underline the common cause binding Puritan and Catholic, Dryden uses the same phrase, "chased from their native walk," to depict how both sides were hunted either into foreign exile or into hiding at home during the Restoration. The Catholics were driven from their "native walk" (1:15) and "native place" (3:729) during the Oates Plot of 1678–1682, when the Hind was "chas'd" throughout the "kingdoms, once Her own" (1:5, 26). In the same way, the Puritans were "chas'd" from their "native walks" during the Tory revenge of 1683–1685, from the time of the discovery of the Rye House Plot to the end of the prosecutions for Monmouth's Rebellion (1:237). By repeating the words "chased" and "native walk(s)," Dryden links Puritans and Catholics as prey-animals hunted into their hiding places and driven from their native land.

In *Britannia Rediviva*, composed in June 1688, Dryden likewise uses the rhetoric of native rights to applaud the king's campaign to repeal the Test. Even when the king is at the nadir of his popularity, Dryden staunchly defends the repeal campaign in print. In an apostrophe to the newborn prince, the poet asks him to "finish what thy Godlike Sire begins," and then explains that James II has just begun "to make us *English-Men* again" (40–41). That is, by using his royal prerogative, the king has started restoring nonconformists to their native inheritance, but only repeal of the Test Acts and penal laws will complete the process. The poet does not have much hope that the next parliament will vote for repeal, but he thinks the birth of James II's son guarantees that nonconformists will at least continue to enjoy their *birthrights*: the smiling "open face" of the royal baby "Assures our Birthrights, and assumes his own" (117). The phrase "his own" refers to the ancient power to dispense from statutes like "the still impending Test" (157). The poet sees the prince as a child of prayers "Drawn down from Heav'n," and the flood of calumnies surrounding his birth as the Dragon's attempt to devour the "son"

6. Cowherd, *Protestant Dissenters*, 46, 53.

born of that woman "clothed with the sun" in Apocalypse 12:4. In his
memoirs, King James blames his two ambitious daughters Mary and
Anne for spreading these slanders about his son's birth that sparked the
revolution.[7]

Shortly after passage of the Test Act of 1673, Castlemaine thanked
Penn for regarding Catholics as "Englishmen," and later, when a crowd
cheered his acquittal in 1681, he wrote that it proved "that no people are
so naturally well pleased with the preservation of a *Fellow-Subject*, as *Englishmen*, and consequently how necessary it is to ferment their passions,
and to put them quite besides themselves, before their humour can turn
bloudy and inhumane."[8] In the 1685–1688 campaign Penn argued that
Catholics want only to stand "upon Native Rights, the Great Charter,
what we all of us call, our Birth-right," and he warned that the "Exclusion
of Roman Catholics" from "all Places of Public Trust, either Civil or Military" is no "Security to our Civil Rights, or to the Fundamental Constitution of our Government. They are English Men as well as we."[9] For defending Catholics, Penn was suspected of being a Jesuit.[10]

Henry Nevil Payne also includes Protestant Dissenters with Catholics
when he appeals to native rights. Like Dryden, he may have converted
only in the 1680s, since Castlemaine calls him a Protestant in his *Manifesto* (1681). But he was a sympathizer long before then, for he was caught
in 1679 with verses he had composed in honor of his friend Edward Coleman, the first man to be convicted as a traitor and executed in the pretended Popish Plot. Along with an invocation to Coleman in which he is
regarded as a saint, the verses include a couplet that perfectly evokes the
sprezzatura of the man: "Not that I hope to equall you in place, / Tho' I
could wish it with the like Disgrace." Payne was also a playwright, best
known for his *Siege of Constantinople* (1675), a finely wrought drama in
which the passage of the Test Act of 1673 was shown as the Turks' captur-
ing of Irene, the Church of England, by the treachery of Shaftesbury. In

7. James II, *Life*, 2:158–62.
8. Castlemaine, *Apology*, 560; *Manifesto*, 81.
9. [William Penn], *A Letter from a Gentleman in the Country to His Friends in
London, upon the Subject of the Penal Laws and Tests* ([London], 1687), 8; and the "First
Letter" of *Three Letters Tending to Demonstrate How the Security of This Nation
against All Future Persecution Lys in the Abolishment of the Present Penal Laws and
Tests* (London: Andrew Sowle, 1688), 12–13.
10. For example, in Maurice's *The Project*, 25, and in *A Letter from a Minister of the
Church of England to the Pretended Baptist* (London: Andrew Sowle, 1688), 6.

this play, to underline the ineffectiveness of the Test, he had one of his characters remark: "Your frankness binds me more than Sacraments."[11] Payne contributed much to the repeal campaign when he refuted the idea of collective guilt, which is the groundwork of the Test Acts.

In the seventeenth century most Englishmen believed that nonconformists were justly deprived of their right to public employment because they had inherited the guilt of crimes committed by former and even foreign members of their churches. Henry Payne, however, struck a truly modern note when he contended that "no Community is answerable for the Rebellious politick Practices of their Members; no, though their Declarations to obtain their purposes be in the name of the whole, provided any number of the same societies protest and act against such Declarations." He added with typical brio that if every community were to be disabled in law for the actions of its particular members, the members of every society in the world would have forfeited "their Title to the protection of those Laws they live under."[12]

This modern argument against collective guilt is found earlier in Castlemaine, but only with respect to Catholics: he writes of the injustice of tarring all English Catholics in perpetuity for the Gunpowder Plot of 1605, when that plot was carried out by a handful of men who were unknown to other Catholics and who were entrapped by government agents acting under the supervision of Lord Robert Cecil.[13] This debunking of collective guilt is also glimpsed in the writings of other opponents of the Test. For example, Bishop Cartwright asks, "[W]hy should the indiscretion of a few incense us against the rest?"[14] Likewise, Penn exclaims, "[S]ocieties must not be condemned for the miscarriages of particular Persons."[15] In the eighteenth century, Lord Taaffe applies this principle to the statements of a particular member of the Catholic religion,

---

11. Payne, *Verses on the Death of Edward Coleman*, in W. H. Hart, *Index Expurgatorius Anglicanus* (London: J. R. Smith, 1872), 198. Also, *The Siege of Constantinople* (London: Tho. Dring, 1675), 42.

12. Payne, *Persecutor Expos'd*, 29.

13. Castlemaine, *Apology*, 401–15. This view of the Gunpowder Plot derives from the petition signed by twenty-five Catholics; see [Richard Broughton], *English Protestants Plea, and Petition, for English Preists and Papists, to the Present Court of Parliament, and All Persecutors of Them* ([St. Omer], 1621; rpt., Amsterdam: Theatrum Orbis Terrarum/Norwood, N.J.: Walter J. Johnson, 1976), 54–58.

14. Cartwright, *Answer of a Minister*, 41.

15. Penn, *Free Reflections*, 14.

as Castlemaine had done: "It is a species of civil superstition as the protestant states of Germany have long since got rid of [to quote] a pope or a Roman doctor who has countenanced rebellious conduct or treachery as if that impugns all Catholics."[16] John Locke, however, in *A Letter Concerning Toleration* (1689), imputes collective guilt to Catholics and wants to deny them toleration because some particular members in former times said that "Faith is not to be kept with Hereticks," and "Kings excommunicated forfeit their Crowns."[17]

Dryden does not take this line of argument against collective guilt; rather, he pleads for Christian forgiveness. In *Britannia Rediviva*, he sees that historical grudges undergird the Test Acts and Penal Laws, and so he warns his fellow Englishmen that their hardness of heart is unchristian: "not daring to forgive, / Our Lives unteach the Doctrine we believe" (283–84). He gives an example of such ready forgiveness when he prays that God will not exact retribution for the blood of Catholic martyrs executed in 1678–1681, but will let that blood be the seed of converts, to produce "A Harvest ripening for another Reign, / Of which this Royal Babe may reap the Grain" (163–64).

In *An Answer to a Scandalous Pamphlet* (1687), written in reply to the Marquis of Halifax's defense of the Test, Payne argues that repeal will be "a Bulwark against the like Law for Destruction of any other Party, [that] may chance to be out of fashion." He adds that the Test strikes at "the Root, and destroys the very foundation of *English* liberty; since against the true intent of *Magna Charta*, it deprives Men of their Birthright, without any Crime or Tryal of their *Peers*; and may be an In-let by *Faction* to all manner of Slavery."[18] His bold phrase "out of fashion" and his use of the word "Faction" hint that age-old birthrights are being sacrificed for the narrow interests of an upstart faction. Now when Payne and other repealers speak of a new "*Magna Charta*," a charter of liberty, or a "universal franchise," they are referring to a proposed law which they hoped would be enacted by the next parliament after the repeal of the Test. This charter

16. Taaffe, *Observations*, 14.

17. John Locke, *A Letter Concerning Toleration* (1689), ed. James H. Tully (Indianapolis, Ind.: Hackett, 1983), 50.

18. Henry Payne, *An Answer to a Scandalous Pamphlet Entituled A Letter to a Dissenter Concerning His Majesties Late Declaration of Indulgence* (London: N[at] T[hompson], 1687), 7. The author of the *Letter to a Dissenter*, who had signed himself T. W., was actually George Savile, marquis of Halifax.

was supposed to guarantee that there would never again be a Test Act by making it a "crime" even for the king himself to try to curtail access to public employment for reasons of religion. The excitement over this charter among the Protestant Dissenters can be glimpsed in the repeal literature of 1688, as when one author who purports to be a high churchman says that the coming "Universal Liberty" will make it "highly Penal, for any Party to infringe it" and will "effectually secure the *Protestant Religion*" against any arbitrary king, the reason being that the new charter will declare any religious test for public office to be evil in itself, and the king of England has no power under the constitution to dispense with something evil in itself. It follows, then, that "this *Magna Charta* is a very great Security" which James II is willing to place beyond the reach of the royal prerogative.[19] The name "Magna Charta" may have been meant to remind the nation that Catholic Englishmen had not always been obliged, for survival, to be friends of the royal prerogative and that "Magna Charta itself, annual elections of our representatives, and the great sanctions of the British constitution, were fought for, and obtained by our Popish ancestors."[20]

In the hopes of repealing the Test and enacting this proposed charter, James II sent his agents to interrogate candidates for the next parliament about whether, if elected, they would vote to repeal the Test. To many, this canvassing appeared to impose a new and opposite Test for public office: it implied that only those who favored equal access to public employment regardless of religion were fit for public office. This canvassing made the king unpopular with the ruling party in the spring of 1688 and brought him no nearer to getting a parliament willing to "take off the Test." In a letter to the dramatist George Etherege, dated February 16, Dryden alludes to this canvassing as counterproductive: "for my minde misgives me, that he will not much advance his affaires by Stirring."[21] While the Protestant Dissenter Shute rejoices in the "new Test" which he sees as against bigotry, the Anglican bishop Cartwright is clearly distressed

19. A. B., *A Letter from a Minister of the Church of England to the Pretended Baptist, Author of The Three Considerations Directed to Mr. Penn* (London: Andrew Sowle, 1688), 4–5. The author of *Three Considerations* was Thomas Comber. Since Bishop Cartwright uses these initials "A.B." for *An Answer of a Minister of the Church of England* (1687), it is possible that he is the author of this reply to Comber, too.

20. [John Curry, M.D.], *Observations on the Popery Laws* (Dublin: T Ewing, 1771), 33.

21. *The Letters of John Dryden*, ed. Charles E. Ward (Durham, N.C.: Duke University Press, 1942), 26.

by signs of a growing backlash, and he tries to allay the majority party's anger by insisting that James wants only to "Treat with His People" about the repeal "for the future," and wants only a "conditional" consent and "terms offered." He tells them coaxingly that no coercion is involved, because the king can only recommend candidates for the next parliament on the basis of their answers about the Test, and the English are still "free after all" whether or not to elect them.[22]

However impolitic the canvassing was, it was not illegal, and, as a modern historian notes, the king did not go "beyond his constitutional rights in his campaign to pack parliament."[23] It is worth mentioning that in 1827 a political instrument closely resembling James II's "Three Questions" was used successfully to finally overthrow the Test: it was called the "Dissenting pledge" and got the candidates for parliament to commit themselves to repeal of the Test before they were elected.

It is often asked what the king's motives were in trying so urgently to repeal the Test. After the 1688 revolution, it was alleged that he had wanted to place Catholics uppermost in England and to tyrannize over the consciences of others. But according to Lord Ailesbury, an Anglican nobleman who was a close friend of James II, the king's private conversation revolved frequently around "liberty of conscience and many hands at work in trade; and that made him receive all the French Huguenots," as well as deplore in Ailesbury's hearing "the King my brother of France's severity" against Protestants.[24]

There was another motive, too, besides this prospect of economic prosperity. When James lost his naval command in wartime, in 1673, as a result of the Test Act, he learned from personal experience about the humiliating incapacity for public office which nonconformists had to endure. In Macpherson's notes, which are based on the complete memoirs of James II lost in the French Revolution, we find that in July 1669, the very year in which he first talked about converting to Catholicism, James had a conversation about liberty of conscience with an anti-Catholic Puritan. It appears from this passage that the secret prospect he now had of becoming a nonconformist himself gave him sympathy for the Protestant

22. Cartwright, *Letter from a Clergyman*, 39; Shute, *A New Test in Lieu of the Old One*.

23. Speck, *Reluctant Revolutionaries*, 153.

24. *Memoirs of Thomas [Bruce], Earl of Ailesbury*, 2 vols. (Westminster, U.K.: Roxburghe Club, 1890), 1:103.

Dissenters: "the duke of York, at Tunbridge, assured Dr. Owen, that he had no bitterness against the nonconformists. He was against all persecution, merely for conscience's sake; looking on it, as an unchristian thing, and absolutely against his conscience."[25] In 1674, about a year after he had lost his own public employments because of the Test, James, then duke of York, instructed Governor Andros of the colony named in his honor, New York, "to leave everyone in peace and quiet on the subject of religion." In 1683, when Thomas Dongan, a Catholic, was governor of New York, James approved without reservation a charter of religious liberty for that colony, and, after he became king, expanded it in 1686 "to include not merely all Christians, but people of all religions, or of none." A year before he extended this religious freedom to Jews in New York, he ordered that Jews in England be "relieved of all restrictions," and he "instructed his attorney general to stop all proceedings against them."[26]

In a work written long after these events and published only after his death, the Anglican lawyer Sir Roger North recalled that the Roman Catholic party in the late seventeenth century was "constant" to protecting the sects from the laws: "and I believe not a few [Protestant Dissenters] were well assured the Duke of *York* would have done it in general, if he could have prevailed so far."[27] Certainly, it was impolitic and risky for King James to try to repeal a Test against religious minorities that was so popular with the majority party, but in his memoirs he says that he thought he had a chance to succeed precisely because the English Catholics were so few they could not reasonably inspire fear. He ponders the charge that he was trying to bring in "popery and slavery" and asks what probability there was "of a Kingdom's being enslaved by a few Catholicks, tho in imployment, or that a handfull of Papists could endanger the Religion and propertie, which millions of Protestants were the keepers of." He wonders how anyone could think him able to establish "Popery with a Protestant army, did he design it, or with a handful of his own people subjugate a nation, which the power of Rome, when it govern'd the world, was never able to make an absolute conquest of."[28]

25. James Macpherson, *Original Papers; Containing the Secret History of Great Britain . . . to Which Are Prefixed Extracts from the Life of James II. as Written by Himself,* 2 vols. (London, 1775), 51.

26. Malcolm V. Hay, *The Enigma of James II,* 72–79.

27. North, *Examen,* 355.

28. James II, *Life,* 2:88.

One historian, who calculates that the ratio of English Catholics to English Protestants was no more than 1:150, thinks that "in assessing James's intentions, it is important for modern historians to recognise that he knew the demographic evidence, and it underscores the unlikelihood of his aiming at anything more ambitious than toleration and access to office for his co-religionists."[29] Another scholar surmises that James wanted mainly to protect his co-religionists from future persecution and leave them "strong enough to escape extirpation under his successor."[30]

The appeal to native rights works in still another way in the repeal literature: the Test is said to sacrifice the "common interest" of all to the special interests of a few. Penn argued that the Test secures the advantage of a small ruling class at the expense of the whole nation: "the continuance of the Test and Penalties" is for the "Interest of a very small part of the Nation," while liberty of conscience is for the "general Interest of the whole." He finds that "Liberty of Conscience is the natural Right of Mankind, and the general Interest of England. Penal Laws and Tests are direct Infringements of that Right and they tend evidently to the ruin of that Interest."[31] Similarly, an anonymous repealer observes that those who oppose James II's charter may use "the Name of Conscience, but upon strict scrutiny, it will appear Pride and Interest," for when they raise "terrible Presages and Apprehensions" over the repeal of the Test, they stand up for "Temporal Jurisdiction and Command."[32]

We find this line of argument in Dryden's poem, too, when the Panther claims that she follows her conscience by defending the Test, and the Hind strips this cloak of conscience from her to reveal the self-interest beneath. The Hind says that surely she uses the wrong word, because a well-informed conscience is ever "the same" and the Panther's is "of the *Camelion* hew" (3:788), first espousing passive obedience to kings and then re-

29. Mark Goldie, "Sir Peter Pett, Sceptical Toryism, and the Science of Toleration," in *Persecution and Toleration*, ed. W. J. Sheils (Oxford: Ecclesiastical History Society/Basil Blackwell, 1984), 270.

30. John Miller, *James II: A Study in Kingship* (London: Wayland, 1978), 128. For James II's aims, see also J. R. Jones, *The Revolution of 1688 in England* (New York: Norton, 1972), 82. Jones compares the English Catholics to the "Jews in twentieth-century eastern and central Europe" (76), which helps to explain James II's concern for their plight.

31. Penn, *Free Reflections*, 6–7, 20.

32. Anon., *The Great Case of Toleration Stated, and Endeavoured to Be Resolved* (London: Andrew Sowle, 1688), 12.

sisting a king who uses his prerogative against the Test. The correct name for such a "*Proteus* Conscience" is "interest" (we would say "self-interest"): "int'rest is her name with men below" (3:824). The Hind clearly gains this round of the argument when the Panther stands exposed and sullenly concedes that interest, not conscience, makes her cling to "our *Test*" and keep all benefit for her own "Tribe":

> Conscience or int'rest be't, or both in one;
> (The *Panther* answer'd in a surly tone,)
> The first commands me to maintain the Crown,
> The last forbids to throw my barriers down
> Our penal laws no sons of your admit,
> Our *Test* excludes your Tribe from benefit.
> (3:825–30)

Arguing in the same vein, a writer sympathetic to James II's project, accuses the established clergy of using the word "conscience" in place of "interest." He tells the English clergy that they call it "conscience" when they refuse to do what the "greatest Number" of their "supposed Friends will be Disobliged by," namely, reading the king's declaration for liberty of conscience from the pulpit. This "Politick Conscience" will not let them do what "may Hurt (your Interest, or as you Term it) the *Church*, and herein our *Conscience* is guided by a frequent Review, and Must'ring up the Numbers on both sides."[33] Bishop Cartwright also argues that *interest*, not *conscience*, prevents the clergy from assisting the king in the repeal campaign. Since the greater part of the ruling class opposes repeal, he points out, the clergy fear to "provoke" them by siding with a king whom they do not fear at all: "As for the King, no body cares how much he be provoked."[34] The Hind makes the same point, saying that when the Panther had proved "by long experience" how far James "cou'd forgive, how well he lov'd," she then crossed his will and with bold presumption joined his foes, "unrestrain'd by fear" (3:799–809).

Those campaigning against the Test argue, in addition, that respecting everyone's native rights will serve the common interest by securing the state against rebellion. One anonymous author, for example, explains that the Test breeds anger against the state: "Those Laws that render Subjects

---

33. Anon., *The Ministers Reasons for His Not Reading the Kings Declaration, Friendly Debated by a Dissenter* (London: G. Larkin, 1688), 10.

34. Cartwright, *Letter from a Clergyman*, 33–34.

incapable of Offices and Places of Profit, beget in their Minds an implacable Aversion towards the Government." Subjects will "consult the ruin of that government, which excludes them from the Comforts and Accommodations of Life, and in some Cases, from a possibility of getting Bread."[35] This right to seek the "Comforts and Accommodations" of life seems like a precursor to the right to the "pursuit of happiness" in the Declaration of Independence. The author of *An Important Query* also argues that repeal will avert rebellion: had such an "intire liberty" been granted by Charles I, he observes, "the Blood which hath been spilt for more then forty years past, might have been prevented."[36]

Those writing for repeal also suggest that the Test works against the common interest of all by preventing the best qualified persons from serving in employments. William Penn laments that "the ablest States man, the bravest Captain, and the best Citizen may be disabled, and the Prince forbid their Imployment to his Service." He claims he knows twenty "Old *Roundheaded* Sea-men" who have had to struggle against their consciences to take the Test so as to serve their country in naval battles.[37] Dryden's Hind takes up this argument in her tale, when the Farmer notices that the Pigeons have passed a statute that debars him from his "Subjects use" (3:1083–84), that is, from employing those best qualified to serve in any employment.

The argument that protecting everyone's native rights equally serves the "common interest" is also found at the end of the Hind's tale, which closes with a grand tableau of the new era of liberty. Apart from the Pigeons, who are to retain separately their "Wealth and State," all the birds on the farm, wild and tame, are now joined in a "common Int'rest." The king promises he will "equally protect" their "sev'ral Kinds" and give them "the same Franchise" and "the like Impartial Grace" (3:1235–55). In *Britannia Rediviva*, likewise, King James is praised for treating all Englishmen with strict equality: "A Prince's favours but on few can fall, / But Justice is a Virtue shar'd by all" (337–38).

This reign of peace which the Hind expects England to enjoy under

35. Anon., *Indulgence to Tender Consciences Shewn to Be Most Reasonable and Christian. By a Minister of the Church of England* (London: Henry Hills, 1687), 2.

36. Anon., *An Important Query for Protestants: Viz. Can Good Com Out of Galilee?* (London: for G. L. and J. H., 1688), 11.

37. Penn, *Perswasive*, 23.

the Indulgence of James II evokes the prosperous garden at the end of
Canticles, where every man brings "for the fruite thereof a thousand
pieces of silver" (8:11). It also glances at the renewed garden of Isaiah
60:22, where "the least shall be [grown] into a thousand." For we now
see a flowering of civilized arts and prosperous trading, which Dryden
hopes will prove the best argument of all for repeal:

> What after happen'd is not hard to guess;
> The small Beginnings had a large Encrease,
> And Arts and Wealth succeed (the secret spoils of Peace.).
>   (3:1264–67)

CHAPTER 6

The Appeal to the Property Rights of Peers

The appeal to native rights was grounded on the idea that every English-man inherited certain immemorial rights at birth and could not lose them except after commiting a crime. This argument was useful for attacking the Test Acts of 1661 and 1673. However, to overturn the Test Act of 1678, it was more useful to appeal to property rights, since this last Test affected at first only the inheritance rights of English noblemen by depriving them of their seats in the House of Lords.

In the repeal campaign of 1685–1688, Dryden and a few high-church opponents of the Test speak of the 1678 statute as the most heinous of the three Test Acts and reserve their most passionate words for it. Indeed, the Hind uses a powerful biblical rhetoric to compare the last Test to Judas's betrayal and to King Saul's persecution of David. This statute, which stripped James of his best friends in parliament, seemed to attack the hereditary principle behind the English monarchy. For if parliament could pass a law to deprive a peer of his seat in the House of Lords merely because of his religious opinions, then what was to prevent parliament from passing another law to deprive the royal heir apparent, again for his religious opinion, of his right to wear the crown. According to one mod-ern historian, the Test of 1678 may have ejected "perhaps as many as 20 per cent of the peerage" from parliament.[1] It was designed solely to exclude Catholics, for it mandated taking an oath that branded Catholic worship as idolatry (and certainly no Catholic could swear to such an oath), and did not target Protestant Dissenters, for it did not impose the obligation of taking the sacrament of the national church, which would have required kneeling.

In part 3 of *The Hind and the Panther,* the Hind argues that regardless of their religious beliefs, the Catholic peers have a property right to sit in the parliament, because the right to legislate was inherited from time immemorial along with their titles and estates. This argument can be identified in the repeal literature by its rhetorical use of the terms "robbery" and "disseisin." The Anglican bishop of Oxford writes that repeal of the 1678 statute would be a "Compensation" to those peers whom Lord Shaftesbury "robb'd of their Peerage" and "stript of the greatest Privilege of their Birth-right."[2] Similarly, James II in his memoirs charges that the 1678 act "rob'd the Peers of their birth right, and without their being guilty of any crime, took that from them which nothing but treason could have done before." The repeal of that statute, he thinks, would have made "some amends" for their being "wrongfully oppress'd" in the sham Popish Plot.[3]

The appeal to property rights was based, like the appeal to native rights, on England's customary law. As Blackstone explained, the term "property" in law did not merely designate physical property, such as land and buildings: a person might have "an estate" in offices and dignities, "an incorporeal hereditament or a right" issuing out of inherited land.[4] Long before the repeal campaign began, Castlemaine had argued that Catholics had a property right to worship privately in England because they were "in possession," that is, their faith was the religion of the land at the time of the Reformation. To illustrate his principle, he said that the first Christians had tolerated "Ancient Heathens because they found them in possession," that King Ethelbert had tolerated British pagans because he found them "in possession," and that the Turkish

1. Speck, *Reluctant Revolutionaries,* 171.
2. Samuel [Parker], Lord Bishop of Oxford, *Reasons for Abrogating the Test Imposed upon All Members of Parliament Anno 1678 Oct. 30* (London: For Henry Bonwicke, 1688), 6.
3. James II, *Life,* 2:145–46.
4. J. W. Erlich, *Erlich's Blackstone* (New York: Capricorn, 1959), 125–30.

emperor himself permitted Catholics to worship privately in Eastern Europe because he had found them "in possession."[5] Since he had studied law at the Inner Temple, Castlemaine deployed the language of property rights shrewdly, as in this passage: "Therefore as a man that is turned out of his house by a stranger, may expect more than the stranger being dispossest can do from the right owner: so Papists may justly expect more liberty from Protestants, then they can upon any pretence from Papists; yet Protestants live to this day freer in Catholique kingdoms then we do under them."[6] Samuel Pepys's diary entry for December 1, 1666, reveals that Castlemaine's *Apology* was greatly in demand, though suppressed by parliament. After getting hold of a copy at someone's house and reading it, Pepys praises its style and gives a summary of its arguments. William Penn also knew Castlemaine's property-rights argument, for he refers to it when he declares that one unanswerable plea against the persecuting laws of England is that they are "against our great Law of Property, and so void in themselves. This has been the Language of every Apology."[7]

The Hind glances at this property-rights argument, too, when she calls the Test of 1678 a wrongful "disseisin" of property. Before the Test, she notes, "Our Peers possess'd in peace their native place," even long before the "First Reformers" (3:728–29). Then came the earl of Shaftesbury, the "great Oppressor," who "disseis'd" his "brother" by a legal trick, a mere "slight of law," while their "common Sire" King Charles II surrendered in a "fright" (3:710–12). Here she depicts the 1678 Test as a legal maneuver by which this leader of the radical Whigs stole the inheritance of the Catholic peers right under the nose of the king, who was powerless to stop the robbery because of the "fright" produced in him by the Popish Plot. The phrase "slight of law" refers to the last Test Act as a magician's trick, while the words "brother" and "sire" evoke a family situation in which a Protestant prevents his older Catholic brother from inheriting the estate to which the latter is entitled by the ancient law of England, while the father stands by helpless.

The Hind argues that if the church party votes now to retain the 1678 statute despite the fact that the frauds of Shaftesbury's party and the Rye

5. Castlemaine, *Apology*, 202, 552–53.

6. Castlemaine, *A Reply to the Answer of the Catholique Apology; or, A Cleere Vindication of the Catholiques of England from All Matter of Fact Charged Against Them by Their Enemyes* ([Antwerp?], 1668), 137.

7. Penn, *Good Advice*, 54–55.

House Plot of 1683 have now been fully exposed, this will amount to a new injustice—their keeping possession of an estate after their "unrighteous title" has been demonstrated (3:713). They will be shown to value de facto possession of property above de jure right. Here Dryden anticipates what will become the refrain of the Jacobite writings in the 1690s, that the dethroned king "Jemmy" will have "his own" again, because his property right to reign cannot, under the ancient constitution, be set aside by parliament's act of giving William de facto possession of the crown.

The property-rights argument provides the legal context for the urgency with which James II tried to repeal the 1678 Test. In common law, according to Blackstone, a wrongful intruder who was actually in possession of property was *presumed* to have a *right* as well as a mere *possession* unless the rightful owner made an entry as soon as possible upon the property. Thus common law required a person who had been unjustly dispossessed of his property to be active and quick to reclaim his own. If the owner was foolish enough to wait till a generation had passed to assert his right, then the heirs of the intruder would already have the actual right, and not just the presumptive right, of possession. Hence, instead of being able to make an entry on his property, now the rightful owner would have to prove his claim in a court of law.[8] Thus, if the rightful owner remained passive, the one who inherited from a de facto possessor became the presumptively rightful owner. As applied to the Test Act of 1678, this interpretation meant that James II had to repeal the statute while the first generation of peers who had been admitted by this Test could still be ejected, for it would be too late when their sons came to inherit those seats in the House of Lords.

From this we see how clever the members of the Tory party were when they tried to preach *patience* to James II, asking him to move slowly in the repeal campaign because the church was in danger. They knew that the common law required him to be quick about reclaiming that property in the *same* generation it was stolen. The author of *A Letter in Answer to Two Main Questions* gives warning about the Tories' plea for patience. He uses a rhetoric of property rights to show that patience with regard to the Test will be fatal: "It were to ask a Man, whether in prudence, he ought to part from the *present possession* of his Estate, and live (*he knows not how*

8. Erlich, *Erlich's Blackstone*, 240–43.

long) without it, upon the *hopes* and *promise* of *he knows not whom?* that the same Estate would be most probably restor'd to him, *he knows not when?*"[9]

The defenders of the Test were indeed vague about how long they expected nonconformists to wait. Henry Nevil Payne finds it "pretty plausible Sophistry, to make Men neglect the present Possession of their Desires, in hopes of a future Possibility of gaining them."[10] Another repealer points out that the church party, because of their "Disturbed Imagination, which is through Prejudice so Darkned," had not found in the course of the past twenty-eight years a single year when they felt secure, and so what hope was there when they said they would be indulgent after the danger was past?[11] Bishop Cartwright, addressing the ruling party, summed up their plea for patience thus: you are saying that Dissenters should "starve while your Grass grows," and you spread "a suspicion" that the king's declaration is a "mere Trap, a Gin, a pitfall," when it is truly the Dissenters' best hope.[12]

Dryden's poem contains a similar passage about how the plea of patience is a conformist stratagem to stop the repeal campaign. The Panther, representing the Tories, confesses that she holds on to the "unjust" Test unwillingly—"Unwilling, witness all ye Pow'rs above"—and only temporarily, until some "happier time" when she feels secure enough to repeal the Test Acts. She pleads with the Hind to "possess" her "soul with patience" and wait for the reign of William and Mary:

Possess your soul with patience, and attend:
A more auspicious Planet may ascend;
Good fortune may present some happier time,
With means to cancell my unwilling crime.

(3:839–42)

9. [T. G.], *A Letter in Answer to Two Main Questions of the First Letter to a Dissenter* (London: For M. T., 1687), 2.
10. Henry Payne, *An Answer to a Scandalous Pamphlet*, 4, 7.
11. Anon., *The Minister's Reasons . . . Debated*, 19–20.
12. [Thomas Cartwright, Bishop of Chester], *A Letter from a Clergy-Man in the Country, to the Clergyman in the City, Author of the Late Letter to His Friend in the Country: Shewing the Insufficiency of His Reasons Therein Contained for Not Reading the Declaration. By a Minister of the Church of England.* ([London], N. pub., 1688). This was an answer to the Marquis of Halifax, but it came out too late to help James II, for it was licensed August 15, 1688.

Seeing through the ruse, the Hind cries out "Hold." Then, using the language of property rights, she calls this plea for patience a swindle:

> You wou'd *postpone* me to another reign:
> Till when you are content to be unjust,
> Your part is to possess, and mine to trust.
> A fair exhange propos'd of future chance,
> For present profit and inheritance.
>
> (3:848–52)

The words "possess," "present profit," and "inheritance" all apply to the Panther's wrongful intrusion on the Hind's estate, that is, the seats in the House of Lords taken from the Catholics.

From across the Channel the French king saw the Tory cry for patience as a trick: on November 29, 1685, he wrote in code to his ambassador that the English parliament would think it had gained much if James undertook nothing in favor of the Catholic religion during his reign and left it in the deplorable state in which he found it when he came to the throne, subject to the Penal Laws and to all that the fury and transports of its greatest enemies could attempt against it in a conjunction favorable to them.[13] William Penn sees the call for patience as a way of bringing in a "connivance," which would be sinful in his view because it would require every "civil Magistrate" to be "Perjur'd that suffers them in that Liberty against Law."[14] That is, the magistrates sworn to uphold the law would violate their oaths of office by shutting their eyes to nonconformist worship that was against the law.

The Hind uses the language of property rights in another way when she charges the Panther's party with having received the Test of 1678 as a "sacrilegious bribe" in return for giving countenance to the lies of Titus Oates. Both the Anglican Roger North and the Catholic John Gother make this point, that at first the Tories encouraged the Oates Plot or allowed it free rein for their own advantage. In his *Examen*, North recalls that "the loyal Gentlemen and Churchmen, that had, at first either given Countenance to the Plot, or passively let it drive, without endeavouring to rectify their furiously mistaken Neighbours, found themselves levelled at . . ." Elsewhere, too, he remembers that the church party, "though they saw clear enough, that *Oates* was an Impostor, and his Tale below *Legend*,

13. Fox, *Appendix,* cxxxii.
14. Penn, *Good Advice,* 45.

yet, for certain prudential Reasons, (as they thought) had a Fancy to let it run on," at which time the national pulpits were used to spread the plot: "the public Prayers had been accommodated to the Plot; which is a common Method of instilling chimeric Dread into the Peoples Imaginations; as if the public Prayers were among the Impliments of *Matchiavel*."[15] Similarly, John Gother relates that pulpits rang from 1678 to 1681 with the perjuries of Oates "as if they had been deliver'd by the *Evangelists*." He cites sermons by Stillingfleet, Tillotson, Sharp, and Jane, among others, that called for speedy and severe punishments against Catholics from "*Solomon's* Rod" even before any trials took place, thereby inflaming legislators, judges, and mobs, he says, with fury and vengeance.[16] Indeed, in his letters to France, ambassador Barrillon reports to Louis XIV that the plot witnesses are believed in advance and Catholics executed without the least proof because of the English predisposition against Catholics.[17]

Henry Payne claims that one segment of the church party was very active in fomenting the Exclusion Crisis, the attempt to exclude the Catholic heir from the crown. He declares that if a church were answerable for the crimes of its particular members, then the national church's face "would perhaps appear as deform'd with Spots, as any she can find to Persecute." His image of a "spotted" Church afflicting "spotted" nonconformists is the very same image Dryden uses two years later in *The Hind and the Panther*. Payne thinks that the church party contracted these "Spots" from having had in its ranks "the most Potent Sticklers for *Exclusion* through the whole Nation" and the "very Heads and Ringleaders of the *Black Box* Party," that is, those trying to assert the legitimacy of the bastard son of Charles II, the Duke of Monmouth, who had converted to Protestantism.[18]

Following this line of argument against the 1678 Test, the Hind depicts Shaftesbury as having set a clever trap for the church party within the trap he set for Catholics:

15. North, *Examen*, 190, 348, 504.

16. [John Gother], *Good Advice to the Pulpits, Deliver'd in a Few Cautions for the Keeping Up the Reputation of Those Chairs, and Preserving the Nation in Peace*. (London: Henry Hills, 1687), 2–6, 8, 16–17, 20–22. In the 1994 edition of the *Short Title Catalogue* this item (Wing 1328) is misprinted as *Good Advice to the Papists*.

17. J. J. Jusserand, *Angleterre, Tome Deuxième: 1666–1690* (Paris: E. de Boccard, 1929), 277–80. This book is from the series *Recueil des instructions données aux ambassadeurs et ministres de France depuis les traités de Westphalie jusqu' à la Révolution Française*.

18. Payne, *Persecutor Expos'd*, 7.

> As I remember, said the sober *Hind*,
> Those toils were for your own dear self design'd,
> As well as me; and, with the self same throw,
> To catch the quarry, and the vermin too,
> (Forgive the sland'rous tongues that call'd you so.)
> How e'er you take it now, the common cry
> Then ran you down for your rank loyalty.
>
> (2:18–24)

The "common cry" in 1680, that is, the newly elected House of Commons, turned against the Panther, the remnant of the Laudian high church, when the Bill of Exclusion against James II failed to pass. Earlier, in 1678–1679, the Popish Plot had been a trap to "catch the quarry," that is, to catch the Catholic peers, expel them from parliament, and imprison them. Then, in 1680, the Popish Plot evolved into the Exclusion Crisis, a trap for the high-church party itself, because the Whigs knew that excluding the heir was against the principle of hereditary monarchy that most of the Tory party embraced.

The Hind says that, before he died, Shaftesbury made a new testament in favor of the Panther. The seats in the House of Lords were "land" which Shaftesbury was allowed to seize and which he gave to the Panther as a "sacrilegious bribe" for the 1678 Test. So now, the Hind argues, if the Panther fails to return the bribe and give back the "land" to the dispossessed peers, she will be less just than Judas:

> Would you to that unrighteous title stand,
> Left by the villain's will to heir the land?
> More just was *Judas*, who his Saviour sold;
> The sacrilegious bribe he cou'd not hold,
> Nor hang in peace, before he rendr'd back the gold.
>
> (3:713–17)

The Hind accuses the Panther in these lines of a betrayal with a kiss. This might be an allusion to the martyrdom of Thomas Howard, Lord Stafford, an elderly Catholic peer who was actually tried in the House of Lords in 1680 for his supposed role in the imaginary papal army and condemned to death by his own friends and kinsmen on the most absurd evidence. In his epithalamium "On the Marriage of the Fair and Vertuous Lady, Mrs Anastasia Stafford," Dryden speaks of his kinsman Lord Stafford as a holy martyr. He affirms that Stafford was under the special care of "sacred Providence" in 1680: "The God that suffered him to suffer here, / Rewards his race, and blesses them below," because he holds "the blood of martyrs dear" (33–40).

The Hind alludes to another potent biblical figure besides Judas when she notices that the "mitr'd seats are full, yet *David*'s bench is bare" (3:733). Her syntax hints that this sight is somehow strange. Indeed, in his *Apology* Castlemaine relates how the Catholic peers had voted unanimously in 1661, against their own interest, to restore the bishops of the Church of England to their rights of peerage in the House of Lords.[19] Ironically, in 1687, most of the Anglican bishops in turn opposed the restoration of Catholic peers to their seats. When the Hind parallels the "bare" Catholic seats with "*David*'s bench," she evokes 1 Samuel 20:25–27, where David's place at the royal table is "empty" because of Saul's persecution caused by his irrational jealousy. Perhaps she uses the word "bench" to underline the idea that the place vacated is an ancient seat of justice, as in the name "King's Bench."

The allusion to David reinforces the Aeneas myth in part 3. For the Panther resembles both Queen Amata and King Saul, in that she is crazed with jealousy and false fears, while the innocent Hind, like Aeneas and David, wants humbly to survive, be of service, and lay the groundwork for distant glory. By their persecutions, Amata and Saul only ensure that the hero and his tribe—the Trojans and the tribe of Judah, respectively— will eventually be established more firmly as a result of present afflictions. By implication, this will happen to the Catholic party in England, too. Shiloh, a messianic name (Gn 49:10), takes away the Panther's "Scepter" just as Yahweh sends his prophet Samuel to tear away Saul's hope of a future dynasty: "For *Shiloh* comes the Scepter to Remove" (3:1258).

Thus Catholic and high-church repealers both described the Test of 1678 in biblical language as a sacrilegious betrayal of the anointed one. For it was James himself who was the chief target of the Popish Plot and the Exclusion Crisis. The Anglican bishop of Oxford argues passionately for repeal of the third Test because of its "Birth" as "the First-born of Oats's Plot, and brought forth on purpose to give Credit and Reputation to the Perjury."[20] The 1678 Test, he insists, was what made the Popish Plot plausible, for when all the Catholic noblemen were immediately charged

19. Castlemaine, *Apology*, 33.
20. Parker, *Reasons for Abrogating*, 5.

with treason, banished from the House of Lords, and imprisoned in the Tower, the populace could not but be driven to panic fears. This evil birth of the last Test is also in the mind of Bishop Cartwright when he pleads for repeal, insisting that this last Test is grounded on a plot now "for the most part acknowledged to be nothing but Shame and Illusion, Cheat and Villany."[21] Arguing in this vein, the Hind wonders what "new delusion" blinds the Panther now that the "Popish Plot," once a "painted Harlot," has been shown to be a "Hag uncas'd, and all obscene with itch" (3:723–27). She means that the purported Popish Plot has turned out to be, after all, the Rye House Plot of the radical Whigs, a plot designed to assassinate the royal brothers. Here the Hind uses the same word "hag" that the Catholic spokesman Henry Nevil Payne does, when he says that after 1685 the ruling party saw revolutionary Whiggism as a "*Superannuated* Hag."[22]

The Hind reproaches the Panther for forgetting those ties of kinship and friendship that should have bound the Catholic and Protestant peers together in the House of Lords. Those ties are what make the Test of 1678 and the condemnation of Stafford such Judas-like betrayals. This point about the English peers being a family is found in the *Apology*, too, for Castlemaine tries to awaken in the peers a sense of mutuality to counterbalance their differences of religion. Because the families of the English nobility had intermarried since the Reformation, he reminds Protestant landowners that Catholics of their "owne flesh and blood" are punished by the Test. Even though they have "as much birth among us as England can boast of," their Catholic kinsmen receive from the Test "an incapacity for Employment, like the Villains as it were in Ancient times, who had no propriety in the Kingdom."[23]

In the Lords' Journal on April 21, 1675, there is a declaration on the property rights of peers that sounds exactly like the property-rights argument used for repeal of the Test in the 1685–1688 campaign. An oath of civil allegiance had been proposed to the peers as a Test, but it was refused in this way: "We the Peers of this Kingdom declare, that the rights of the Nobility, and the Customs of Parliament are weakened, by the bare putting the question, Whether this oath shall be taken? For the right of

21. Cartwright, *Letter from a Clergyman*, 30.
22. Payne, *Persecutor Expos'd*, 7.
23. Castlemaine, *Reply*, 165.

voting in Parliament does not depend upon certain conditions, but descends by inheritance; neither can there be any loss of it, but that by
which the honour of the Nobility is forfeited; and that can be forfeited
only by Treason."[24] The same House of Lords later voted not to reinstate
the Catholic nobles who made the very same argument. In his memoirs
James II laments that the Test of 1678 took from the peers those rights
"which nothing but treason could have done before, which made the
Peers reject it in the year 1675."[25]

Bishop Cartwright wanted the 1678 Test repealed because it removes
"*ancient Land-marks*," a phrase that reminds us of the Panther's "But" or
"butt" (3:759), which could be interpreted as an ancient boundary stone.
Those seats in the House of Lords had been an inheritance of the peerage
from time immemorial in Britain. Cartwright is especially grieved at the
injustice of the 1678 law because the Catholic families afflicted by it were
"*greater Sufferers*" than others in the Civil Wars and so "might modestly
have expected to have been *restored* to their Privileges of *True English
Subjects* before now, and to have been rais'd above *Contempt* and *Danger*."[26] The phrase "greater sufferers" hints at Cartwright's acquaintance
with the list of Catholic war heroes in Castlemaine's *Apology*.

On the other side, the prevailing view in the church party is well captured in *The Lay-Mans Answer* (1687), where a Tory poet warns those
counting on repeal of their imminent punishment. Alluding to the rhetoric and imagery of *The Hind and the Panther*, the author predicts that
those who "grow wanton in these days of Sun-shine," that is, under King
James's dispensing power, will soon feel the Panther's wrath when the
king is out of the way. He then tells the story of a Panther who fell into a
pit, suffered the cruelty of certain people, escaped, and then returned to
wreak a bloody revenge on those who had shown contempt for her:
"Shepherds and Flocks were undistinguish'd slain, / And raging Vengeance foam'd around the Plain."[27] This fable is in the very same spirit as
the Panther's tale, and it proves how well Dryden had gauged the inten-
sity of "the *Panther's* hate" (2:645).

24. *The History and Proceedings of the House of Lords* [from 1660], 8 vols. (London:
E. Timberland, 1742), 1:138.
25. James II, *Life*, 2:145.
26. Cartwright, *An Answer of a Minister of the Church of England*, 36–37, 51.
27. Anon., *The Lay-Mans Answer to the Lay-Mans Opinion* (London: N. pub.,
1687), 6–11.

The property-rights argument, then, was used mainly against the 1678 Test by Catholics and high churchmen. Giles Shute adumbrates a different property-rights argument, designed for Protestant nonconformists, when he says the Test and Penal Laws became "Legal Pick-Locks" and "Legal Thieves" during the three years of rigorous enforcement, and now the king is calling certain persons to account "for all the Moneys and Goods which they have taken from the *Dissenters* of all sorts, of late years." This rhetoric implies that the Test was used in 1683–1685 as an aggressive shibboleth to find out Dissenters and bring them under the penalties of the Test. It seems that the church party reproached the nonconformists for seeking restitution from those who had oppressed them (apparently beyond the letter of the statutes) in 1683–1685. Shute sums up their argument: "*this bringing the Persecuters before the Commissioners, looks like Revenge; and we ought rather to forgive them.*" Conceding that Dissenters should have no "Personal Prejudice" against the "Persecuting Spoiling Thieves" they are bringing to justice, Shute states that since the disease was civil as well as religious, the remedy should have "a Purge and a Vomit too,"[28] that is, both repentance and restitution. The project to compensate the Protestant Dissenters for their unwarranted pecuniary losses during the Tory revenge was surely a risky strategy for the king in 1688, and the fact that it was carried forward at all reveals how far the coalition between Protestant Dissenters and Catholics had come by that time.

28. Shute, *New Naked Truth*, 45–48, 38.

CHAPTER 7

The Appeal to the European Context: The Dutch Test

A further strategy in the repeal campaign was to appeal to the European context in order to put the Test Acts in perspective. After all, the idea of a religious test as a prerequisite for civil employment had not originated in England, and the practice had spread to several parts of Western Europe during the seventeenth century. To bring about change in the English laws, opponents of the Test Acts argued that religious minorities were treated better elsewhere and, in a related tactic, attempted to demonstrate that the English were no better than those they professed to despise. For this reason, the repeal campaigners repeatedly compared England to Holland and France.

In Canticles 7:2 the Bridegroom praises his Bride for the grace and beauty of her manner of walking. The Septuagint and the Vulgate render the Hebrew literally: "How beautiful are thy steps [or goings] in sandals." It was generally agreed by ancient expositors that Christ was here commending missionary work to his Church-Bride. Her "goings" were the journeys of missionaries who went to proclaim the Gospel in distant lands (RFL, 303). In Dryden's poem, the Panther is a national church "confin'd" to "her own labyrinth" at home (1:403). The Hind rebukes her for letting the East India Company send out immoral men, such as thieves and panderers, to be the only English "Missionaires" in the Far East (3:555). At least, though, the English are not as bad as the Dutch, who send forth men who "improve their traffick" by denying the very name of Christian:

> They run full sail to their *Japponian* Mart:
> Prevention fear, and prodigal of fame
> Sell all of Christian to the very name;
> Nor leave enough of that, to hide their naked
> shame . . .

(2:572–75)

Here Dryden alludes to Japanese fears that Christianity threatened their traditional society; a consequent Japanese demand that Dutch traders repudiate belief in Christianity by carrying out such symbolic acts as trampling upon a crucifix; and the Dutch willingness to accede to Japanese demands in order to secure their lucrative Japanese trading monopoly.

The charge of Dutch apostasy in the Far East had been the key theme of the war literature of 1672–1673, to which Dryden had contributed his play *Amboyna* (1673). Although two previous Anglo-Dutch wars had been fought in the seventeenth century, it was the first time Dutch irreligion was the theme of the war literature, some of it written by Protestants like Giovanni Stoppa.[1] This literature, still within memory in 1685–1688, was the background of the anti-Dutch argument in the repeal campaign: it was said that the Test which the high churchmen defended as the "bulwark" of their establishment was identical to the practice of the irreligious Dutch republic.

According to one modern historian, Holland began to use a religious test for office around 1619. Until then Dutch Calvinists had attempted to exclude upper-class Catholics from public employments, but "not too systematically," but from around 1619 they "systematically excluded" them from commissions and appointments even in country districts.[2] A contemporary Dutch historian confirms that there were "countless cases in which provincial States or town magistrates required membership of the Calvinist Church as a condition for nomination in specific offices,"

---

1. Giovanni Battista Stoppa [or Stoupe], *The Religion of the Dutch,* trans. John Davies (London, 1680), 51. This work first appeared in 1673. See my essay "Swift and the Dutch East India Merchants: The Context of 1672–73 War Literature," *Huntington Library Quarterly* 54 (1991): 235–52.

2. Pieter Geyl, *The Netherlands in the Seventeenth Century, 1609 to 1648,* 2d ed. (London: Benn/New York: Barnes and Noble, 1966), 17.

but he finds no "Test Act in the Republic," no "general law" such as that enacted in Britain.[3] Thus the English Test Acts codified into law what was a systematic practice in Holland.

According to the high churchman Peter Heylyn, to whose history of Calvinism Dryden refers approvingly in the margin of *The Hind and the Panther* (1:180), the Huguenots also excluded Catholics from civil offices after 1619. The French king protested that their refusal to admit "those of the *Roman Catholick* Religion unto Civil Offices in any of their Towns and Territories" violated "the Articles of Pacification" to which they had bound themselves.[4] After 1619, too, it appears that Swiss Calvinists used a test, because one of the repeal campaigners laments that in Bern, Zurich, and Geneva "they would needs . . . shut out young Men from Employments, or impose a Test upon them, which perhaps some have Signed not without struglings in their Consciences."[5] Yet even though use of a religious test was a common practice among European Calvinists, the repeal campaigners linked it chiefly to the Dutch, the commercial rivals of the English.

In "The Banished Priests Farewell," an anonymous poet ridicules the English parliament for imitating the "acts" done by the Dutch state in the Test statute of 1673:

> Alas! poor fools, for you to imitate
> The acts done by that great and proudest State
> Who neither principle nor valor have,
> Nor faith, nor anything above a slave,
> Makes but your folly to appear the more.[6]

In these lines, we see an echo of the contemporary war literature in the scoff that the Dutch have "no faith." In Holland the Test had paved the way for toleration by disempowering religious minorities. William Penn relates how someone told him that Holland was a place "where only one

---

3. A. H. Huussen, professor of modern history at the University of Groningen, in a letter dated 14 May 1990, in response to my inquiry.

4. Peter Heylyn, *Aerius Redivivus; or, The History of the Presbyterians Containing the Beginnings, Progresse, and Successes of That Active Sect. From the Year 1536 to the Year 1647*. 2d ed. (London and Oxford, 1672), 418. Pages 418–19 occur twice in succession, and this is the second one.

5. *Indulgence to Tender Consciences*, 3–4.

6. Anon., "The Banished Priests Farewell," in *Poems on Affairs of State, 1660–1714*, 7 vols., ed. George de F. Lord (New Haven, Conn.: Yale University Press, 1963), 1:205.

Perswasion has the Government, tho the rest their Liberty," that is, where a test is used to control access to all public employments, but where others besides Dutch Calvinists are allowed to worship. Penn does not think freedom of conscience should have to come at the cost of political liberty. He retorts that liberty of conscience in Holland is a mere expedient to trade, but in England it ought to be a right, a part of fundamental law.[7] Like him, Shute thinks that the "swearing *Sacraments*" of Holland should not be imitated by the English because the Dutch give freedom of worship only out of "civil policy," and they now oppose England's having a "Magna Charta" in religion only for fear that it may "interfere with their Worldly Secular Interest" should the English exiles return home; for this reason, they send over "their Pamphlets that are stuft with frightful Notions" about Catholic "Designs" and claim they are "willing to afford us a *Liberty of Conscience*, which is but just next door to a greater Captivity."[8] Thus Shute sees William of Orange's offer of a toleration without the repeal of the Test Acts and Penal Laws as an invitation to virtual slavery.

Although it imitated Dutch practice, the English Test was harsher because it also barred nonconformists from service in the military. When William of Orange sought to gain the goodwill of the English, he told them through *Fagel's Letter* (1688) that he would maintain their version of the Test and keep nonconformists out of the military. King James regarded *Fagel's Letter* as illogical: it said that Dutch Catholics, unlike English Catholics, could serve in the military "because of their services and smallness of their numbers." But King James II argued that this reason held "much better" for English Catholics, whose "merit was full as great, and their number much fewer in proportion," for Dutch Catholics were about one-fourth of the population, while English Catholics were at most one-twentieth, and "only formidable because some people were resolved to be afraid."[9] When James spoke of "merit," he probably had Castlemaine's list of war heroes in mind.

Since the Dutch test was more lenient than the English one, some timid opponents of the English Test proposed a version of the Dutch test as a compromise. The author of *Advice from a Dissenter* urges the English to let nonconformists serve in the military because the Dutch case proves

7. Penn, *Good Advice*, 59.   8. Shute, *A New Naked Truth*, 24–28.
9. James II, *Life*, 2:135.

that giving such "a share" in liberty is "agreeable to the Practice of other Protestant Countries."[10] Later on, a Catholic spokesman calls the Dutch way with "dissenting subjects" mild by comparison to the British system and praises the American colonies for following the "*Dutch* plan."[11]

Another strategy employed in arguments against the Test was to argue that repeal was an "Expedient" that would improve trade and do great harm to Holland, England's economic rival. The author of *A Letter from Holland* declares that the English have greatly hurt their own economy by "Oaths and Tests" which forced many of their nonconformist business-men to seek refuge in Holland. According to this author, the Dutch have reaped so much profit from these exiles that they now hate to see them go home and are using all their arts to stop England from instituting liberty of conscience, fearing it will do their trade more harm than a seven-year war with Britain.[12] The Hind glances at this argument at the end of her tale when she shows that the English farm prospers greatly when all the birds, wild and tame, are equally protected by the owner (3:1265–66).

It is in the context of these attacks on the Dutch during the repeal campaign of 1685–1688 that the Hind compares the English to the Dutch for using the Test Acts as dikes against an imaginary Catholic "flood." First, though, the Hind opens this part of the debate by calling James's indulgence to nonconformists a "floud of mercy that o'erflow'd our Isle." She compares the king to "the *Nile*," which floods in a "Calm" way to make Egypt "fruitfull" (3:802–3). The Panther replies by advising her to be satisfied with the "all-dispensing pow'r" that protects her "now" and to give up hope of repeal, because the church party will never consent to pulling down its banks when there is a threat of a disastrous "flood." The Panther changes the Hind's image of a benign, life-giving flood to that of a destructive flood, a great tidal wave. She insists that repeal would be like pulling down her "banks" and "barriers" and letting a huge wave "sweep the Pastors and their flocks away" (3:831–34).

10. Anon., *Advice from a Dissenter in the City to His Friends in the Countrey. Shewing It to Be Their Duty and Safety, to Concur with Those Who Are for Abolishing the Penal Laws and Tests* (London: N. pub., 1688), 6. This supposed Dissenter, whose last-ditch plea was licensed on September 7, uses the same rhetoric as Dryden, because he speaks of persecution as "scorpions" and "rods," sees "spots" on the national church, and calls Tests "shibboleths."

11. Curry, *Observations on the Popery Laws*, 51–52.

12. C[ornelius] D[e] W[itt], *A Letter from Holland Touching Liberty of Conscience* (London: For E. R., 1688), 1, 3–4.

In her ensuing rebuke, the Hind compares the English to the Dutch because of this fear of floods and inundations:

> Your care about your Banks, infers a fear
> Of threatning Floods, and Inundations near;
> If so, a just Reprise would only be
> Of what the Land usurp'd upon the Sea;
> And all your Jealousies but serve to show
> Your Ground is, like your Neighbour-Nation, low.
> T'intrench in what you grant unrighteous Laws,
> Is to distrust the justice of your Cause.

(3:860–67)

On the literal level, the Hind says that the English and the Dutch both devise banks and trenches against her universal faith because the ground they build on is low. This word "low" evokes the 1672–1673 literature about Dutch irreligion, and the implication is that there is a void of faith in England, too, that invites an influx of the Hind's religion. She implies that the two nations are fearfully trying to stave off a "flood" of conversions by their tests against Catholics.

On a deeper level of the text, the Hind's joining of the words "floods" and "inundations" in line 861 glances at two biblical passages about the testing of a church, for there are only two places in Scripture where the words "fluvius" and "inundatio" are in proximity. First, in Isaiah 59:19–60:6, in a vision of the last times, a violent "flood" arrives to give recompense or repayment to the coastlands. Such a repayment is echoed in the Hind's phrase "just Reprise." After the flood, the inundation comes: it turns out to be an "inundation" of camels, or great prosperity like that caused by the flooding Nile. Curiously, in the Catholic version of this text, it is the Lord himself who comes in like a flood, as the Hind suggests, but in the Protestant versions, both the Geneva and the King James, it is "the enemy" that "shall come in like a flood," as the Panther fears.

This rhetoric, then, suggests the biblical testing of a people or a church. In Luke 6:48 and Matthew 7:24 Christ speaks of his church as a house founded so firmly upon the rock of his word that when the inundation and the flood arrive to test it, the house will remain standing. Dryden alludes to this text when he deplores the Panther's weak foundation in the first part of *The Hind*:

> O solid rock, on which secure she stands!
> Eternal house, not built with mortal hands!
> Oh sure defence against th'infernal gate,
> A patent during pleasure of the state!
>
> (1:493–96)

In the above lines, the words "rock," "built," and "infernal gate" resonate with Christ's promise to Peter: "and upon this rock I will build my church; and the gates of hell shall not prevail against it" (Mt 16:18). The poet scolds the Panther for not building upon the rock of Christ's promises but instead, like the Dutch, on the lowlands of the Test. He hints that her weak foundation makes the Panther's insecure and incites her deep fears of "Threatning Floods, and Inundations near" (3:861). Of course, this biblical imagery suggests her fears may be warranted, though she is in error concerning the Hind. For the house that was not built on rock could not resist the floods and inundations, and "the ruine of that house was great" (Lk 6:49). The Panther's danger arises not from the Hind but from the Presbyterian Wolf whom she is inciting against the Hind. The poet remembers only too well the ruin of the Panther's house in the great flood of his youth, when the Book of Common Prayer was proscribed and most of the English people took the Puritan Covenant.

In Canticles 8:7 we find the most ancient of the sources for the Hind's imagery of "floods." There the Bridegroom assures his Bride that she need not fear to be drowned by floods: "Manie waters can not quench charitie, neither shal flouds overwhelme it" (8:7). Christian commentators interpreted the "waters" and "floods" in this verse to mean threatened or actual persecutions, which they said would never quench the Bride's love for God and for neighbor (RFL, 363). This is what Dryden shows in his poem: though threatened with imminent persecution, the Hind never ceases to "woo" the Panther's "Kindness to the last" (3:892). But the Panther raises false fears of persecution because her jealousy is "hard as hel" (Sg 8:6). This jealous zeal quenches her charity and makes her so insecure that she is willing to maintain her barrier of "unrighteous Laws" against the Hind's calm and fruitful flood.

CHAPTER 8

The Appeal to the European Context: The Edict of Nantes

Those who campaigned for repeal of the Test could not help but write against the background of persecution in France. After all, the French refugees were streaming into England and Ireland. In *The Hind and the Panther* Dryden places the current campaign to repeal the Test in a French context for two reasons: first, to distinguish James II from Louis XIV, and second, to show that the Panther's rigor against nonconformists is just as bad as that of the French king.

The poet recognizes that what is happening in France puts James II in danger, so he appeals to the English to admit that the two kings are different in character. In the preface to *The Hind and the Panther*, he shows the revocation of the Edict of Nantes to be contrary not only to the measures that James II has taken with nonconformists, but also to the example of Christ himself: "'Tis not for any Private Man to Censure the Proceedings of a Foreign Prince: but, without suspicion of Flattery, I may praise our own, who has taken contrary Measures, and those more suitable to the Spirit of Christianity." The poet pleads that religion is beyond the regulatory powers of the state: a person is "absolute in his own Breast, and accountable to no Earthly Power, for that which passes only betwixt God and Him. Those who are driven into the Fold are, generally speaking, rather made Hypocrites then Converts."

Since his countrymen virtually mythologized Catholic kings as persecutors, Dryden begins his defense on a mythical level. He creates a vivid embodiment of the persecutor in the figure of the conqueror Nimrod, whom he sees as a prefiguration of the Antichrist. Nimrod imposes his dominion over the consciences of others by use of exterior force. The good shepherd Pan is the very opposite of Nimrod: he not only protects his own flock, but he also draws and tames wild, predatory creatures as he restores the blessed Garden in the Wilderness, that is, the new Jerusalem. In the following passage Louis XIV is, by implication, a modern embodiment of Nimrod, while James II and Pope Innocent XI are embodiments of the divine Pan:

> Thus persecution rose, and farther space
> Produc'd the mighty hunter of his race.
> Not so the blessed *Pan* his flock encreas'd,
> Content to fold 'em from the famish'd beast:
> Mild were his laws; the Sheep and harmless Hind
> Were never of the persecuting kind.
> Such pity now the pious Pastor shows,
> Such mercy from the *British Lyon* flows,
> That both provide protection for their foes.
>
> (1:282–90)

As in the preface, Dryden reveals that Louis XIV is not following the model of Christ or the Catholic Church when he uses persecution instead of fragrant persuasion to bring in converts. Instead, he drives out potential converts, forcing them to seek asylum in other countries. Both the "harmless Hind" and her beloved shepherd Pan disapprove of such coercion of conscience. Later on, in her tale, the Hind says that the Buzzard whom the high-church Pigeons choose to be their "Captain of the *Test*" (3:1192) will bring in more "feather'd *Nimrods*" like himself (3:1274) and prey on the Pigeons themselves. Thus, the coercion of conscience represented by Nimrod is found in those eager to enforce the Test against the English Catholics.

While Nimrod subjugates others, the British king protects even his "foes" (1:290), following Christ's command to "love your enemies: do good to them that hate you" (Mt 5:44). The poet here implies that James is hated by some of the refugees to whom he extends his protection. Indeed, a modern historian notes that among the arriving Huguenots, "many exiles asked William for help . . . to lead them in rebellion" against the English king.[1] Later on in the poem, to rebut the charge that James will persecute Protestants if the Test is repealed, the Hind points to the fact that he is welcoming the Panther's friends:

> Behold! how he protects your Friends opprest,
> Receives the Banish'd, succours the Distress'd:
> Behold, for you may read an honest open Breast.
> (3:876–78)

The phrase "your Friends," like the word "foes" in 1:290, implies that the arriving Huguenots immediately side with the Panther against James. Even so, the Hind praises James for having compassion on them as the "oppressed," "banished," and "distressed." In the above lines, the word "succours" alludes to the king's "letters patents" issued early in 1686 to collect money for Huguenot refugees.

The problem for James and his small band of writers in the repeal campaign was that the effort to "take off the Test" started in 1685, the very same year Louis XIV revoked the Edict of Nantes. Since the Test was imaged as the chief rampart around the national religion, James's campaign to revoke the Test could plausibly be compared to Louis XIV's revocation of the Edict of Nantes. In both cases what was being repealed was a "security" for Protestants. Of course, the parallel did not really hold because the two laws were diametrically opposite: the Edict of Nantes of 1598 granted liberties to Huguenots, while the Test Acts of 1661, 1673, and 1678 took away liberties from English nonconformists. Indeed, it was the revocation of the Edict of Nantes, not its promulgation, that resembled the enactment of the Test Acts. By that revocation, conformity to the national religion became the new prerequisite for French citizenship, the new mark of national identity. By 1688 the French situation had helped to sabotage the English repeal campaign. The same thing would happen again a century later. In 1786 there was a new campaign to revoke the Test because of the "expanded civil rights of Protestants in France" and "the steps taken by Emperor Joseph II to remove civil disabilities imposed on

---

1. Hubert P. H. Nusteling, "The Netherlands and the Huguenot Emigrés," in *La Révocation de l'Edit de Nantes et les Provinces-Unies,* ed. J. A. H. Bots and G. H. M. Posthumus Meyjes (Amsterdam and Maarssen: APA Holland University Press, 1986), 46.

individuals for their religious opinions." Four years later, when the French National Assembly attacked church property, the Tories cried out that repeal of the Test would endanger church property in England, too.[2]

The name of France became synonymous with Catholic persecution of Protestants in 1685–1688, but it had not always been so. The much-traveled Castlemaine had written in 1668 that Protestants in France and the Empire had more liberties than Catholics did in England, and he warned that English persecution of Catholics might give the French and Austrian monarchs a pretext to use "the like severity to dissenting Sub-jects." He pointed out that Huguenots in the France of the 1660s could worship in "open Churches" and take "publick employments," while no Catholics under "Reformed" governments had any of these liberties.[3] In 1672 Dean Cressy reminded his readers that Huguenots were able to pub-lish books of controversy in France, while English Catholics were barred from recourse to the press to advance or even to defend their religion, though publicly challenged in defamatory books to reply.[4] In 1673, too, John Milton lamented that "French and Polonian protestants enjoy all this liberty among papists," including the liberty of "arguing, preaching in their several Assemblies, Publick writing and the freedom of Printing," freedoms that Protestant Dissenters are denied "among Protestants" in England.[5] Thus the liberties of the Huguenots under the Edict of Nantes (1598) had long been the measure by which English nonconformists cal-culated their own misery.

Louis XIV also looked to England and Holland during those decades to re-evaluate the Edict of Nantes. In a 1663 letter addressed to Charles II, he complained about the laws against Catholics in England, saying, "you know with what gentleness and moderation the Catholic princes treat all those in their estates." As early as 1670, he seemed to be looking for a pre-text to suppress dissent: he asked why he needed to grant so much liberty "while the Dutch Calvinists refused to allow Catholics in the Netherlands to practice their religion publicly."[6] It was no coincidence that Louis

<hr />

2. *Repeal Committees*, ix, xvi.
3. Castlemaine, *A Reply*, 265–67.
4. Cressy, *Fanaticism Fanatically Imputed*, 183.
5. Milton, "Of True Religion" (1673), in *Complete Prose Works of John Milton*, 8 vols., ed. William Alfred et al. (New Haven, Conn.: Yale University Press, 1962–1982), 8:426–27. Castlemaine cites this very passage to bolster his argument in *Apology*, 306.
6. J. B. Wolf, *Louis XIV* (New York: W. W. Norton, 1968), 385, 215.

XIV's persecution of the Huguenots began in 1680, the third year in which Catholics were dying in England for the pretended Popish Plot. In those very years there was a secret alliance between the king of France and the English opposition leaders who were fomenting the Popish Plot. The common political goals of the two parties were these: to reduce Charles II's authority, to demobilize the standing army, and to create domestic turmoil in Great Britain. Perhaps politics never made stranger bedfellows than the absolutist French monarch and the revolutionary Whig leaders. Yet both of them accepted the idea of religion as a form of national identity. As will be shown, by giving heavy subsidies in 1678–1682 to those who were fomenting the Popish Plot, Louis XIV helped to create the context in which his repression of Protestants would be popular in France. In a coded letter of 22 August 1680, ambassador Barrillon told Louis XIV that the laws against the English Catholics were now equivalent "to a revocation of the Edict of Nantes." He added that the English Catholics were soon going to be utterly banished, just as the Moors had been from Spain.[7] Since the revocation of the Edict of Nantes was still five years away and the dragonnades, that is, the forced quartering of dragoons on Huguenot families, were only starting, Barrillon's words suggest that he knew his king aimed at persecution, and so he offered him the pretext of an English example.

Louis was probably inviting opinions favorable to his design, as when he was urged to retaliate against the Huguenots for the way the Dutch and the English oppressed Catholics, especially with the Test for public employment: "England and the northern Protestant countries," said Jacques Bainville, "had set an example by suppressing what remained of Catholicism, and excluding Catholics from employment," and so, if the king of France should decide on an action similar to that which had taken place in England, "public opinion was certain to approve."[8] Indeed, at the time, popular opinion was on the French king's side, just as in England the Test Acts were supported by popular opinion.

In 1688 an Anglican clergyman on the side of repeal remarked that it was strange how the same people who "inveigh against the French king" for persecuting Huguenots are angry at James II for not letting them per-

7. Jusserand, *Angleterre*, 278.

8. H. Daniel-Rops, S.J., *The Church in the Seventeenth Century*, trans. J. J. Buckingham (London: Dent/New York: Dutton, 1963), 204.

secute the English Catholics.[9] From April 1685, the church party kept calling for the strict execution of the Penal Laws and Tests. They raised fears
that if these laws were suspended or abolished, the old religion would
somehow become the state religion again by default, legally recovering its
first rights.[10] The Hind rebukes the Panther for her hypocrisy in railing
against Louis XIV for his "causeless rigour" against Huguenots when she
herself is constantly calling for the severe laws against nonconformists to
be executed. In a passage referring to the revocation of the Edict of
Nantes, the Hind tells the Panther she should not "throw the stone" at
the French king. By this phrase "throw the stone" the Hind alludes to
John 8:7, where Jesus tells the Pharisees that the one among them un-
tainted by sin should throw the first stone at the adulteress. Like Jesus
wounding the self-righteous Pharisees to the quick by forcing them to ex-
amine their own souls, the Hind lays bare the Panther's guilt:

> If you condemn that Prince of Tyranny
> Whose mandate forc'd your *Gallick* friends to fly,
> Make not a worse example of your own,
> Or cease to rail at causeless rigour shown,
> And let the guiltless person throw the stone,
> His blunted sword, your suff'ring brotherhood
> Have seldom felt, he stops it short of bloud:
> But you have ground the persecuting knife,
> And set it to a razor edge on life.
>
> (3:680–88)

The word "mandate" in line 681 refers to the revocation of the Edict of
Nantes. From 1680 to 1685, Louis had driven the Huguenots to hide behind the veil of supposed conformity by threats of dragonnades and offers
of bribes, so that when he revoked the Edict of Nantes, he might claim
that the Huguenots had all been converted. But his "mandate" in 1685
"forc'd" them to "fly," since now they were expected to take the Sacrament
of the Altar kneeling, as a test of their conversions. The Hind insists that

9. James Paston, *A Discourse of Penal Laws in Matters of Religion* (London: For the
author, 1688), 26. Paston was the chaplain of Sir Robert Wright, Lord Chief Justice.

10. Charles James Fox, *Appendix*, lxvi–lxxxi. Fox includes many valuable letters
that were exchanged between Louis XIV and Barrillon in 1685, but he misreads them
badly. When James II uses the phrase "etablissement d'une libre exercice," i.e., to secure
freedom of worship, Fox repeatedly mistranslates this to mean that James II intends to
"establish the Catholic religion."

the Panther gave a "worse example" than the French king: for Louis held a "blunted sword" and stopped his persecution "short of bloud" when he oppressed the "suff'ring brotherhood" of the Huguenots. That is, French Protestants at least, were not martyred like English Catholics. It was the Panther who put a "razor edge" on the "persecuting knife" both in the Popish Plot years, when conformists carried out the trials of English Catholics, and in the repression of 1683–1685, when Charles II allowed the laws against Protestant nonconformists to be enforced in all their severity.

There is another aspect to the Hind's warning to the Panther not to "throw the stone." In John 8:7 the Pharisees set a trap for Jesus, whom they see as too merciful to sinners; they want him to prove he respects the Mosaic law by consenting to the stoning of the adulteress. Likewise, the Panther who will not "cease to rail" against the French king is setting a trap for James, whom she sees as too merciful toward nonconformists; she wants him to prove he upholds English law and will maintain her establishment by allowing her to enforce the Penal Laws and Tests against nonconformists, as in 1683–1685.

The Hind asks God to avert the entry of "Tyrannick force" into England. She means that the sight of the Protestant refugees awakens a desire for retaliation against English Catholics:

> Tyrannick force is that which least you fear,
> The sound is frightfull in a Christian's ear;
> Avert it, Heav'n; nor let that Plague be sent
> To us from the dispeopled Continent.
> (3:870–73)

The Hind calls the persecution of religious minorities a "plague" because it is a contagion transmitted from one country to another with the displaced populations, whose plight creates a reactive intolerance. Indeed, a modern historian notes that there were repercussions against Catholics in the Netherlands as well as in England in the wake of Louis XIV's persecution.[11] Again, the Hind insists that Louis XIV and James II are at opposite poles from each other, and that persecution from the English king is the least of the Panther's fears.

The Popish Plot and the revocation of the Edict of Nantes were related parts of Louis XIV's larger design to create a nationalized religion in

---

11. Nusteling, *The Netherlands and the Huguenot Emigrés*, 46.

France. It is impossible to gauge how reasonable and moderate Dryden's views were in this period without understanding the international background of England's turmoil. Thanks to the survival of thousands of dispatches written in numerical code between 1678 and 1688, we have a complete account of an ongoing secret relationship between the English Whig leaders and Paul de Barrillon d'Amoncourt, marquis de Branges, the ambassador from Versailles. This marquis was a highly cultivated emissary who had Madame de Maintenon for his patron, a bishop for his brother, and such literary figures as La Fontaine, Madame de Sévigné, and Madame de Lafayette for his friends. His subtle, informative reports were deciphered interlinearly for Louis XIV to read and are now deposited in the Quai d'Orsay archives in Paris.[12] It was the Whig historian Sir John Dalrymple who first made Barrillon's dispatches known in his *Memoirs of Great Britain*. He did so with profound regret because it was his own political party that had, a century earlier, taken bribes from France to disband the army and stymy the king.

On November 13, 1677, a year before the Popish Plot broke out, the opposition party in England sought connections with France; soon Barrillon and the Huguenot envoy Ruvigny arranged to give bribes to a number of them, including the Duke of Buckingham and Algernon Sidney.[13] The sums went as high as 300,000 French livres, a bit less than 30,000 pounds sterling, for distribution to members of parliament. Modern historians and biographers generally concede that the Whig leaders received bribes from France at the time. One of them tells how Shaftesbury and his colleagues crossed the Channel many times to negotiate with France in 1677, but acknowledges that "none of the biographies of Shaftesbury, Buckingham, Locke, or of any of the other principals involved have shed much light on what these secret intrigues accomplished."[14] The French bribes are so embarrassing that many historians

12. Paul de Barrillon, *Correspondance politique-Angleterre*, vols. 125–68, in Les Archives Diplomatiques (Ministère des affaires étrangères), quai d'Orsay, Paris. There are some forty volumes, and from my readings of volumes 133–34 for 1679 I would estimate that each volume contains about 300 sheets written on both sides. Much of what Barrillon's papers contain is presented in digest form in Dalrymple (see next note) and Jusserand's *Angleterre*.

13. Sir John Dalrymple, *Memoirs of Great Britain and Ireland*, 3 vols. (Rpt., Farnborough, U.K.: Gregg, 1970), 1:164–67, 183, 380–83.

14. Richard Ashcraft, *Revolutionary Politics and Locke's Two Treatises of Government* (Princeton, N.J.: Princeton University Press, 1986), 129.

simply ignore them. The same historians, however, will delve in much detail into Charles II's secret subsidies from France earlier in this reign. Dryden is correct when he writes that Charles II, in his last years, had to deal with a furious "Tempest" created by "Foreign and Domestick Treachery" (*Threnodia*, 321).

There were two interrelated plots in 1678–1682, the Popish Plot and the Exclusion Crisis: the Popish Plot involved an imaginary papal army in which all the important Catholics in England were supposed to have commissions; the Exclusion Crisis involved the imposing of a religious test for kingship, which would exclude James from the throne. The Popish Plot was the first half of the Exclusion Crisis: it incited the panic fear about a Catholic invasion that made it possible to mount the campaign to exclude the legitimate heir, a Catholic, from the throne. Lord Dalrymple states that the Whig leader Lord Shaftesbury "framed the fiction of the popish plot in order to bury the Duke [of York] and perhaps the King under the weight of the national fear and hatred of popery."[15] The revolutionary Whigs drove both these plots forward and kept the country in continual turmoil for four years. Since Dryden believed that the British government required a balance of power, it is understandable that he would satirize in some of his best poetry the parliamentary leaders whom he saw as wilfully creating turmoil in order to encroach upon the power of the executive branch. However, Dryden was no defender of arbitrary power, as some have charged, for he applauded the Habeas Corpus Act, which was brought in at that time by the Whig party and confirmed by the king.

Barrillon never told Louis XIV plainly that French bribes paid for the judicial murders of over forty Catholics in England, including some priests who were hanged for the "crime" of merely being priests. In letters in the Quai d'Orsay archives, we can trace Barrillon's role in British affairs as he informs the French king over and over again that the persecution of Catholics under the Popish Plot is being carried out by the English king and his Tory party for their own advantage. This was partly true, of course, since only conformists held offices and implemented the laws, but it was the Whig leaders who managed the plot from above with French money, who put on the pope-burning parades, who suborned witnesses with large bribes, and who tortured Englishmen in the king's

15. Dalrymple, *Memoirs*, 1:170–71.

prison, as for example the hackney coachman Francis Corral, whose horrid interrogation was conducted by Lord Shaftesbury himself and who was tortured for about forty-five days.[16]

Lord Dalrymple is surprised that in Barrillon's letters there is no "encouragement given by France to the popish plot, though that was the great engine made use of by the popular party against Charles."[17] What puzzles Dalrymple is the absence of a paper trail connecting Louis XIV to the Popish Plot, when those who were driving the plot from 1678 to 1682 were receiving his huge bribes. Indeed, in his letters Barrillon maintains a subtle, artificial separation between the Popish Plot and the Exclusion Crisis and presents the Whigs as engaged only in the latter event: demobilizing the army, excluding James from the crown, and reducing Charles II's authority to a veto. This wall of separation between the Popish Plot and the Exclusion Crisis is reflected also in Dalrymple and Jusserand, when they draw their narrative from Barrillon's dispatches. Reading these reports, one would not suspect that the Popish Plot and the Exclusion Crisis were happening simultaneously and were managed by the same people. Louis was unlikely to have been duped by Barrillon's polite dissimulation.

The crisis of 1678–1682 was pure artwork, a revenge play so complicated as to make most Jacobean tragedies look puerile. Louis XIV wanted to punish King Charles and his brother James for what he saw as their perfidy. In 1677 James's daughter had married William of Orange, an enemy of France, and Charles II had told the French ambassador that he would join the war against France, thereby canceling his secret treaty with Louis. By January 1678 the Duke of York was asking to be appointed as the general of the army against France, in the hope, Barrillon reported, of regaining the popularity he had lost in England by his conversion to

16. Jusserand, *Angleterre*, 278; on Francis Corral, see Roger L'Estrange, *A Brief History of the Times* (London: R. Sare, 1688), 102–7. Lord Shaftesbury personally supervised this extended torture in solitary confinement, but the heroic coachman never consented to perjure himself for fear of "a more Dreadful Hearing for me, at the Lord's Bar." L'Estrange interviewed him in 1688 and could still see deep scars. Mrs. Elizabeth Cellier was imprisoned for several years and pilloried chiefly for saying in her book *Malice Defeated* (1680) that she knew the Whig leaders had tortured people in the king's prison to make them perjure themselves. At one point Corral was offered five hundred pounds, very likely from the French king's money, to be a perjured witness in the Popish Plot.

17. Dalrymple, *Memoirs*, 1:291.

Catholicism. In August of 1678, just before the Popish Plot was revealed, James again offended Louis by opposing the peace treaty between France and Holland and urging that the war continue. Barrillon gloated in his letters that James was hated for being a Catholic despite his efforts to lead the popular war against France.[18] At this point Louis XIV began to carry out his plan against the royal brothers. It was a macabre sort of joke when Edward Coleman, who stood accused of secret dealings with France, was examined by a committee "composed entirely of men who appear on Barrillon's list as being in receipt of French bribes."[19] Coleman, a close friend of James, was made the first victim of the Popish Plot by the agents of the French king himself.

In 1679, while English Catholics were dying, the French king was fixated in his correspondence with Barrillon on the demobilization of the English army, carefully noting its dwindling numbers in code, while the trials of Catholics were handled as a matter of course in script. After Charles II signed a treaty with Spain in June 1680, Louis offered Barrillon all the money he could use to bribe the members of the English parliament that fall, when the Exclusion Bill would come up for a vote. Roger North was mystified about the source of all the money being spent by the drivers of the plot. He remarked that there were "Purses, of the first Magnitude" behind the plot, for huge sums were being disbursed to suborn false witnesses, to publish anti-Catholic propaganda, and to finance such public displays as lavish anti-Catholic processions, in one of which the pope's "car" alone cost a hundred pounds.[20] He was puzzled over what could possibly be the "Bottom" of all the complex machinery of the plot, which, like a besieged city, had walls within walls, plots within plots. At the bottom of all the turmoil there was indeed an army, but not the imaginary papal army: it was an army of *louis d'or* marching into the pockets of Whig leaders so they could rid Britain of its standing army.

Again, we find a macabre sort of joke when the king of France, at the time of the Exclusion Bill, secretly promises to support both sides in case of civil war: Dalrymple reports that on November 15, 1680, Louis XIV in the same letter tells Barrillon to let James know he will back him in a civil

18. Jusserand, *Angleterre*, 258.
19. Francis S. Ronalds, *The Attempted Whig Revolution of 1678–1681* (Totowa, N.J.: Rowman & Littlefield, 1974), 35.
20. North, *Examen*, 395.

war and also to let the republican party in parliament know that he will protect the privileges of the nation. A month later, in a letter dated December 13, Louis expresses "his satisfaction at the divisions in England." Thus, Dalrymple exclaims, he deceived both "separately" and played them "against each other."[21] Five years later the French king played the same game, ordering Barrillon to start negotiating with the opposition party if the new Catholic king should dare to make an alliance with Spain.[22]

Portrayed in England as the very model of a Catholic king, Louis XIV was actually in conflict with the pope and was privately excommunicated on 16 November 1687.[23] His religion was a national, rather than a universal, faith. By 1686 he was prepared to send the now supposedly conformist Huguenots to kneel for communion as a test of citizenship. From the Huguenot point of view, this amounted to enforced idolatry; from the universal Catholic Church's point of view, this amounted to outright sacrilege. One historian notes that Pope Innocent XI, when he was "informed of the true nature of the mass conversions in France, abhorred and showed open disapproval; his relations with Louis, already bad, deteriorated even more, and he drifted, if not into the enemy, Protestant camp, at least into uncompromising neutrality."[24]

Although maligned as being supporters of France, English Catholics seem actually to have been jealous of Louis XIV's territorial expansion. In 1674 Castlemaine complained that the English Penal Laws and Test Acts prevented Britain from peacefully annexing those parts of the "*Low-Countries*" Spain could no longer defend, as well as "our old *Provinces in France*, and especially *Normandy*," places having "natural Inclinations for us" because of the British form of government, but afraid to join Britain because of "our strange severity" against Catholics.[25] Curiously, three years later, Barrillon informed Louis XIV that Spain was making offers along those very lines, telling Charles II that the allies would conquer

21. Dalrymple, *Memoirs*, 1:353.
22. Fox, *Appendix*, cxxx.
23. Daniel-Rops, *The Church in the Seventeenth Century*, 223. But the church historian Ludwig Freiherr Von Pastor questions whether the pope actually meant to excommunicate the French king or rather merely to warn him that he would incur excommunication by his violent acts against the Church of Rome. See *The History of the Popes*, translated by Dom Ernest Graf, O.S.B. (London: Kegan Paul, Trench, Trubner, 1940), 32:361–62.
24. Nusteling, *The Netherlands and the Huguenot Emigrés*, 43.
25. Castlemaine, *Apology*, 562.

Calais or Dunkirk for the English, or even return Normandy if Great Britain joined the war.[26] Like Castlemaine, Dryden is jealous of France's expanding borders. In *Threnodia* (1685), written soon after James II's accession, he envisions France and Holland as having to crouch at the feet of a martial James II:

> *Gaul* and *Batavia* dread th'impending blow;
> Too well the Vigour of that Arm they know;
> They lick the dust, and Crouch beneath their fatal Foe.
> > Long may they fear this awful Prince,
> > And not Provoke his lingring Sword . . .
>
> > > (478–82)

The phrase "lick the dust" refers to the Messiah's subjugation of inveterate foreign enemies in Isaiah 49:23, Psalm 71:9, and Micah 7:17. Both Holland and France are depicted as the anti-Christian foe. The poet's phrases "impending blow" and "lingering sword" imply that James will have the martial posture to command their respect but will not initiate war. Indeed, James tried to keep England neutral as much of Europe moved toward a long war against France; he hoped to play France and Holland against each other for the economic advantage of England.[27] Unfortunately, Spain and Austria were persuaded that James was the secret ally of Louis XIV, and so these Catholic powers abetted William of Orange's descent upon England to dethrone him in 1688.

In Canticles 1:7–8 the Bride asks where her beloved Shepherd feeds his flock at "midday," lest she "wander" after the flocks of his "companions." Ancient expositors said that the true Shepherd's face "is the noon" and that those "companions" are not his friends but false shepherds who will lead the Bride astray (RFL, 28–30). In part 3, the Hind asks the Panther to "behold" her king's "honest" countenance (3:878), and in her tale, too, she invites her to visualize James as a "Plain good Man," a Farmer not at all like Nimrod. This Farmer resembles the divine shepherd Pan because he draws the wild "Republick Birds" by sweet persuasion to dwell tamely with "Domestick Birds" on his estate. So now the decision is up to the Panther, whether to abide trustingly in her king's perennial solstice or to "wander" in wintry darkness after the flocks of his "companions."

26. Jusserand, *Angleterre*, 211.
27. J. P. Kenyon, *Robert Spencer, Earl of Sunderland* (London: Longmans, 1958), 126.

CHAPTER 9

The Test and the Imputation
of Idolatry

It is no coincidence that the Test Acts of 1673 and 1678 contained an oath against the Catholic Eucharist and that in the same period thousands of pages were printed concerning the supposed idolatry of Catholics who adored Christ in the Blessed Sacrament. In Canticles 1:6 the Bride declares that she is "black"; she complains that the sons of her mother have fought against her and made her keeper of the vineyards, but her own vineyard she has not kept. Ancient interpreters agree that this is the infant Church of Christ speaking of her sufferings; although the oppression of the Church of the Law has been the involuntary cause of the spread of Christ's Church into every area of the world, she still feels like a stranger in her own vineyard, the Jewish homeland (RFL, 23–24). In part 3 of Dryden's poem, we see the milk-white Hind oppressed with "black detraction" (3:258) in her own motherland. The sons of the legal Church make her seem like a stranger to the English by accusing her of gross idolatry.

The cry of idolatry from 1671 to 1688 was strange, considering that during the Restoration there was far more danger of lewdness and irreligion than of idolatry. It was strange, too, because many English Catholics were remarkable for their learning and abilities and were hardly the sort to trip unawares into idolatry. Further, it was strange because the

200

adoration of Christ as really present in the Sacrament of the Altar, which was here called "idolatry," was a worship given in the greater part of the Christian world, both Orthodox and Catholic. But the cry of idolatry amounted, on one level, to calling English Catholics *fools*, at a time in England when people much preferred to be called libertines. It was a way of ending the debate on the issues, especially on the Real Presence and its *modus* of transubstantiation, for no one would bother to read books written by idolaters. On this point, the Franciscan Canes remarked in 1672: "idolatry is such a terrible thundering charge . . . men therefore choose rather to be accounted Atheists than Idolaters. For the first argues wit, the other stupidity." He added that this "blasting imputation" causes that not "one man in a hundred will bother to read a book by a Catholic" written to defend his religion against that "enormous crime."[1] On another level, however, the charge of idolatry was dangerous, since it was meant to inflame the populace against a defenseless minority.

According to Bishop Samuel Parker, the Test Acts of 1673 and 1678 were both intended to brand Catholics as idolaters. This high churchman reports that as soon as James was suspected of having converted to Catholicism in 1673, the earl of Shaftesbury exhorted the members of parliament to rise up against idolatry by passing the Test Act: "First of all he inveigh'd against the Papists, that unless speedy care was taken to prevent it, the Protestant Religion would be destroy'd: That every thing look'd in favour of *Rome*: That he would rather lose his life, than his Religion: And therefore exhorted all who had their Religion at heart, that they would rise with one consent against idolaters. . . ." After this speech he was attended by a great body of the nobility and became popular in the Commons, though recently under danger of impeachment there. Elsewhere, Parker says that Shaftesbury put the term "idolatry" in the Test Act of 1678 as a "stabbing and Cut-Throat word" specifically pointed at James duke of York, because the least punishment for idolatry in the Bible is "Death and Damnation."[2]

Bishop Cartwright agrees with Bishop Parker that Shaftesbury intended to "brand" James "publiquely" as "an Idolater" by the Test Act of

1. [John Vincent Canes], *An Account of Dr. Stillingfleet's Late Book against the Church of Rome* [N. pl.: N. pub., 1672], 11.

2. Samuel Parker, *History of His Own Time* (1686), translated from the Latin by Thomas Newlin (London: Charles Rivington, 1727), 321; Parker, *Reasons for Abrogating the Test*, 71.

1673 and to make the mob "turbulent" against him. Cartwright says that he knows "zealous Protestants" who hold "Idolatry to be a Crime punishable with Death by Christian Magistrates; and some worse than that, that every Mans Hand is to be upon them to put them to Death." And so, the Test of 1673 jeopardized the duke's life, first by stigmatizing him as an idolater, and second by forcing him to take into his service only those who would take "such Oaths, as imply him to be an Idolater."[3] It is no wonder, then, that James called the Test an "intollerable yoake."[4]

Opponents of the Test said that some clergymen had been heralds of the Test by raising a cry of idolatry against Catholics in 1671–1672. In a modern study of the Restoration church we learn that "the tone and agenda for the church's theological and spiritual life were set by a coterie of controversialists, preachers and devotional writers, based in London and the two universities." Edward Stillingfleet was one of those "champions" especially admired by the provincial clergy.[5] Writing in 1673, Castlemaine depicts this London "coterie" as sounding the drum shortly before the Test Act: "But what Sermons, what Books, what Cabals, what travelling over Sea and Land have there been by five or six of your worthy Doctors, to incense our fellow-Subjects against us, as Idolaters?"[6]

A noted Presbyterian remarked in 1672 that Stillingfleet's book called *A Discourse Concerning the Idolatry of the Church of Rome* (1671) had indeed made "mocking" at Catholics "catching."[7] Baxter, another Presbyterian, mentioned in 1673 that Stillingfleet had "greatly animated them [parliament] and all the nation against Popery." Latitudinarians like Stillingfleet, Baxter explained, were "ingenious men and scholars . . . abhorring at first the imposition of these little things [i.e., bowing, kneeling], but thinking them not great enough to stick at when imposed." They were "Cambridge men, Platonists or Cartesians, and many of them Arminians with some additions, having more charitable thoughts than others of the salvation of heathens and infidels. . . ."[8] Baxter's last point

3. Cartwright, *A Letter from a Clergy-Man*, 32.
4. James II, *Life*, 2:147–48.
5. John Spurr, *The Restoration Church of England, 1646–1689* (New Haven, Conn.: Yale University Press, 1991), xv.
6. Castlemaine, *A Full Answer* (1673), 1.
7. *A Letter from Dr. Robert Wild to His Friend Mr. J. J. upon Occasion of His Majesty's Declaration for Liberty of Conscience* (London: T. Parkhurst et al., 1672), 13–14.
8. *The Autobiography of Richard Baxter*, ed. J. M. Lloyd Thomas (1931; rep., London: Dent/Totowa, N.J.: Rowman and Littlefield, 1974), 227.

was that Stillingfleet extenuated pagan idolatry. It was actually a major theme of his *Discourse of Idolatry* that the idolatry of ancient heathens was more excusable than that of Catholics, and so heathens might well be saved, while Catholics had certainly been damned for their idolatry for more than eight hundred years.

In a witty reply to that *Discourse of Idolatry*, the Jesuit Henry Beaumont points out that Stillingfleet ushers in a "real Idolatrie" under color of casting out an imaginary one when he claims that St. Paul referred to Jupiter as the "unknown God" (Acts 17:23) and when he asserts that all the Church fathers except Origen admitted the divinity of Jupiter. Such great errors, Beaumont says, open "a high way" for each libertine to bring in "Heathenisme without check, so hee be but disguised under the Visard of a Champion beating down Popish Idolatrie."[9] Beaumont's point, that Stillingfleet opens a "high way" to libertines, reminds us that the Hind speaks of Stillingfleet and other Latitudinarians as the Panther's "broadway sons" (3:229). By the word "broad-way," the Hind glances at Canticles 3:2, where the Church-Bride seeks for her Beloved in the "broad ways" of the city at night and fails to find him. Concerning this verse, ancient expositors said that there is only one way to Christ, and it is "Himself" (RFL, 116). Christ also warns his disciples that the "broad way" leads to destruction (Mt 7:13). The Latitudinarian clergy took a broad way in matters of faith because they tried to make the national church inclusive by reducing the element of doctrine and mystery in religion. When it came to exterior conformity, however, they took a narrow way, for they were strict supporters of the Test Acts and Penal Laws.

In *A Defence of the Third* [*Duchess's*] *Paper*, Dryden ponders whether Stillingfleet has a "Cloven-foot" under his "Cassock," so great is his "Talent" for "subtle Calumny and sly Aspersion." The poet notes his huge following in England and calls him "Legion" because ten thousand speak in his person: "I have treated him as one single Answerer, tho' properly speaking his Name is *Legion*; but tho the Body be possessed with many evil Spirits, 'tis but one of them who talks." Likewise, in *The Hind and the Panther*, the poet has the Hind link Stillingfleet, because he commits "Homicide of names," to the "perjur'd murtherer" Titus Oates, who has killed both names and bodies. The implication is that the two men are

9. [Henry Beaumont, S.J.], *Jupiter, Doctor Stillingfleets True God* [N. p.: N. pub., 1674], 2–6, 11–12, 23.

leaders in the campaign of "black detraction" against the Hind in Restoration England:

> But *Imprimatur*, with a Chaplain's name,
> Is here sufficient licence to defame.
> What wonder is 't that black detraction thrives?
> The Homicide of names is less than lives;
> And yet the perjur'd murtherer survives.
>
> (3:256–60)

In this passage the Hind implies that the Panther has given Stillingfleet and her other pretended sons a "license" to defame Catholics.

John Gother, a Catholic spokesman, lists a number of Restoration clergymen who followed Stillingfleet's lead and made Catholics "so odious to the people" for their supposed idolatry that the English would tolerate Jews and atheists "with less regret" than Catholics.[10] The root of this attack on Catholics seems to have been a surge of iconoclasm within the Restoration Church. For example, we see iconoclastic zeal in Bishop Barlow's public letter to John Evelyn, originally written in 1669: noting that English Catholics still sing the ancient hymn "Vexilla Regis," composed in 569 by Fortunatus, Barlow says it shows that they still adore two "*rotten sticks*" and "*a despicable wooden* Cross with Divine Worship."[11] An Anglican writing from Oxford informs us that the walls of churches were then adorned with "holy admonitions" against idolatry.[12] According to Dr. Nicholas Harpsfield, the churches in the reign of Edward VI, when iconoclasm was rampant, were likewise decorated only with scriptural warnings against idolatry, "to make the world believe that to pray to the saints, to pray for the dead, to worship Christ's body in the blessed sacrament, was nothing but plain superstition and idolatry."[13]

In her tale, which telescopes the history of the Test Acts, the Hind shows that Stillingfleet's defamation of Catholics in the *Discourse of Idol-*

10. [John Gother], *Reflections upon the Answer to the Papist Misrepresented* ([London], 1686), 19.

11. Thomas Barlow, *A Letter Concerning Invocation of Saints, and Adoration of the Cross, Writ Ten Years Since, to John Evelyn of Depthford, Esq, by Dr. Barlow Then Provost of Q. Colledge, and Now Lord Bishop of Lincoln* (London, 1679), 19–22.

12. [James Harrington, the Younger], *Some Reflections upon a Treatise Call'd Pietas Romana & Parisiensis* (Oxford: At the Theatre, 1688), 28.

13. Nicholas Harpsfield, L.L.D., *A Treatise on the Pretended Divorce between Henry VIII and Catharine of Aragon*, ed. Nocholas Pocock (Westminster, U.K.: Camden Society, 1878), 282.

atry paved the way for the Test Act of 1673. We see in the following lines that before the "deadly *Shibboleth*" of the Test was enacted, the "*Pigeon-*house" created a "hideous Figure" of Catholics as idolaters. Although this "Grotesque design" had no resemblance at all to real Catholics, it pleased the crowds. They came to "*Pigeon-*hall," that is, into the churches, to view the new freakish "Figure," that is, to hear sermons about the Catholics as unheard-of monsters:

> An hideous Figure of their Foes they drew,
> Nor Lines, nor Looks, nor Shades, nor Colours true;
> And this Grotesque design, expos'd to Publick view.
> One would have thought it some *Aegyptian* Piece.
> With Garden-Gods, and barking Deities,
> More thick than *Ptolomey* has stuck the Skies.
> All so perverse a Draught, so far unlike,
> It was no Libell where it meant to strike:
> Yet still the daubing pleas'd, and Great and Small
> To view the Monster crowded *Pigeon-*hall.
> There *Chanticleer* was drawn upon his knees
> Adoring Shrines, and Stocks of Sainted Trees,
> And by him, a mishapen, ugly Race.
>
> (3:1042–54)

By the phrase "Garden-Gods" is meant the body and blood of Christ in the Eucharist under the signs of bread and wine. The phrase "*Aegyptian* Piece" alludes to Stillingfleet's remark that Catholic adoration of Christ in the sacrament is worse than the Egyptian adoration of the leek. By the phrase "Great and Small" the Hind reveals how popular the scapegoating was shortly before the Test was enacted.

John Gother uses almost the same rhetoric and imagery as the Hind to describe the effect of Stillingfleet's *Discourse on Idolatry* on the nation in 1671–1673, saying that this book imposed "upon the Multitude with artificial Monsters" and showed Catholics praying "before stocks and stones" and "Breaden Gods" in a worse than "Heathenish Idolatry." Afterward, the Test Acts of 1673 and 1678 simply gave legal form to this caricature, condemning Catholics "to all those horrid shapes." Stillingfleet taught the English that all Catholics had been damned for idolatry: that "the Learned and Unlearned, Laity and Clergy, all Ages, Sects and Degrees of Men, and Women, and Children of whole Christendome have been at once drown'd in abominable Idolatry, the space of Eight hundred years and more." [14] The Hind alludes to Stillingfleet's *Discourse* when she says that "piety" should forbid the Panther to think

> That seav'n successive ages should be lost
> And preach damnation at their proper cost;
> That all your erring ancestours should dye,
> Drown'd in th'Abyss of deep Idolatry.
> (2:630–33)

She implies that respect for her ancestors as well as faith in the divine promises should give the Panther kinder thoughts of the Middle Ages.

To make things worse, Catholics could not easily get access to the press to clear themselves of charges of idolatry. Stillingfleet issued a public challenge, saying that they had to reply to his charge in the "open field" or admit that his book was unanswerable. Canes reports that an all-out effort was immediately made to prevent Catholics from replying, the presses being suddenly "so frequently invaded, so violently searched night and day, especially by the industry of one of them, who entring in to the Printing-houses, cried out aloud, *And what! have ye here anything against the Doctor Stillingfleet?*" Thus, Canes says, Stillingfleet "imperiously challenged" Catholics to clear themselves of idolatry but gave them no "*open field*" except Tyburn.[15] Serenus Cressy regards Stillingfleet's book as "Ominous," "ill-boading," and "fore-running some expected mischief." Like Canes, he is amazed that the presses have been "walled up" by "Partizans" ever since the printing of the *Discourse of Idolatry*, so that now "*Stationers* apprehend greater danger in publishing *Answers* to his *Book*, than any *Books* of Sedition or *Treason*." Cressy gives us a measure of Stillingfleet's importance in London when he writes that "*Searches* into the *Presses* have been more sollicitously exact, and more frequent dayly and hourly," than at any time since 1660, with "*Inquisitors*" turning over every small paper, "examining whether any thing has been written against *Doctour Stillingfleet*."[16]

The Anglican bishop of Oxford regards Stillingfleet as the precursor

---

14. [John Gother], *Papists Protesting against Protestant-Popery* (London: Henry Hills, 1686), 7, 12, 14, 22.

15. Canes, *An Account*, 3.

16. Cressy, *Fanaticism*, 7, and "To the Reader." See also [Richard Ashby], "Address to the Reader," in *Some Generall Observations upon Dr Stillingfleet's Book* (N. p.: N. pub., 1672), where it is charged that Stillingfleet attacks Catholics and is "interpreting this our silence to be an argument of our weakness."

of the Test Act of 1673. He says that this man's "Modern Zeal" went far beyond the teachings of the true Church of England and caused Catholics to lose their birthrights "for no higher act of Recusancy, than not swearing to the Truth of Dr. Stillingfleet's Unlearned and Fanatique Notion of Idolatry; that in reality is the bottom of all this Mischief and Madness."[17] By his use of the words "zeal" and "fanatic," Bishop Parker implies that Stillingfleet remained a Puritan at heart even after he conformed at the Restoration. He is one of those "sons of Latitude" whom the Hind describes: they have intruded into the Panther's line but belong to the Wolf in the hidden "hinder parts" (3:160–70).

Dean Cressy understands Stillingfleet in a different way. He sees him not as a secret Puritan but as a skeptic, one who "methodized" William Chillingworth's *Religion of Protestants*. Cressy explains that men like Stillingfleet can persecute others because they detach outward conformity from inward belief: "The misery is, None are more eager in usurping a Magisteriall and Tyrannicall Power over other mens consciences, then such as renounce all Authority internally obliging in the Church: Because having no tye upon mens consciences, or security in their Subjects Obedience, they find externall violence the only Means to support them, which surely argues a horrible depravation in the minds, especially of Ecclesiasticks."[18] Concurring with Cressy on this point, Abraham Woodhead, in his work *Dr Stillingfleet's Principles* (1671), singles out this tenet which Stillingfleet adopted from Chillingworth, that the Thirty-nine Articles do not have to be *believed,* only *not opposed.* All that is required to be Anglican is "outward submission for Publick Peace sake."[19] Thus, Stillingfleet can hollow out the mystery of the Real Presence while maintaining all the panoply of ceremony that betokens the Real Presence. This is what the Hind complains about when she tells the Panther, concerning the Restoration Church, "Your churches substance thus you change at will, / And yet retain your former figure still" (2:50–51).

Catholics urged the high churchmen not to stand by silently while Stillingfleet contradicted the teachings of Henry Hammond, Herbert Thorndike, and Jeremy Taylor, three among the many Anglican divines

17. Parker, *Reasons for Abrogating the Test*, 35.
18. Cressy, "To the Reader," in *Fanaticism*, 96, 99, 167–68, 179.
19. [Abraham Woodhead], *Dr Stillingfleet's Principles, Giving an Account of the Faith of Protestants, Considered by N. O.* (Paris, 1671), 5–6.

who had exonerated Catholic adoration of Christ in the Eucharist from the charge of idolatry. It seems that some high churchmen did intercede for Catholics to be allowed to answer Stillingfleet's charge of idolatry, but in vain. Bishop Parker gives one high-church answer much later, in 1684, when he makes an implicit parallel between the ancient Donatists and the Latitudinarians: the Donatists hated liberty of conscience, they spread sedition against Constantine when he granted it, and they had a "Natural Faculty of Canting" by inveighing against the "Idolatry" of Catholics. Parker adds that it is "the custom of all Fanaticks to improve everything into Idolatry."[20] The Hind makes a similar point in her tale when she shows how some Pigeons "had learn'd to Cant" and were impugning their patron as a "gross Idolater" (3:1208, 1227).

The Hind suggests that the Test Acts of 1673 and 1678, which were based on this imputation of idolatry, were handed to the Anglican clergy to be used as a deadly "weapon" against James and against the hereditary principle in monarchy. Bishop Cartwright recalls how many in the Church of England became "divided from the Loyal" after the Test and tried to intrude the Duke of Monmouth, Charles II's illegitimate son, into the succession. Cartwright says that even if these "Excluding Members" of the church recovered their "Loyalty" in 1685, the Monmouth rebellion came out of the spirit they had "conjur'd up."[21]

The Hind rebukes the Panther for finding so much "innocent" security in the Test that she flies into a "rage" whenever anyone talks of repeal:

> To name the *Test* wou'd put you in a rage,
> You charge not that on any former age,
> But smile to think how innocent you stand
> Arm'd by a weapon put into your hand.
>
> (3:698–701)

The Panther will not renounce a Test which she says parliament put in her hand, but she knows well that the makers of the Test Acts were the king's "foes" and "hers," that is, foes of high-church worship as well as foes of the age-old hereditary monarchy:

> Yet still remember that you weild a sword
> Forg'd by your foes against your Sovereign Lord,

20. Parker, *Religion and Loyalty* (London, 1686), 282.
21. Cartwright, *A Letter from a Clergy-Man*, 23.

Design'd to hew th' imperial Cedar down,
Defraud Succession, and dis-heir the Crown.
T' abhor the makers, and their laws approve,
Is to hate Traytors, and the treason love.
What means it else, which now your children say,
We made it not, nor will we take away?

(3:702–9)

In other words, if the Panther loathes the radical Whigs for having con-
spired to kill James bodily in 1683, then she should give back the weapon
Shaftesbury bequeathed her in his will, because the Test was designed to
murder James in his public capacity. This point is often made in the repeal
tracts: one anonymous repealer states that "the late Impious *Tests*" were
"contriv'd designedly to Exclude the present *King*"; we find the same
point in William Penn; and Bishop Parker notes that Shaftesbury was in
"fierce Pursuit of Princely Blood" when he devised the 1678 Test.[22] In addition, the Jesuit Darrell calls the Test a weapon against James which the Tories want to hang up in Westminster Hall, to intimidate the king, "as a Tro-
phy of so infamous a Victory past, and as a Terror for the time to Come."[23]

King James writes in his memoirs that the cry of idolatry in the pulpit
campaign began, by 1686, to have overtones of rebellion. The clergy
started making "immaginary dangers a good pretence to encourage a real
Sedition." On November 16, 1686, "one Samuel Johnson, a Clergieman"
published "a most Seditious libel," he says, in which he told the soldiers
and seamen they should not suffer themselves to be yoked "with Idolaters
and bloody Papists, who fight for the Mass book and to burn the Bible."[24]
Johnson was inciting those soldiers and seamen to violence against Catholic officers, the prescribed biblical punishment for "Idolaters" exempted
from the Test. In her tale the Hind seems to refer to the mood of 1686
when she portrays the Pigeons as "drunk" with "Popular Applause" as
they publicly oppose their Patron's plan to repeal their "unnatural" Test:

But still the *Dove*-house obstinately stood
Deaf to their own, and to their Neighbours good:
And which was worse, (if any worse could be)

22. Anon., *A New Test of the Church of England's Loyalty* (London: For N[at]
T[hompson], 1687), 6; Penn, *Good Advice*, 15; Parker, *Reasons for Abrogating the Test*, 9.
    23. W[illiam] D[arrell], S.J., *The Lay-Mans Opinion, Sent in a Private Letter to a
Considerable Divine* (N. p.: N. pub., 1687), 6.
    24. James II, *Life*, 70.

Repented of their boasted Loyalty:
Now made the Champions of a cruel Cause,
And drunk with Fumes of Popular Applause;
For those whom God to ruine has design'd,
He fits for Fate, and first destroys their Mind.
(3:1087–94)

In the phrase "repented of their boasted loyalty," the Hind shows the sedition in the Pigeons' popular stand against repeal.

One opponent of the Test declares that the clergy see the repeal of "this Parliament-Test" as "parting with their Hearts Blood."[25] As a result, Bishop Cartwright says, many of them have become "the *Standard-Bearers of Sedition*." Cartwright complains that his fellow Anglican clergymen are teaching the people from the pulpit that St. John regards idolaters as no better than "*Murderers, Dogs, Sorcerers, and Whoremongers*," and worshippers of "*Devils*" (Rv 22:15, 9:10) and that "St. *Paul* ranks them with *Sodomites and Thieves*" who "shall *not inherit the Kingdom of Heaven*" (1 Cor 6:9–10). This pulpit campaign is making the king "*vile to the People*" exactly as the "*Primitive Christians*" were made vile by being dressed in "Beasts skins" before being killed.[26]

The Jesuit Darrell says that he hears a call to revolution in the sermons on idolatry. He finds it less mischievous to draw a weapon against the king, as the Whigs did in the Rye House Plot, than to tell "500 People at a time in the Name of God that the Religion their King Professes is rank Idolatry." When Darrell pleads with the clergy that James has been beaten "sufficiently" by the "Rod" of the Test, he implies that their cry of idolatry is a strategy to save the Test.[27] In the same period, John Gother describes the Anglican "pulpit" as a battlefield, with the clergy striking "blindly" at the king with their Bibles and beating an alarm "upon their Cushions."[28]

Dryden's poem, begun in 1686 and completed in the first part of 1687, alludes more than once to the harsh sermon campaign against the king. In the tale of the Swallows, the Panther represents King James as a sun who is "eclips'd in his way" by an infant moon and is stripped of "the small

25. Anon., *Plain Dealing Concerning the Penal Laws and Tests Delivered in a Dialogue between a Country Man and a Citizen* (1688), 6.
26. Cartwright, *An Answer of a Minister*, 23–25.
27. Darrell, *Lay-Mans Opinion*, 6, 8.
28. [John Gother], *Good Advice to the Pulpits*, "To the Reader" and 49–50.

remainders of his day" (3:601–2). This eclipse which blackens the king's light is the pulpit campaign against the king for his supposed idolatry. The Panther depicts her pretended sons as an infant moon because they are the growing part of the national church. The Panther unwittingly undercuts herself, however, by depicting her sons as a crescent moon, because the imagery evokes the Ottoman Turks, then at war with the Holy League of nations in Hungary.

It is worth noting that Bishop Cartwright uses the very same imagery and rhetoric found in the Panther's tale for the pulpit campaign against the king in 1685–1688. He compares the effect of all those sermons on idolatry to a darkening of a light in the sky: their "undutiful" words from the pulpit "eclipse his Honour" by "interposing" a "thick Body between him and his Peoples Hearts." The "thick body," of course, is the imputation of idolatry. Cartwright is shocked that a sermon on idolatry has recently been given in the precincts of the court itself and asks "cannot we *abhor Idols*, without *flying into his Face?*" It seems a clergyman actually preached against idolatry within the Protestant chapel at court. Cartwright rebukes those who want to "prop" the church by these "*unwarrantable Arts*" and, like the Hind, urges them to "trust" in the king's promise.[29]

In the Hind's tale a Buzzard is called in by the Pigeons to carry out their revenge, and this creature declares from the pulpit within the Patron's own Yard that the Patron is "a gross Idolater" (3:1227). In this scene, the Hind refers to the same event Cartwright took note of. This sermon on idolatry seems to have been given in the court precincts on the eve of the Act of Indulgence in 1687. Darrell also speaks of this occurrence, saying that in a pulpit at court the king's religion was branded "with Idolatry it self, a Mark, like that one of Cain, to invite every body to do him a mischief." After this sermon, he notes, many people suddenly flocked to that Protestant chapel; though they had previously been "Strangers" to "Zeal," now they hurried to worship God "for spite." Darrell adds that the pulpits all over the land have begun sounding a weekly alarm about "the approaching Inundation," so that it seems like a prelude "to Arms."[30] The rhetoric of "inundation" which the Panther uses in Dry-

---

29. Cartwright, *A Letter from a Clergy-Man*, 35.
30. Darrell, *Lay-Mans Opinion*, 6–7. But on the other side, a modern historian writes that when James II urged Archbishop Sancroft to stop the pulpit campaign

den's poem (3:830–34) is thus copied from life. Like Darrell, the Hind refers to a sudden swarming of "Atheists" and "Birds of ev'ry feather" within the Pigeons' chapel located in the Patron's own yard:

> The House of Pray'r is stock'd with large encrease;
> Nor Doors, nor Windows can contain the Press:
> For Birds of ev'ry feather fill th' abode;
> Even Atheists out of envy own a God.
>
> (3:1209–12)

Here the Birds who never came to worship before come in droves, so they can join in the sport of persecuting the Catholic Hens (3:1214–16).

But, on the other hand, a supporter of the Test answers Darrell's tract and tries to cast doubt that any such event took place in the Protestant chapel at court. He demands to know the name of the preacher who branded the king there with the "Mark of Cain."[31] It is possible, of course, that this particular personage was someone too powerful for Cartwright, Darrell, or Dryden to identify any more clearly.

Historians have wondered why James II, after all this, commanded the clergy of the national church to read his declaration on liberty of conscience from the pulpit in the spring of 1688. His impolitic command sparked the revolution. Cartwright explains that the king wanted his declaration read in the same place where he had been slandered to the people. Instead of being read aloud, however, the "Indulgence" was simply branded as evil in itself, as "*Malum in Se*, as a Pest to the Publick, as an Abomination and Prophanation of our Churches, and not fit to be heard by Christian Ears."[32] One repealer suggests that the clergy refused to read it because they wanted "to *Conceal*" from the people "the Matter of the Declaration," lest they approve it.[33]

In the Hind's tale the Farmer is not harmed by the Pigeons' rebellious-

---

against his religion, this amounted to a "concerted attempt to gag and humiliate the Church of England." See John Miller, *Popery and Politics in England, 1660–1688* (Cambridge: Cambridge University Press, 1973), 209.

31. Anon., *The Lay-Mans Answer to the Lay-Mans Opinion* (London: N. pub., 1687), 7.

32. Cartwright, *A Letter from a Clergy-man*, 7. Herbert Croft, bishop of Hereford, also urged the Anglican clergy to support the king and read his declaration from the pulpit; see *A Short Discourse Concerning the Reading His Majesties Late Declaration in the Churches* (London: C. Harper, 1688), 5–14.

33. Anon., *The Ministers Reasons . . . Debated*, 11.

ness. Indeed, he gains a moral victory after the pulpit campaign has reached his own yard: "He strove a temper for th' extreams to find, / So to be just, as he might still be kind" (3:1231–32). After seeing how much his own Hens have been slandered, the Patron begins to pity all the other Birds that the Pigeons have reviled. He issues a "Gracious Edict" that removes only the Pigeons' "licence to oppress," but none of their wealth and state. At first, the Pigeons revile him to his face, but they are finally silenced by the great prosperity that ensues as a consequence of the Patron's grant of liberty. This prosperity, which the repealers hoped they would have time to bring home, is conceived as the most effective argument of all against the Test Acts.

CHAPTER 10

The Test as Sacrilege: MPs and the Real Presence

The argument that the Test was a sacrilege had two facets. First, the re-pealers argued that Charles II's parliament had usurped the authority of a church by defining the Lord's Supper in the Test and by so doing had isolated England from the rest of Christendom, past and present. Sec-ond, they argued that parliament had defiled the sacred mysteries by re-quiring people to receive communion merely as a qualification for secu-lar employments.

When it is expressed satirically, the first argument is recognizable by a key word like "certainty," "almighty," or "infallibility" applied to the English parliament. One repealer speaks of the Test as that "new Point of Faith lately broach'd by a famous *Act of an Infallible* English *Parliament* conven'd at *Westminster*, and guided by the Holy Spirit of *Shaftsbury*."[1] The Jesuit Pulton writes that the English dare not "question the Cer-tainty and Truth of a Religion prescrib'd by so *Wise, Sincere, and Learn'd* an Assembly."[2] Likewise, in *The Medall* (1682), Dryden speaks of the par-

1. Anon., *A New Test of the Church of England's Loyalty*, 8.
2. [Andrew Pulton, S.J.], *A Full and Clear Exposition of the Protestant Rule of Faith, with an Excellent Dialogue Laying Forth the Large Extent of True Protestant Charity against the Uncharitable Papists* ([London]: N. pub., c. 1687), 6–7.

liament that voted in the Test as an "Almighty Crowd" that changed the national religion in its own "*Pindarique*" way, that is, without consulting the ancient rules or the deposit of faith:

> Almighty Crowd, thou shorten'st all dispute;
> Pow'r is thy Essence; Wit thy Attribute!
> Nor Faith nor Reason make thee at a stay,
> Thou leapst o'r all eternal truths, in thy *Pindarique* way!
>
> (91–94)

In the phrase "Wit thy Attribute," Dryden glances at the ease with which parliament passed the Test against the Real Presence. It shortened "all dispute" in the sense that it abruptly ended the debate that had lasted since Luther's time on the meaning of the phrase "This is My Body." A hundred and forty years later, in 1827, the Protestant Committee to Repeal the Test repeated the plea that there was indeed a "pretension to infallibility" in the parliament that enacted the Test.[3]

Bishop Parker makes this same argument without a satiric edge when he says that by imposing the "State Test" parliament encroached on the Church's "Prerogative" with "prophane Levity" and made "Decrees concerning Divine Verities." In these statutes, the members of parliament (MPs) invaded "our Saviour's own Kingdom" and gave an "Affront to Almighty God." Although he concedes that bishops were sitting in the House of Lords when the Tests Acts were passed, he points out that they were there only as "Temporal Barons" and that their ecclesiastical authority could not be exercised lawfully with "lay-concurrence." The Test is thus a "Law of an Ecclesiastical Nature made without the Authority of the Church."[4] In his memoirs, King James II echoes the rhetoric of Bishop Parker when he says that it is "not in the power of Parliaments to make decrees about divine veritys" because only the clergy "vested with the Ecclesiastical power" can devise oaths, which parliament may then vote to accept.[5]

The other side of this argument is that parliament's unlawful assumption of church authority has had the effect of separating England from the rest of Christendom, past and present. In this plea, the Test Acts are said to have made the English Church a purely local affair. In *The Medall*

---

3. *Repeal Committee Minutes*, 67.   4. Parker, *Reasons for Abrogating*, 8–11.
5. James II, *Life*, 2:147.

Dryden attacks the Test for reducing the ancient faith of England to a local fashion:

> The common Cry is ev'n Religion's Test;
> The *Turk*'s is, at *Constantinople*, best;
> Idols in *India*, Popery at *Rome*;
> And our own Worship onely true at home:
> And true, but for the time; 'tis hard to know
> How long we please it shall continue so.
>
> (103–8)

In these superbly oblique lines, the "common Cry" is the clamor of the House of Commons for "Religion's Test." Here the poet makes a point often made in anti-Test literature, that the new statutes sever the national church from the universal faith of Christendom, for now it is "onely true at home" and "true, but for the time." The "*Pindarique*" legislature, whose MPs follow their momentary whim, might alter the national worship again at any time (91–92). And so, in 1682, when he was still a Protestant, Dryden warns that parliamentary votes are no discerning test for the tenets of Christ's faith, for by the same token other sovereign states could impose their own local, temporary fashions in religion. When Dryden rebukes the Panther for being an insular church that does not obey Christ's command to send out missions—"In her own labyrinth she lives confin'd. / To foreign lands no sound of Her is come" (1:403–4)—he echoes a well-established line of argument against the Test.

William Penn attacks the Test in the same way, using almost the same words. He says that the English now give their religion "into the Magistrates Hand," and it amounts to this: "at Rome a Papist, at London a Protestant, at Constantinople a Mahometan." This principle vindicates the king of France in his Revocation of the Edict of Nantes, he contends, because it makes being a "Calvinist at Paris" just as much "a fault" as being "a Papist at London." In accepting the Test, the Church of England is "Hobbist," even though she "clamours against the Leviathan." Like Dryden, Penn rebukes the English Church for confining herself to one place and avoiding the "Pains and Perils" of sending out the missions that Christ commanded. He laments that his countrymen "Believe as the State requires" without thinking of universal truth: "all our Faith and Worship must be submitted to the Political reason of the community, we are of, hit or miss."[6] Similarly, Henry Payne sees a new insularity in English religion resulting from the Test, arguing that parliament has now confined "truth" to "one single Church in an Island," in communion with no other in the world.[7]

The convert Edward Sclater tries to show that the Test Acts separate the national Church not only from the Church of Rome but also from the Greek Orthodox Church. He writes about a council convened at Constantinople in 1639–1642, at which the Eastern bishops adopted the term "transubstantiation" from the Western church to condemn the teaching of an Eastern Calvinist. In their decree the Greek bishops restated their ancient belief that "the honour we are to render to these terrible mysteries, ought to be the same as to Jesus Christ himself." Sclater points out that no one in England condemns the Greeks for idolatry, even though they teach the same thing as the Catholics in Britain.[8]

Making a similar plea, Robert Fuller says that the Test Acts separate the people of England from the Christians of Tartary, Persia, India, Armenia, Greece, and Ethiopia, who believe in the "Transmutation" of the elements of bread and wine and consequently adore the Real Presence of Christ in the sacrament. The statutes that impute "idolatry" to Catholics and cut them off from public employment as misbelievers thus isolate the English themselves from all other Christian nations. In addition, the English cut themselves off from most other Protestants, because Luther and Calvin were "far from condemning such Adoration, or making it Idolatry."[9] Fuller's point about Lutherans, who comprised half the Protestants in those days, is found in other Catholic responses to the charge of idolatry in the Test. For example, Castlemaine exclaims: "And if that shocking *Article* to flesh and bloud, and reckon'd also by our *Enemies* as our most dangerous *Tenet*, (I mean *the real and substantial presence of*

6. [William Penn], *A Defence of the Duke of Buckingham's Book of Religion and Worship* (London: A. Banks, 1685), 13–14, 19–20; and *Good Advice to the Church of England*, 13.

7. Payne, *The Persecutor Expos'd*, 30.

8. Edward Sclater, *Consensus Veterum; or, The Reasons of Edward Sclater Minister of Putney, for His Conversion to the Catholic Faith and Communion* (London: Henry Hills, 1686), 87–91.

9. R[obert] F[uller], *Missale Romanum Vindicatum; or, The Mass Vindicated from D. Daniel Brevents Calumnious and Scandalous Tract* (N. pl.: N. pub., 1674), 2, 128–29, 161.

Christ in the Sacrament) blots not a *Lutheran* out of the *Book of Life*, why should it me? 'Tis true, we differ in the *Mode* or Manner of his being there, but not in the *Reality*."[10] Castlemaine's phrase "shocking . . . to flesh and bloud" is close to Dryden's phrase for the Real Presence: "The lit'ral sense is hard to flesh and blood" (1:428). Still another convert's rhetoric on the Real Presence is close to Dryden's: "I know it is hard, for flesh and blood to relinquish sense," that is, sensory perception in the eucharistic mystery.[11] This phrase "hard, for flesh and blood" alludes to the Capernaites who rejected Jesus in John 6:61 with the comment that his words on the Real Presence were too "hard." Catholics and Lutherans understood the Capernaites to be carnal men unwilling to receive the doctrine of the Real Presence because it was beyond their sensory perception.

Another opponent of the Test goes a little further and adds that parliament, when it enacted the Test, not only detached England from Christendom but joined it to Islam: "I should think that this new *Tenet*, which makes it *Idolatry* to adore the *Divine Body of Christ* (whether there be a *Transubstantiation* or not) must certainly savour more of a *Mahometan* than of *Christian* Doctrine."[12]

The Anglican bishop of Oxford also takes up the argument that the Test has confined the religion of England to one island by renouncing a mystery "unanimously received" in Christendom. Parliament did not know the difference between the terms "Real Presence" and "Transubstantiation," he claims, when it branded nearly all Christians past and present with idolatry. Moreover, when the English now take the oath that transubstantiation is idolatry, the proposition is completely unintelligible to them, for unless they have studied medieval realism and nominalism it is "morally impossible for them to understand" the term "substance" in "transubstantiation." Bishop Parker thinks the Test amounts only to this: that the landed class of England must swear to anything "rather than lose any worldly Interest."[13] In his memoirs, King James repeats Parker's phrasing when he says that the Test forced the English "to abjure what it was morally impossible for them to understand," and forced them "to de-

10. *The Earl of Castlemain's Manifesto*, 122–23.

11. Sclater, *Consensus Veterum*, 97.

12. Anon., *A New Test of the Church of England's Loyalty*, 8.

13. Parker, *Reasons for Abrogating*, 64–70.

termine solemnly in the Presence of God, the truth of certain metaphysical notions, which all the subtilties of the Schooles" could not decide.[14]

Parker also thinks that the Test separated the Church of England from its own roots, which were Calvinist, not Zwinglian. According to him, the legislators who voted in the Test were *nominal* Anglicans who did not know what the Church of England had taught concerning the Lord's Supper before the Civil Wars. In the Interregnum, Parker explains, the sacrament was reduced to a bare sign, to Zwingli's idea of a "meer Sacramental Figure and Representation and a Participation only of the Benefits of the Body and Blood of Christ by faith." At that time "the only Measure of Truth with them, was Opposition to the Church of Rome" and the two most "frightful" topics were "Transubstantiation and Idolatry." After the Restoration, the same "Zwinglianism" continued to be preached in the newly settled Restoration church by the very same clergymen. Although they outwardly conformed to the Book of Common Prayer, they kept this idea of the Sacrament of the Eucharist as nothing more than a metaphor.[15]

In a similar vein, Henry Payne contends that the bulk of the clergy from the time of Cromwell remained in place at the Restoration: during the Interregnum, he says, out of "Nine Thousand Benefic'd Parsons, not above Three Hundred, besides the Dignitaries, quitted their Spiritual Preferments. But all conform'd to that is now call'd *Phanaticism*." Subsequently, the clergy that had become Presbyterian under Cromwell went on to conform to Anglicanism under Charles II.[16] This is Dryden's argument, too, that the high-church Panther who suffered loss of income and exile during the Interregnum represented only a small portion of the national clergy; she was and remains outnumbered by a "pretended race" of clergymen who conformed to Puritanism under Cromwell and to Anglicanism at the Restoration. A modern historian agrees with Payne that there was continuity in the clergy from 1641 to 1662, but he claims that at most 70 to 75 percent of the national clergy took the Puritan Covenant in 1643 and the Engagement in 1650.[17] Obadiah Walker believes that the

---

14. James II, *Life*, 2:147.

15. Parker, *Reasons for Abrogating*, 65–66.

16. Payne, *Persecutor Expos'd*, 8. On p. 40, Payne says that nine-tenths of the nation were what "we now call Phanaticks."

17. Robert S. Bosher, *The Making of the Restoration Settlement: The Influence of the Laudians, 1649–1662* (Westminster, U.K.: Dacre, 1957), 5.

Zwinglian view of the sacrament as a metaphor, a view which was imposed during the Interregnum, remained the teaching of the Restoration Church. When Archbishop Wake and Dean Henry Aldrich deny the Real Presence in their pamphlets, he says, they only prove they are "of the modern or present Church of England."[18]

Edward Sclater, however, sees not continuity but a sharp decline in respect for the Lord's Supper since the Interregnum. He contends that the sacrament, for the Presbyterians, was at least a *sign* of Christ's presence, but after the Restoration the sacrament dwindled to nothing at all: from the "Womb of Separation," he says, sprang "the Denial of Christs real and substantial Presence, and the making the Elements bare signs and figures: From these a Generation worse than them, that makes them meer Cyphers."[19] Sclater hints that the sacrament that was the basis of the Test Acts was regarded as having no Real Presence of any sort. The parliament that passed the Test seemed to think there was nothing sacred in the Lord's Supper capable of being defiled. If he is correct, Sclater gives us an insight into the rationalist indifference toward embodiments in religion out of which the sacramental Test arose.

Indeed, the low churchman Gilbert Burnet defends the Test against the charge of sacrilege in just the way Sclater leads us to expect. Burnet insists that there is nothing in the sacrament capable of desecration. When we partake of the sacrament as prescribed by the Test for "Imployments," he explains, we receive Christ's "*dead Body*, which is not now actually in being" but only conceived as presented to us.[20] Burnet's phrase, "*dead Body*, which is not now actually in being," makes the sacrament a memorial of the Crucifixion, a reconceiving of an historical event. The implication here is that no *bodily* rising occurred on Easter morning, because Christ's body is not now "in being." It was the mark of the Socinian in the seventeenth century thus to present the symbols of bread and wine as reminders of death.[21] Likewise, in his *Discourse* about idolatry, Still-

18. [Obadiah Walker], "Appendix 2," entitled "Animadversions upon the Reply to the Two Discourses Concerning the Adoration of Our B. Saviour in the Holy Eucharist," to [Abraham Woodhead], *A Compendious Discourse* (Oxford, 1688), 191.

19. Sclater, *Condensus Veterum*, 97.

20. G[ilbert] Burnet, *A Discourse Concerning Transubstantiation and Idolatry. Being an Answer to* [Samuel Parker] *the Bishop of Oxford's Plea Relating to Those Two Points.* (London: N. pub., 1688), 4–6, 33–35.

21. Daniel-Rops, *The Church in the Seventeenth Century*, 357.

ingfleet says that Christ is no more to be worshipped in the sacrament "than in a turf." He adds that even if the body of Christ were actually present and if the bread were indeed converted into his body, "what then? is that the object of our adoration? do we terminate our Worship upon his humane nature?"[22] Stillingfleet implies that there was never a hypostatic union between Christ's human nature and his divine nature, and so, even if he were visibly present in his humanity he could not be adored. This is the view that Dryden, in *The Hind*, finds "impious" and "graceless" in the Socinian Fox, the rationalist who cannot descry "God" or "Natures king" in the Child of Bethlehem (1:59).

In St. John's Apocalypse 13:17, we read that in the days of Antichrist a person will not be able to buy or sell unless he wears the mark of the Beast. Everyone will be told to wear on his body, for carnal reasons, "the character, or the name of the beast, or the number of his name." The word "character" can mean a letter of the alphabet. In her tale, the Hind implies that the Test is this character of the Beast. The champions of the Test want to impose the wearing of the "B," that is, the mark of the Beast, as the condition for being publicly employable in England. For this reason, the Hind depicts those who support the Test as already wearing the letter "B" on their chest, the seal or medal of Antichrist. This is a parody of Canticles 8:6, "Put me as a Seale upon thy hart." In the Apocalypse, there is a larger and a smaller Beast, a military Antichrist and his prophet in the clergy. Likewise, in the Hind's tale, the Buzzard whom the Pigeons summon to be their avenger has two sides: he is a prince and a prophet. The letter "B" is perhaps also meant to glance at the prince of Holland, for Dryden refers to Holland poetically as *Batavia* (*Threnodia*, 478), and at the churchman Burnet. The Hind speaks of Burnet as a carnal "Prophet" and shows that in his life, an inversion of the life of Christ, he served as his own herald (3:1146, 1157). The Hind dubs the Buzzard "the Captain of the *Test*" (3:1192), a name that fits both Burnet and the prince of Batavia. As we have shown, Burnet's idea of the sacrament in the Test was of something carnal and incapable of being desecrated, or as he put it, a "*dead body*, which is not now actually in being." Thus the Hind can depict Burnet's Test as a perfect antithesis to the ancient communion rite, which makes the living presence of Jesus Christ accessible to his followers.

22. Stillingfleet, *Discourse*, 98–99.

During the debate on the 1673 Test in the House of Lords, the Trea-
surer Thomas Clifford, Dryden's patron, gave a passionate speech in
which he called the Test Act a "dirty Bill" and a "*Monstrum horrendum*"
because Commons had dared to meddle in "what one ought to believe at
Communion." Subsequently, there was talk of impeaching him for treason for that speech. Even though he had been signing orders to enforce
the Penal Laws against Catholics and receiving the Anglican sacrament
up to the end of 1672, Lord Clifford resigned on 19 June 1673 and became
a Catholic rather than take the Test which he saw as a sacrilege.[23] At the
same time that Clifford and James duke of York resigned their offices in
1673, an anonymous poet was writing this complaint to parliament:

> Are you, poor drunken noddies, fit to define
> God's sacred worship and things most divine,
> Which learned councils trembled how to do
> Though God and Church have call'd them thereunto?

He grieved that secular men had presumed to act as a learned council of
the Church to define the "holy mysteries" of the faith.[24]

There was a second line of argument about the sacrilege of the Test,
namely, that it encouraged the unworthy receiving of communion. From
1673 until 1827, this was the most passionate argument of all for repeal, because it was urged that the most sacred rite of Christianity was being defiled by using it for a mere qualification for worldly, secular employments.

One repealer claimed that military men "very prophane in their Lives"
have been swallowing without hesitation "all these Tests you speak of."[25]
Likewise, Henry Care warned that the Test is "prostituting" the sacrament
and "exposing it to Secular Ends and Designs."[26] Castlemaine reported
that within a year of the enactment of the 1673 Test the talk of the town
was all about sacrilege: "What abominations have we also seen [since] the
other day, when besides Swearing, *Communicating too was enjoind all
Persons in any Office or Employment. . . .* Are not those known, & of Qual-

---

23. Cyril Hartmann, *Clifford of the Cabal* (London: Heinemann, 1937), 261. The
attempt to impeach him for high treason for this speech is described in *A Relation of the
Most Material Matters Handled in Parliament: Relating to Religion, Property, and the
Liberty of the Subject* ([London]: N. pub., 1673).

24. Anon., "The Banished Priest's Farewell," in *Poems on Affairs of State*, 1:207.

25. Anon., *Plain Dealing*, 6.

26. Care, *Draconica*, 17.

ity too, *that from Wenches & Brothel houses went to performe the Obligation of this Law?* Have not some drunk over night, & early wakend with heat & thirst, calld their Companions to go to Church, *because Communion wine was the best mornings draught after a Debauch?* Have not others revelling all Saturday even 'till Sunday it selfe cry'd; *That the Act enjoind no preparation, & that they reciev'd now to save their Offices, & not their Souls;* nor was there any thing more ordinary at London, *than to finde Bread, which the Communicants had thrown under foot.* Twould be long enough before I end, were I to reckon all the strange Profanenesse committed, even such, that several (who were far from being Bigots or Precisians) stood amaz'd at, & the common Pastime in all Companies (during the thus *preventing the dangers from Popery*) was to relate these, & the like stories."[27]

When he was still a Protestant, Dryden satirized the sacrilegious use of the Test in the case of Lord Howard of Escrick: "And Canting *Nadab* let Oblivion damn, / Who made new porridge for the Paschal Lamb" (*Absalom*, 575–76). Howard was imprisoned in the Tower in 1681 when he took the sacrament for the Test in "Lamb's-Wool," that is, in "ale poured on roasted apples and sauce." To underline his impiety Dryden calls him "*Nadab*" because this son of Aaron, in Leviticus 10:1–2, dared to offer a "strange fire" to the Lord.[28]

Taking a slightly different approach in part 1 of *The Hind*, the poet depicts an atheistic type of courtier taking the Test. This is a man who ridicules all forms of Christianity in Britain and joins in no worship, yet who does not hesitate to kneel and receive the sacrament as a Test for secular preferment:

Next her the *Buffoon Ape*, as Atheists use,
Mimick'd all Sects, and had his own to chuse:
Still when the *Lyon* look'd, his knees he bent,
And pay'd at Church a Courtier's Complement.
(1:39–42)

Dryden shows that while the Test repels those who sincerely diverge in their beliefs, it does not stop those who have only contempt for the Sacrament of the Altar from coming forward to receive it. These men receive the

27. Castlemaine, *Apology* (1674), 103.
28. See the note to lines 575–76, in the California edition, 2:261.

holy mystery of Christianity only as a "Courtier's Complement." Dryden's point is well illustrated by the case of a famous Deist who took the Test not long afterward and excused himself with this very word "compliment." Judge Heywood reports that "Anthony Collins, Esq. who wrote several treatises against Christianity, was in the commission of the peace; and being obliged to qualify himself according to the Test Act, is said to have given notice of his design in the following ludicrous manner: *Sir, I design to take a bit of bread and a cup of wine with you*; and when he was pressed by a friend upon the impropriety of a person professing his principles, receiving the Sacrament, he answered, *I only do it to pay a compliment to the custom of my country*."[29]

Giles Shute pursues the same line of argument, calling the sacramental Test the "mystery of iniquity," that is, the seal of Antichrist and the mark of the Beast, because Christ never "never Instituted and Appointed" his Supper for any "such base, low, secular End" as for merchants to get "a License to sell Ale" or for "drunken debaucht Fellows" to be qualified "to bear Arms in the Trained Bands." He alleges that even though Article 29 commands the clergy to separate the worthy from the unworthy receivers, the sacramental Test is given without hesitation "to whole droves of the vilest of men." In this way, he says, the Test changes divine food into "so much Rats-bane," "spiritual Poyson," and "fretting Leprosie."[30]

Perhaps the most powerful contribution to the argument about sacrilege is the Hind's passionate statement about the English Test as the "unfaithfull" touchstone that does not discern the worthy from the unworthy receiver:

> But that unfaithfull *Test*, unfound will pass
> The dross of Atheists, and sectarian brass:
> As if th' experiment were made to hold
> For base productions, and reject the gold:
> Thus men ungodded may to places rise,
> And sects may be preferr'd without disguise.
> (3:738–42)

In these lines Dryden alludes to a passage about sacrilege in St. Paul which was often cited in seventeenth-century debates as a proof of the Real

29. Heywood, *The Right of Protestant Dissenters*, 73.
30. Shute, *A New Test in Lieu of the Old*, 27; *New Naked Truth*, 12–13, 21, 34–35, 44.

Presence. St. Paul tells the Corinthians that the body of Christ in the sacrament is a test or touchstone that will separate the worthy from the unworthy receiver before God: "whosoever shall eat this bread, or drink the chalice of the Lord unworthily, shall be guilty of the body and of the blood of the Lord. But let a man prove himself: and so let him eat of that bread, and drink of the chalice. For he that eateth and drinketh unworthily, eateth and drinketh judgment to himself, not discerning the body of the Lord" (1 Cor 11:27–30). St. Augustine's comment on these verses, cited in the 1582 edition of the Rheims New Testament, is that the receiver who does not discern and adore Christ in the Eucharist shall be damned (Epistle 118, c. 3). St. John Chrysostom is also cited for his warning that the unworthy receiving of the Eucharist makes a man guilty of villainy to Christ's own person. In her lines about the Test as a false touchstone, the Hind's word "unfaithful" reinforces her term "ungodded." This language implies that the sacramental Test amounts to a kind of anti-Christian apostasy. It is like the Fumie Test by which the Dutch merchants deny their Christianity and trample the crucifix in Japan for the sake of a trade monopoly. It is the opposite of St. Paul's discerning touchstone, for it passes infidel "dross" and throws out nonconformist "gold." The Test is an invitation to "men ungodded" to trample the mysteries for profit. Such men of "no conscience" (3:748) easily get a certificate for public employment, as do the "sectarian brass" who conform hypocritically.

Using almost the same image of the "unfaithful touchstone," William Penn warns concerning the Test that "to over-value Coyne, and rate Brass to Silver, Beggers any Country; and to own them for Sons she never begat, debases and destroyes any Church." The modern Test creates only "*disguised Enemies*" and "Friends in *Masquerade*."[31]

A century later, William Cowper attacks the Test as a sacrilege with the same passionate rhetoric used by the repealers of the 1680s:

Hast thou by statute shov'd from its design
The Savior's feast, his own blest bread and wine,
And made the symbols of atoning grace
An office-key, a pick-lock to a place,
That infidels may prove their title good
By an oath dipp'd in sacramental blood?

31. Penn, *A Persuasive to Moderation*, 37.

A blot that will be still a blot, in spite
Of all that grave apologists may write,
And though a Bishop toil to cleanse the stain,
He wipes and scours the silver cup in vain.[32]

Cowper's word "infidels" echoes the Hind's "ungodded." His horror at the indelible "stain" in the communion cup evokes Lord Clifford's cry of "*Monstrum horrendum.*"

On the other hand, the Protestant Repeal Committee concedes, in 1827, that the ministers of the established Church have all along been placed in a "dangerous dilemma" by the Test Acts. They have had no legal right to stop sacrilegious communions, despite their ecclesiastical obligation to do so: "In the rubric and by the canons, they are enjoined to call upon any notorious evil liver (they having full knowledge thereof) so presenting himself and to warn him against presuming to come to the Communion until he shall have openly declared himself to have truly repented of and amended his evil life; and are authorized, if not absolutely commanded, to repel him until he shall have so done." But since a minister would be "liable to an action for damages" for refusing communion to one "appointed under the king's authority," it happens that "no one presenting himself to receive the sacrament as a qualification for office is ever rejected, and thus the Church and religion itself suffer injury and disgrace severer than any which the attacks of the most determined infidel could inflict."[33]And so it seems that the Test was a Procrustes's Bed for the established clergy as well as for those nonconformists elected to corporate offices, until 1767, to make them liable to the penalties of the Test Acts.

A modern historian gives a thoughtful overview of the entire argument about the sacrilege of the Test: "[T]he price paid for the security of Protestantism was too high. The Test Act relegated the most sacred rite of the English Church to the rank of a political formula. Men known to have no religious belief, who openly scoffed at Christianity, were admitted, compelled indeed if they wished to hold office, to a performance of sacrilegious hypocrisy. The consequences of thus interfering with conscience by legislation were fully realized only in the following century. 'There can be no doubt,' wrote [the Protestant historian William] Lecky, 'that the

---

32. William Cowper, "Expostulation (1782)," in *Poems by William Cowper: 1748–1782,* ed. John D. Baird and Charles Ryskamp (Oxford: Clarendon Press, 1980), 306.
   33. *Repeal Committee Minutes,* 83–84.

Sacramental Test, besides its political results, had a very serious influence in lowering the religious sentiments of England.'"[34] In 1828 the argument about sacrilege persuaded the bishops to vote unanimously against the Test, against the advice of the ultra-Tories, and help to ensure repeal.

34. Hay, *The Enigma of James II*, 68. Hay cites William E. H. Lecky, *History of England in the 17th Century*, 8 vols. (New York: Appleton, 1878–1890), 1:317.

CHAPTER 11

The Mating of Panther and Wolf: A Test for a Rubric

The ecclesiastical groundwork for the three Test Acts and for the campaign against Catholic "idolatry" from 1671 to 1688 seems to have been a single rubric inserted into the Book of Common Prayer in 1661. If Dryden is correct, that single rubric had an immense importance in the history of the Test Acts from 1661 to 1687. In *The Hind and the Panther* Dryden offers a unique, seventh argument against the Test Acts based on that rubric. No one else seems to have reflected as deeply on the root of the Test Acts as Dryden did.

In *A Letter from a Person of Quality* (1675), Lord Shaftesbury, the architect of the Test Acts, said that the Church of England's Book of Common Prayer was "not so sacred, being made by Men the other day." He then spoke of former changes made in the liturgy "as might the better unite us," alluding to the rubric added to the communion service in 1661[1] Shaftesbury's phrase "better unite us" echoes the preface of the Book of Common Prayer published in 1662, in which the bishops write that they made such revisions as "might most tend to the preservation of peace

---

1. *The History and Proceedings of the House of Lords*, 149.

228

and unity in the church." His phrase "not so sacred" reveals that, in his opinion, the addition of that rubric proved that other canons might also be changed. He was not the only one to think so.

One church historian explains that the "Post-Communion Rubric, known popularly as the Black Rubric," was the "most important" change in the 1662 Book of Common Prayer because "it removed from the Rubric the phrase 'real Presence'" and it "made adoration of ANY Presence IN the elements contrary to the doctrine of the Church of England." He points out that the rubric was restored from a prayer book of the previous century. It had been inserted with an accompanying article in the 1552 Book of Common Prayer of Edward VI, after John Knox had raised a storm in London by preaching against the idolatry of kneeling for communion.[2] In the 1662 edition, the newly incorporated rubric appears at the end of the unpaginated chapter on communion:

Yet, lest the same Kneeling should by any persons, either out of ignorance and infirmity, or out of malice and obstinacy, be misconstrued and depraved; It is here declared, that thereby no Adoration is intended, or ought to be done, either unto the Sacramental bread and wine, there bodily received, or unto any Corporal Presence of Christs Natural Flesh and Bloud. For the Sacramental bread and wine remain still in their very natural substances, and therefore may not be adored, (for that were Idolatry, to be abhorred of all faithful Christians). And the Natural Body and Bloud of our Saviour Christ are in heaven and not here; it being against the truth of Christs Natural Body, to be at one time in more places than one.[3]

This rubric asserts that Christ is bodily in heaven, which is at a distance from us, and so he cannot be adored as if he were "here" at communion, for to adore him "here" would be "Idolatry."

Dryden argues, as we will show, that this rubric was the groundwork of the three Test Acts. The rubric's words saying that Christ was "not here" at communion legitimized the use of the sacrament to qualify men for secular employments, for, as Lord Shaftesbury says, it proved that the liturgy was "not so sacred." Moreover, the rubric gave the Anglican

---

2. Dyson Hague, *The Story of the English Prayer Book*, 2d ed. (London and New York: Longmans Green, 1930), 233.

3. *The Book of Common Prayer* (London: John Bill and Christopher Barker, 1674). The rubric is in gothic lettering at the end of the communion service.

Church authority to attack Catholics as supposed idolaters of the sacrament. Indeed, the rubric states explicitly that any adoration of the Real Presence as "here" is idolatry.

The Black Rubric was drawn from the teaching of Zwingli, the most rationalistic and iconoclastic of the first Protestants. Zwingli had a horror of embodiments in religion, and especially of the Real Presence in the sacrament. His position on the Eucharist was that the Ascension of Christ precluded any Real Presence in the Lord's Supper. Zwingli said that Christ, after the Ascension, was locally present at the right hand of the Father at a great distance from us and would be confined there until the Second Coming. Thus, "Real Presence" could have only a figurative sense and the sacrament had no mystery or power in itself. Both Luther and Calvin found Zwingli too reductive on the issue of the Lord's Supper. Indeed, after the Marburg Colloquy of 1529, concerning the phrase "This is My Body," Luther would not even give Zwingli the fraternal handshake.[4]

Zwingli's point, that the Ascension contradicts the Real Presence, is the same one that was raised by Berengarius in the eleventh century, when five successive councils were convened to restate the ancient doctrine in the light of his new challenge. It was in the course of those councils that the term "transubstantiation" was defined. Thomas Fuller, in his history of the Anglican Church up to 1648, notes that Wycliff denied the Real Presence, employing the same reasons as Berengarius, when he said the Ascension confined Christ's body to one place and that "God could not, though he would, make his body to be at the same time, in several places."[5] Thus, Berengarius, Wycliff, and Zwingli all made Christ's Ascension into an instrument to re-interpret Real Presence as a metaphor. Their characteristic cry of "not here" was now introduced into the 1662 Book of Common Prayer by way of Edward VI's Zwinglian rubric of 1552.

There was, however, one phrase in the Black Rubric changed between 1552 and 1661. The words "Real and Essential" were altered to "Corporal" in the statement "no Adoration is intended or ought to be done unto any Real and Essential Presence of Christ's natural Flesh and Blood." But this alteration seems to have made no difference in the meaning of the rubric,

4. Hermann Sasse, *This Is My Body: Luther's Contention for the Real Presence in the Sacrament of the Altar* (Minneapolis, Minn.: Augsburg, 1959), 285.

5. Fuller, *Church History*, 133.

because the phrase "Corporal Presence" was used by Lutherans at the time to mean the Real Presence held in common with the Catholics. In the 1552 Book of Common Prayer, Article 29 accompanied the rubric and explained it with Zwingli's characteristic argument about the Ascension. Although this article was not reinserted in 1661, it still reveals what the rubric means by the charge that it is "Idolatry" to adore Christ as "here" at communion.

For as much as the truth of Man's Nature requireth, that the Body of one and the self same Man cannot be at one time in divers places, but must needs be in one certain place; therefore the Body of Christ cannot be present at one time in many and divers places: and because, as Holy Scripture doth teach, Christ was taken up into Heaven, and there shall continue unto the end of the World; a faithful Man ought not either to believe, or to confess, the Real and Bodily Presence, as they term it, of Christ's Flesh and Blood in the Sacrament of the Lord's Supper.[6]

Here the Ascension is used as the instrument to deny the possibility of a Real Presence, as in Berengarius, Wycliff, and Zwingli.

When the Savoy Convocation inserted the Black Rubric into the Book of Common Prayer in 1662, the Presbyterians rejoiced because, as their leader Richard Baxter observed on that occasion, the sacrament of the Church of England had now been freed from "all suspicion of idolatry." Baxter hinted at coercion, for he said that parliament had imposed the rubric on the Church over the objections of high churchmen. He himself had been meeting, under royal command, with the episcopal leaders from April to July 1661 to talk about ways of revising the Book of Common Prayer so as to open membership in the national church to Prebysterians. In a later tract Baxter said that the high churchmen, especially Herbert Thorndike, continued to "disown [even in 1676] the New Rubrick of the Common-Prayer Book which saith, Our Lords Body is in Heaven, and not on the Altar." They had no basis to reject it, he added, because the "*New Rubrick* is but the *Old* restored." It was only the return of Edward VI's prayer book of 1552.[7]

6. Cited in [Abraham Woodhead,] *Two Discourses Concerning the Adoration of Our B. Saviour in the Eucharist. The First: Animadversions upon the Alterations of the Rubrick in the Communion-Service in the Common-Prayer-Book of the Church of England* (Oxford: O. Walker, 1687), 1–2. This will hereafter be cited as *Animadversions.*

7. *Rel. Baxterianae* (1696), cited in Rev. N[athaniel]Dimock, *The History of the Book of Common Prayer in Its Bearing on Present Eucharistic Controversies* (New York:

Bishop Burnet reports that the Savoy Convocation inserted the rubric at the insistence of Bishop John Gauden, a Presbyterian sympathizer, and that the Duke of York called it a "puritanical thing."[8] The Cambridge Platonist Henry More approved of the rubric because it showed that in the sacrament there is a "Real Absence of that Body and Bloud that was crucified and shed on the cross."[9] His striking phrase "real absence" implied that he read the insertion of the rubric as a total repudiation of Real Presence.

At the same time that the Savoy Convocation inserted the Black Rubric into the Book of Common Prayer, in December 1661, parliament passed the first Test Act, the Corporation Act, which was a concession offered to the yet-unsettled Church of England. The Corporation Act (1661) made the receiving of communion according to the rite of the national church, that is, in a kneeling posture, a necessary qualification for holding local office. As we will show, Dryden sees the rubric and the Test as the quid pro quo that forged the ruling alliance of the Restoration, a centrist party enjoying access to public employments. It joined the conformist Presbyterians, who were willing to overcome their "scruples" over kneeling, to the Latitudinarian Anglicans, who were willing to broaden the eucharistic doctrine of the Anglican Church for the sake of including, or "comprehending," moderate Presbyterians.

This seventh argument against the sacramental Test—that the first Test Act of 1661 amounted to a secret quid pro quo between Presbyterians and Anglicans, in Dryden's terms, a secret mating between the Panther and the Wolf—appears to be Dryden's original contribution to the repeal campaign. It is so important to him that it pervades his entire poem, for we are constantly reminded of the Panther's earlier deflowering by the Wolf and her renewed adultery with him in 1685–1688. Dryden thinks that this is what is turning the high churchmen into the enemies of the king and making them defend the Test Acts with all their might. Her secret adultery with the Wolf is what causes the aging Pardelis to be

---

Longmans Green, 1910), 44; Spurr, *The Restoration Church*, 31–32; [Richard Baxter], *Roman Tradition Examined* (N. p.: N. pub., 1676), 12.

8. Dyson Hague, *Story of the English Prayer Book*, 233–34.

9. [Henry More], *A Brief Discourse of the Real Presence of the Body and Blood of Christ* (London: Walter Kettilby, 1686), 1, 5. More insists (38–40) that we eat spiritually the "Eternal Logos, to whom appertains the universal Divine Body," which is the same "Spiritual Food" as in the Manna!

"salvage." Besides, this mating has caused the Panther to be surrounded by "pretended" sons who are wolfish below the waist, who rejoice at the signs of her aging, and who gape eagerly for the grandame gold.

Canticles 8:4 describes the deflowering of the mother: "Under the apple-tree I raysed thee up: there thy mother was corrupted, there she was defloured that bare thee." Ancient expositors saw here, as we explained earlier, both the deflowering of Eve under the Tree in Eden and that of the Jewish Church under the Cross. In Part I, we saw that the "Ancient Mother" of the Panther had been "compress'd" in a "shade," that is, deflowered under the Rood-Tree by Henry VIII, who made himself the Church's shade by the Act of Supremacy. Afterward, the national church became branches hugging the monarchy, "tender branches" twining round the royal "Poplar" tree (1:440). However, since her adultery with the Wolf, the Panther finds shelter behind the Test Acts. In these statutes she wields a sword "Design'd to hew th' imperial Cedar down" (3:704). She now has the power to cut down the tree of monarchy that has long shaded and given strength to her vine.

In his history of the Test Acts, a Presbyterian judge explains that the power of the kingdom had been in the hands of the Presbyterians when Charles II assumed the throne in 1660. At that time the Church of England was only "tacitly re-established," and the "Presbyterian clergy were allowed to retain their livings." Although the king had promised toleration at Breda, this course was rejected by parliament. Instead, the Presbyterians were given "hopes of such alterations being made in the liturgy and discipline of the church of England, as should comprehend them within the establishment; and the proposed alterations were actually under consideration at the time [1661] the Corporation Act was passed."[10]

It is easy to see what those alterations had to be. Ever since the reign of Edward VI, the Puritans had raised scruples about kneeling for communion. But by the early seventeenth century they were beyond scrupling, and they charged that kneeling for communion was a form of idolatry. Calvinists and Zwinglians abroad had long since stopped kneeling for communion: Calvin had instituted an ambulatory communion, and Zwingli a seated one. In 1661, however, the Anglican convocation added a rubric to explain kneeling in such a way that moderate Presbyterians like

10. Heywood, *Right of Protestant Dissenters*, 8.

Baxter were convinced there was no longer any danger of idolatry. Thus, a quid pro quo at the start of the Restoration seems to have created a centrist alliance from which the Act of Uniformity could then be enforced. For as soon as the new prayer book was revised, Charles II sent the House of Lords a letter on February 25 recommending its enforcement by the forthcoming Act of Uniformity.

When the Hind rebukes the Panther for declaring against her former teachings in the rubric of 1661, the English Church does not deny that this is what she did. She pleads only that she was "push'd, against a wall" (2:33). She implies that she was coerced and deflowered, and that this removes the blame: "Tortures may force the tongue untruths to tell" (2:38). The Hind suggests that the mother's rape was also a seduction, that there was an element of assent when the Panther chose to yield her faith rather than be martyred:

> I freely grant you spoke to save your life,
> For then you lay beneath the butcher's knife.
> Long time you fought, redoubl'd batt'ry bore,
> But, after all, against your self you swore;
> Your former self, for ev'ry hour your form
> Is chop'd and chang'd, like winds before a storm.
> Thus fear and int'rest will prevail with some,
> For all have not the gift of martyrdome.
>
> (2:52–59)

At the end of this passage the Hind charges that there were two motives for adding the rubric: "fear and int'rest" (2:58). That is, the Panther was offered the sacramental Test to promote her "int'rest," and thus worldly advantage was one reason she agreed to insert the rubric. The phrases "against a wall" and "redoubl'd batt'ry" (2:33, 54) both remind us that in Canticles 5:7 the keepers of the walls smite and wound the Church-Bride when they find her searching for her Bridegroom. Ancient expositors interpreted this passage as concerning persecution endured faithfully for the sake of the Bridegroom.

Like Dryden, Obadiah Walker believed that there was political coercion when the "Rubrick against the Real Presence" was inserted over the "great opposition" of the clergy in December 1661. Walker claimed that a "Higher Power" prevailed in bringing about a "complying with the Presbyterians." He called the rubric a "new-devis'd Absence of the Lord from his People."[11] What makes the idea of coercion plausible is that the restored bishops had been moving in a totally opposite direction before the Savoy Convocation reconvened on November 21. They had met for several weeks at Ely House and had decided to revise the Book of Common Prayer in a Laudian direction. In the margins of the "Durham Book," a 1619 edition of the Book of Common Prayer still in the library of Durham Cathedral, they wrote the proposed Anglo-Catholic revisions that would have included a "sacrifice" offered on the altar, a commemoration of the faithful departed and of the saints, an "Agnus Dei" sung during communion to acknowledge the Real Presence, and the elements veiled after communion. All this would have restored the very high-church prayer book of 1549. But, "the Laudian influence is barely apparent" in the 1662 revised prayer book.[12] For in the weeks between November 21 and December 20, the bishops made a complete reversal: instead of adding rubrics that would have emphasized the Real Presence of Christ in the sacrament, they re-inserted a Zwinglian rubric from the Puritan prayer book of 1552 that declared kneeling for communion free of "Idolatry" because Christ is "not here."

The Hind remarks that the Panther had been "dumb" on the topic of the Real Presence before she inserted the rubric: the English church had kept "some forms, and ceremonies some" but had "stood in the main question dumb." She had kept kneeling and bowing but had been reticent about preaching on the modus of the Real Presence. But suddenly, the Hind says, the first Test gave her the power of speech. She was now able to say that she had all along believed the same thing as the Wolf:

> Dumb you were born indeed, but thinking long
> The *Test* it seems at last has loos'd your tongue
> And, to explain what your forefathers meant,
> By real presence in the sacrament,
> (After long fencing push'd, against a wall,)
> Your *salvo* comes, that he's not there at all:
> There chang'd your faith, and what may change may
>   fall.
>
>   (2:27–35)

11. Walker, "Appendix 2," 208–10.

12. Bosher, *Making of the Restoration Settlement*, 244–47; F. E. Brightman, *The English Rite* (London: Rivingtons, 1915), cxcv, ccviii, cited in Bosher, 247.

Here, by the phrase "he's not there at all," the Hind echoes the most important line in the Black Rubric: "And the Natural Body and Bloud of our Saviour Christ are in heaven and not here." The Hind asserts that the rubric "chang'd" the "faith" of the Panther. It did not just deny the modus of transubstantiation, but stated that Christ's body was absent at communion. So now the Zwinglian idea of the sacrament, which had been prescribed by the Puritan Directory in the Interregnum, became the Panther's doctrine.

In saying that the Test "loos'd" the "tongue" of one who was "born dumb," the Hind hints that the quid pro quo of the rubric for the Test parodied Christ's healing of the man born dumb (Mk 7:35). The Panther had previously taught that Christ's body was present in the Lord's Supper by *modus ineffabilis,* that is, in an *inexplicable* manner. Calvin, from whom Hooker and Andrewes drew their eucharistic doctrine, had also stressed ineffability.[13] The very high-church Launcelot Andrewes drew "all the devotional implications of the full Catholic position without admitting all its doctrinal bases."[14] This is Dryden's point in Part I when he says that the old Elizabethan and Laudian high churchmen had accepted self-contradictory teachings on communion because they had not spelled out the doctrinal basis for the Real Presence:

> A real presence all her sons allow,
> And yet 'tis flat Idolatry to bow,
> Because the god-head's there they know not how.
>
> (1:414–16)

At the touch of the Test in 1661, however, the Panther declared by the rubric that Christ's body is "not here." The Hind suggests with irony that there must be a *miracle* when the silence of *modus ineffabilis* is so quickly changed to this certitude about real absence: "Your *salvo* comes, that he's not there at all." In the Gospel story, Christ cured the man born dumb with his finger, and the parallel suggests that the Test was the parodic finger of Antichrist that opened the ears and lips of the Panther with the same sort of bodily immediacy.

---

13. Kilian McDonnell O.S.B., *John Calvin, The Church, and the Eucharist* (Princeton, N.J.: Princeton University Press, 1967), 83.

14. Maurice F. Reidy, S.J., *Bishop Lancelot Andrewes, Jacobean Court Preacher* (Chicago: Loyola University Press, 1955), 137.

In her reply to the Hind's charges, the Panther minimizes the importance of the Black Rubric, but she never denies that she inserted it as a
quid pro quo for the Test. She excuses herself not only on the ground of
coercion, but also on the ground that she never claimed to be "infallible"
(2:38–39). The Hind retorts that the rubric has robbed the English
Church of her identity, for now her form is chopped and changed by
every wind. The Panther desubstantiated herself as well as her sacrament
by proclaiming Christ's absence at communion. For now she is like the
dog in Aesop's fable who dropped his meat and reached for its reflection
in the water:

> For *real*, as you now the word expound,
> From solid substance dwindles to a sound.
> Methinks an *Aesop*'s fable you repeat,
> You know who took the shadow for the meat:
> Your churches substance thus you change at will,
> And yet retain your former figure still.
>
> (2:46–51)

With this rubric, then, the Panther has begun to lose her Elizabethan
form: "But after all, against your self you swore; / Your former self"
(2:55–56). Hooker was probably alluding to the rubric of 1552 when he
wrote that there had been a danger for a time that the sacrament of the
Church of England would become a mere shadow, void of all substance,
but that time had passed by the 1590s, and now the only controversy remaining was whether Christ's Real Presence was "*within man only*" or
also in the Sacrament of the Altar.[15] The new rubric seemed to declare
that Christ was absent both on the altar and within man.

In Part I of *The Hind*, Dryden again hints with different imagery that
the high-church Panther (i.e., that one-fourth of the clergy who refused to
take the Covenant) was as "undaunted as an *Indian* wife" in the Interregnum, but she began to lose her identity at the beginning of the Restoration:

> . . . but some souls we see
> Grow hard, and stiffen with adversity:
> Yet these by fortunes favours are undone,

---

15. Robert Hooker, "The Sacrament of the Body and Blood of Christ," in *Ecclesiastical Polity*, 2 vols., ed. Ernest Rhys (London: Dent/New York: Dutton, 1922),
2:319–20. Hooker mentions Zwingli here.

Resolv'd into a baser form they run,
And bore the wind, but cannot bear the sun.

(1:443–47)

The Panther's soul was like a frozen form that kept its shape in the winds of 1641–1659, but since the return of Charles II it has been "resolv'd" into a "baser form" by the sun. The Hind's tale ends with the same image of the Panther's form melting away "Like Snows in warmth" during the open-ended peaceful reign of James (3:1271). This imagery ties in with her being a cold, half-darkened moon, partly captured by the forces below her.

In the Hind's tale at the end of the poem, we see the quid pro quo of 1661 virtually repeated in 1685–1687, only this time the deflowering occurs without any coercion. A Pigeon-adviser suggests that the Buzzard would be glad to end his hostility toward the Pigeons and to join them in attacking the Catholic Poultry—provided that the Pigeons give up their "Forms" to satisfy his scruples: "But all his hate on trivial Points depends, / Give up your Forms and we shall soon be friends" (3:1126–27). The Hind plays on the word "form," which can mean either a liturgical action or the identity of a church. She warns that the Pigeons will end up having no soul, no substance at all, if they continue to reach for an ever lower common denominator in doctrine and liturgy in the hope of including all the Dissenters in their church, instead of repealing the Test Acts and Penal Laws and letting everyone worship independently.

Abraham Woodhead, a spokesman for Restoration Catholics, wrote a treatise against the Black Rubric entitled *Animadversions upon the Alterations of the Rubrick in the Communion Service, in the Common-Prayer-Book of the Church of England*. Composed early in the Restoration, this work was published in 1687 at Oxford, under a special royal license allowing Obadiah Walker to publish the many works of Woodhead.[16] The king

---

16. It has not been noted, to my knowledge, that this extraordinary license lists only works by Abraham Woodhead, while not even mentioning his name, including some works now lost. William Sancroft, archbishop of Canterbury, had a copy of the license in his papers (Tanner MS 460, f. 54) which I saw at the Bodleian Library, Oxford. Thomas Clancy, S.J., informs me that this license is printed in J. Gutch's *Collecteanea Curiosa* (Oxford: Clarendon Press, 1781), 1:288–89. James II intended to raise a monument to Woodhead at University College, Oxford. This saintly man, dubbed "the Invisible Man," was admired also by high-church Protestants like Anthony Wood and Thomas Hearne. The latter called him "one of the greatest Men that ever this Nation produc'd." Catholics claimed that Woodhead had composed *The Whole Duty of Man* before his conversion. His life is given in [Simon Berington], "The Preface: Giv-

was so impressed with Woodhead's writings that he wanted him to honor him with a monument at Oxford. Since Dryden's son was studying with Walker at the time the latter was publishing Woodhead's works, the poet would very likely have known about this project and may well have seen this pamphlet before it was published. Woodhead—who had been ordained in the Church of England long before his conversion in the 1650s—argued passionately that the Black Rubric contradicted everything the Church of England had taught about the Eucharist since Elizabethan times.

Woodhead says that the rubric makes natural philosophy the new ground of the sacrament: for when it declares that Christ's "*natural Body and Blood*" are "not here" in the sacrament, it urges "for that Nonpresence there, this reason or ground out of National Philosophy, *that it is against the truth of a Natural Body, to be in more places than one at one time*; here seeming to found their Faith in this matter on the truth of this position in Nature."[17] He thinks it ought to have said that adoration is due to "*the real and essential presence of Christ's natural Flesh and Blood*," which is here not "*after a natural manner*," but rather "*in its true reality and essence, after some other manner effected supernaturally by divine power*," a power that allows Christ's body to be "*at one time in more places than one.*" In other words, Woodhead recommends a stress on ineffability again. His tone of mild and patient rebuke is exactly that which the Hind takes with the Panther in Dryden's poem. What the Church of England has embraced in the rubric, Woodhead mourns, is "a bare *Zuinglianism*," an "*absolute non-presence of Christ's Body in the Eucharist*," except in its "*vertue, and effects.*"[18]

This word "vertue" had a great importance in the debate over the Real Presence. Zwingli had used the word to denote real absence in the sacrament. For this reason Dryden italicized the term *vertue* in the following passage where the Panther claims that the quid pro quo of the Test for the rubric did not amount to any real change in her doctrine on the Lord's Supper because she had always taught that the communicant receives a "real *vertue*" rather than the body of Christ:

---

ing a Succinct Account of Mr. Woodhead's Writings and Life," prefixed to Abraham Woodhead's *Ancient Church Government, Part III* (N. p., 1736), xxvi–lix.

17. Woodhead, *Animadversions*, 4.

18. Woodhead, *Animadversions*, 33.

Reply'd the *Panther*, grant such Presence were
Yet in your sense I never own'd it there.
A real *vertue* we by faith receive,
And that we in the sacrament believe.

(2:40–43)

The Hind pounces on the Panther's joining of the words "real" and "vertue" and exclaims that this is not what you formerly taught: "For *real*, as you now the word expound, / From solid substance dwindles to a sound" (2:46–47). She sees the word "vertue" in this context as indicating Zwingli's nonpresence. And indeed the word "vertue" or "virtual" at that time was used to denote a figurative sacrament, as when Dean Aldrich wrote from Oxford that Christ's presence in the sacrament is "virtual" and that the worthy receivers "figuratively eat that body and drink that blood, when they really eat and drink the symbols of them."[19] This Zwinglian idea of the sacrament had been the Puritan position, but now it replaced the Calvinist idea of the sacrament in the Restoration church.

Woodhead mentions how the most "learned" of the Anglican writers such as Ridley, Hooker, Andrewes, and Taylor had maintained a Calvinist Real Presence, that is, the presence of Christ's *natural body* to the worthy receiver's soul at communion. And so, he says, the rubric of 1661 opposes not only the "general Tradition and Doctrine of the Fathers" and the Catholic, Greek, and Lutheran Real Presence, but even the former Calvinist teaching of the Church of England.[20]

On the other side, however, Archbishop Tenison declares that "this Rubric doth in effect charge the church of Rome with gross idolatry."[21] The rubric also rested on the "Homily of Idolatry" of the previous century, which was recommended in Article 35 of the Church of England. But this homily had not been binding on belief in the same way that the newly inserted rubric was.

19. [H. Aldrich], *A Vindication of the Oxford Reply to Two Discourses* [by Woodhead] *There Printed A.D. 1687 Concerning the Adoration of Our Blessed Saviour in the Eucharist, from the Exceptions Made to It in the Second Appendix* [by Walker] *to a Compendious Discourse on the Eucharist Published by the Same Press* (Oxford: At the Theater, 1687), 71.

20. Woodhead, *Animadversions*, 9. Woodhead cites only the *learned* clergy among the Presbyterians and Anglicans, preferring to make the strongest case for his opponents before rebutting.

21. Dimock, *History of the Book of Common Prayer*, 56.

From his hidden hermitage at Hoxton, Abraham Woodhead attacked the Black Rubric, using a subtle line of reasoning that also undergirds Dryden's attack on it. Woodhead meekly urged his countrymen to distinguish transubstantiation from Real Presence, to distinguish the modus (or metaphysical explanation) from the mystery itself. He explained that Catholics "ground their Adoration not on Transubstantiation, . . . as if, Transubstantiation defeated, Adoration is so too; but on a Real Presence with the Symbols; which in general is agreed on by the Lutherans together with them." He argued that even if transubstantiation could be proved an error, "yet as long as not confuted in the point of Real Presence, they [Catholics] would never the less continue to adore the self same Object, as now, in the same place, namely, the Body of Christ still present there with the Symbols and therefore there adorable. . . ." Like Dryden, Woodhead pleaded with his countrymen to have more charity, saying that even if Real Presence could be proved an error, yet Catholics were still "excusable from Idolatry," since they believed that "no other there but Christ may be worshipped, that nothing visible in the sacrament is He or his Body." If mistaken, their adoration would still be directed to an adorable object, and they would only be mistaken about where Christ is to be found.[22]

Thus, the Black Rubric, with its declaration that adoration of Christ at communion was idolatry, was the basis from which Stillingfleet and others stigmatized Catholics as the worst idolaters the world had ever known. This rubric set the stage for the campaign of defamation against Catholics in 1671–1688 for their supposed "idolatry" of the sacrament. The rubric was the groundwork for the Test Acts, which used the Panther's sacrament as a rite of qualification for public employment. This rubric and the Test Act formed the cornerstone, laid in 1661, for the Revolution of 1688.

At the end of *Threnodia* (1685), Dryden dismisses the Test Acts as needless. The only test the English have to pass is one of trust in Divine Providence: "Faith is a Christian's and a Subject's Test, / Oh give them to believe, and they are surely blest" (502–3). That poem closes with a splendid tableau, in which God is enthroned above and parliament is assembled in

---

22. [Abraham Woodhead], *The Second Discourse, The Catholicks Defence, for Their Adoration of the Body and Blood of our LORD, as Believed Really and Substantially Present in the Holy Sacrament of the Eucharist* (Oxford: O. Walker, 1687), 21–22.

mid-sky, gazing at the Book of Destiny. The lower part of the tableau opens out to the world's seas, to a future awaiting the choice of the English nation. On their choice depends the glorious mastery of the circling oceans and the spread of peace around the globe. Two years later the English are still poised to make their choice. In *The Hind*, the divine artist unfolds his great design once again for the British and asks only to bless them with the worldwide destiny he has held in abeyance for them since their "Mother" strayed under the "Tree," in 1529 and again in 1661. First, though, they must pass the test of faith in Providence. They must consent to see their king as a divinely appointed shepherd and their history as hand-shaped divine art.

Epilogue

Thus, in the design of *The Hind and the Panther*, Dryden uses the imagery, characters, and narrative line of the Canticle of Canticles as a key with which to decode God's artistic plan for English history. From ancient times a line of expositors had found in Canticles a universal Bride summoning a national Bride back into an inclusive marriage with Christ. This idea of Canticles provides the outline for Dryden's plot, where the Hind summons the high-church Panther back into the Catholic Church. Even though the Panther refuses the summons, Dryden plants the seed of hope in his design that the next English generation, the "little sister" of Canticles, will indeed enter in. For then Britain will have a slow rise, like ancient Rome, to her appointed destiny as the arbiter of world peace.

The Hind's invitation to the Panther in part 2 is framed in spiritual terms: it is a welcome to enter into the eucharistic mysteries and become the Bride of the fourth age, the one who will lead the war against Antichrist. However, the refusal of the Panther in part 3 is framed in political terms: it is a defense of the Test Acts, under which the eucharistic mysteries of the universal Bride are defamed as "idolatrous." The Panther does not argue for her own eucharistic doctrine when she rejects friendship with the Hind; rather, she upholds the Test Acts, statutes that make her sacrament merely a qualification for public employment and ensure that only those who outwardly conform to her communion rite will have civil and military power. These are the laws in which she finds security when she rejects the Hind. Dryden shows that her rejection of the Bride is a rejection of the Bridegroom for whom she speaks, and that her rejection of the Catholic king's campaign for repeal is a rejection of the call of Divine Providence. In the imagery and design of *The Hind*, the Panther renews her secret adultery with the Wolf when she conducts her pulpit campaign against the "Idolatry" of the king during the reign of James II.

The second plane of Dryden's design is apocalyptic. The Bride's statement in Canticles 8:2, "I will take hold of thee, and wil bring thee into my mothers house," was believed to refer to the conversion of the Jews in the last times. The Hind is figured as the Christian daughter coming into her Jewish mother's house and summoning her to lead the church of the fourth age in the war against Antichrist and his prophet. It is ironic that the Panther of the present generation collaborates instead with Antichrist, with some of her own sons wearing the "character" of "B" for the Beast on their breast, so great is their eagerness to maintain the carnal security of the Test Acts.

The third plane of Dryden's design, as we have shown in this study, is the parallel between the Hind and Aeneas. The Hind is portrayed as the gracious exile, the conduit of ancient civilization whose descendants are destined to bring peace to all mankind. She is the world-wanderer whom heaven has guided by signs and wonders back to the ancient mother country so as to inaugurate the reign of peace. On first arrival, though, the exile is persecuted by the wild inhabitants as a dangerous foreign intruder, but only because the native queen, jealous of the exile's ancient "Pedigree," incites the barbarians to attack her and her tiny camp, forcing the Trojan heroes into an alliance with their former enemies the Greeks. At the end of her tale, the Hind justifies the alliance between the Greeks and the Trojans, that is, between the Dissenters and the Catholics for the purpose of overthrowing the Test Acts, and she portrays it as a sign of the coming Pax Romana. Within this part of the design, Dryden embeds hope for the English Catholics that the marriage of Aeneas with Lavinia, which presages the next generation of English people, is assured and they will never need to be exiles again.

In part 3 of his poem, Dryden reveals that he is deeply engaged in the repeal campaign of 1685–1688. All six arguments for repeal that are found in the pamphlets of that age are also found in his poem, chiefly enunciated

by the spotless Hind, but also occasionally by the Panther, who grudgingly admits that the Test Acts are "laws unjust." We have also shown that
the poet contributes a unique, seventh argument by tracing the origin of
the first Test to the quid pro quo of December 1661, the exchange of the
Black Rubric for the Corporation Act. These were the mutual concessions that formed the foundation of the ruling party in the Restoration,
the party comprised of moderate or conformist Presbyterians and Latitudinarian Anglicans. This secret origin of the ruling party is figured
throughout *The Hind and the Panther* as the result of a secret adultery
between the Panther and the Wolf. It is called adultery because the Panther, after passage of the Act of Supremacy, was officially "married" to
the king of England, but now she secretly embraces the antiroyalist party.

Thus Dryden parallels the reign of James to the marriage song of Canticles to reveal that 1687 could well be the beginning of the end for England's harsh treatment of nonconformists, but only if the nation consents
to obey the summons of Providence that speaks through the king.
Springtime has arrived, and now the heavenly Bridegroom calls the English Bride into his garden for renewal and labor: "Arise, make hast my
love, my dove, my beautiful one, and come. For winter is now past, the
rayne is gone, and departed. The flowers have appeared in our land, the
time of pruning is come" (Sg 2:10–12). In *Britannia Rediviva,* written
the next year, Dryden prays that the Panther may indeed lose her spots,
that the English who oppose King James may come forth at last and be
reborn in the sacramental springtime. He also prays that the selfish "In-
t'rest" which is badly disguised as "Conscience" in the acrimonious debate over the Test Acts may be wiped away like Original Sin: "Let Conscience, which is Int'rest ill disguis'd, / In the same Font be cleans'd, and
all the Land Baptiz'd" (190–91).

Bibliography

Abingdon, James [Bertie], Earl of. "James Earl of Abingdon's Discourse with King James the Second, Nov. 18th, 1687, from His Own Memorandum of It." In *H. M. C. Lindsey*, ed. C. G. O. Bridgeman and J. C. Walker. London, Historical Manuscripts Commission, 1942.

Advice from a Dissenter in the City to His Friends in the Countrey. Shewing It to Be Their Duty and Safety, to Concur with Those Who Are for Abolishing the Penal Laws and Tests. London, 1688.

Ailesbury, Thomas [Bruce], Earl of. *Memoirs of Thomas, Earl of Ailesbury.* 2 vols. Westminster, U.K.: Roxburghe Club, 1890.

Ainsworth, Henry. *Solomons Song of Songs in English Metre: With Annotations.* 1623. N. p., 1642.

Albert the Great. *Man and the Beasts.* Translated by James J. Scanlan, M.D. Binghamton: State University of New York, 1987.

[Aldrich, Henry]. *A Vindication of the Oxford Reply to Two Discourses There Printed A.D. 1687 Concerning the Adoration of Our Blessed Saviour in the Eucharist, from the Exceptions Made to It in the Second Appendix to a Compendious Discourse on the Eucharist Published by the Same Press.* Oxford: At the Theatre, 1687.

Ashcraft, Richard. *Revolutionary Politics and Locke's Two Treatises of Government.* Princeton, N.J.: Princeton University Press, 1986.

Barlow, Thomas. *A Letter Concerning Invocation of Saints, and Adoration of the Cross, Writ Ten Years Since, to John Evelyn of Depthford, Esq, by Dr. Barlow Then Provost of Q. Colledge, and Now Lord Bishop of Lincoln.* London, 1679.

Barrillon, Paul dé. *Correspondance politique—Angleterre.* Vols. 125–68 of the coded manuscript reports from England, in *Les Archives Diplomatiques,* Ministère des affaires étrangères, Quai d'Orsay, Paris.

Bartlet, J. Vernon. "Worship (Christian)." In *Encyclopaedia of Religion and Ethics,* 13 vols., ed. James Hastings, 12: 764–68. Edinburgh, U.K.: Clark, 1921.

Basile [Dubois] de Soissons. *Defénce invincible de la vérité orthodoxe de la Présence Réele de Jésus- Christ en l'Eucharistie.* Paris: Pierre Compain, 1680.

Baxter, Richard. *The Autobiography of Richard Baxter.* Edited by J. M. Lloyd Thomas. 1931. Reprint, London: Dent/Totowa, N.J.: Rowman and Littlefield, 1974.

[Baxter, Richard]. *Roman Tradition Examined.* N. p., 1676.

[Beaumont, Henry, S.J.]. *Jupiter, Doctor Stillingfleets True God.* N. p., 1674.

Bernard of Clairvaux. *The Works of Bernard of Clairvaux.* 4 vols. Translated by Kilian Walsh and Irene Edmonds. Kalamazoo, Mich.: Cistercian Press, 1971–1980.

The Bestiary: A Book of Beasts, Being a Translation from a Latin Bestiary of the Twelfth Century. Translated by T. H. White. New York: G. P. Putnam, 1960.

The Bible. London: Robert Barker, 1615.

The Holie Bible. 2 vols. Doway: John Cousturier, 1615.

Biblia Sacra, Vulgatae Editionis. Milwaukee, Wis.: Bruce, 1955.

Birrell, T. A. "John Dryden's Purchases at Two Book Auctions, 1680 and 1682." *English Studies* 42 (1961): 193–217.

The Book of Common Prayer. London: John Bill and Christopher Barker, 1674.

Bosher, Robert S. *The Making of the Restoration Settlement: The Influence of the Laudians, 1649–1662.* Westminster, U.K.: Dacre, 1957.

Bossuet, Jacques Benigne, Bishop of Meaux. *Oeuvres.* 11 vols. Edited by Abbé J. P. Migne. Paris: Migne, 1857–1875.

Bossy, John. *The English Catholic Community, 1570–1850.* New York: Oxford University Press, 1976.

Boyer, Richard E. *English Declarations of Indulgence 1687 and 1688.* The Hague and Paris: Mouton, 1968.

Brightman, Thomas. *A Commentary on The Canticles or The Song of Salomon.* Latin edition, 1614. English edition, London: Henry Overton, 1644.

Broughton, Richard. *English Protestants Plea, and Petition, for English Preists and Papists, to the Present Court of Parliament, and All Persecutors of Them.* [St. Omer], 1621. Reprint, Amsterdam: Theatrum Orbis Terrarum/Norwood, N.J.: Walter J. Johnson, 1976.

Budick, Sanford. *Dryden and the Abyss of Light: A Study of "Religio Laici" and "The Hind and the Panther."* New Haven, Conn.: Yale University Press, 1970.

Buisson, Ferdinand. *Sebastien Castellion.* 2 vols. Paris: Hachette et Cie, 1892.

Burnet, G[ilbert]. *A Discourse Concerning Transubstantiation and Idolatry. Being an Answer to the Bishop of Oxford's Plea Relating to Those Two Points.* London, 1688.

[Canes, John Vincent]. *An Account of Dr. Stillingfleet's Late Book against the Church of Rome.* N.p., 1672.

C[are], H[enry]. *Draconica; or, An Abstract of All the Penal Laws Touching Mat-*

ters of Religion; and the Several Oaths and Tests Thereby Enjoyned. London: George Larkin, 1687.

[Cartwright, Thomas, Bishop of Chester]. A. B. *An Answer of a Minister of the Church of England to a Seasonable and Important Question, Proposed to Him by a Loyal and Religious Member of the Present House of Commons.* London: J. L., 1687.

——. *A Letter from a Clergy-Man in the Country, to the Clergyman in the City, Author of the Late Letter to His Friend in the Country: Shewing the Insufficiency of His Reasons Therein Contained for Not Reading the Declaration. By a Minister of the Church of England.* [London], 1688.

——. A. B. *A Letter from a Minister of the Church of England to the Pretended Baptist, Author of The Three Considerations Directed to Mr. Penn.* London: Andrew Sowle, 1688.

[Castlemaine, Roger Palmer, Earl of.] *A Reply to the Answer of the Catholique Apology; or, A Cleere Vindication of the Catholiques of England from All Matter of Fact Charged against Them by Their Enemyes.* N. p., 1668.

——. *The Catholique Apology with a Reply to the Answer Together with a Clear Refutation of the Seasonable Discourse, Its Reasonable Defence, & Dr. Du Moulins Answer to Philanax; as Also Dr. Stillingfleet's Last Gunpowder Treason Sermon, His Attaque about the Treaty of Munster, and All Matter of Fact Charg'd on the English Catholiques by Their Enemies.* 3d ed. N. p., 1674.

——. *The Earl of Castlemain's Manifesto.* N. p., 1681.

Certain Sermons or Homilies Appointed to be Read in Churches. 2 vols. in one. Reprint of the 1623 edition. Introduction by Mary Ellen Ricke and Thomas B. Stroup. Gainesville, Fla.: Scholars' Facsimiles and Reprints, 1968.

Clancy, Thomas H., S.J. *English Catholic Books, 1641–1700.* Cambridge: Cambridge University Press, 1996.

Challoner, Richard. *Memoirs of Missionary Priests.* London, 1742.

Committees for Repeal of the Test and Corporation Acts: Minutes 1786 and 1827–8. Introduced by Thomas W. Davis. London: London Record Society, 1978.

Considerations on the Penal Laws against Roman Catholics in England, and the New Acquired Colonies in America. London: R & J. Dodsley, 1764.

Cowherd, Raymond Gibson. *Protestant Dissenters in English Politics.* Philadelphia: University of Pennsylvania Press, 1942.

Cowper, William. *Poems by William Cowper: 1748–1782.* Edited by John D. Baird and Charles Ryskamp. Oxford: Clarendon Press, 1980.

Crashaw, Richard. *The Complete Poetry of Richard Crashaw.* Edited by George Walton Williams. New York: Norton, 1970.

Cressy, Hugh Paulin de, or Serenus. *Exomologesis.* 1647. 2d ed., Paris, 1653.

[——]. *Fanaticism Fanatically Imputed.* N. p., 1672.

Croft, Herbert, Bishop of Hereford. *A Short Discourse Concerning the Reading*

His Majesties Late Declaration in the Churches. London: Charles Harper, 1689.

Cudworth, Ralph. *The True Intellectual System of the Universe.* 1678. 3 vols. London: Thomas Tegg, 1845.

[Curry, John, M.D.] *Observations on the Popery Laws.*Dublin: T. Ewing, 1771.

Dalrymple, Sir John. *Memoirs of Great Britain and Ireland.* 3 vols. 1790. Reprint, Farnborough, U.K.: Gregg, 1970.

Daniel-Rops, H[enri], S.J. *The Church in the Seventeenth Century.* Translated by J. J. Buckingham. London: Dent/New York: Dutton, 1963.

D[arrell] W[illiam], S.J. *The Lay-Mans Opinion, Sent in a Private Letter to a Considerable Divine.* N. p., 1687.

D[e] W[itt], C[ornelius]. *A Letter from Holland Touching Liberty of Conscience, April 27, 1688.* London: E. R., 1688.

Dimock, N[athaniel]. *The History of "The Book of Common Prayer" in Its Bearing on Present Eucharistic Controversies.* New York: Longmans Green, 1910.

Dryden, John. *Hymns Attributed to John Dryden.* Edited by George Rapall Noyes and George Reuben Potter. Berkeley and Los Angeles: University of California Press, 1937.

———. *The Works of John Dryden.* 20 vols. Edited by H. T. Swedenberg. Berkeley and Los Angeles: University of California Press, 1956—. (Some volumes have not yet appeared in the California Dryden edition.)

———. *The Works of John Dryden.* Edited by Sir Walter Scott. London: Miller, 1808.

———. *The Letters of John Dryden.* Edited by Charles E. Ward. Durham, N.C.: Duke University Press, 1942.

Dryden: A Collection of Critical Essays. Edited by Bernard N. Schilling. Englewood Cliffs, N.J.: Prentice- Hall, 1963.

Erlich, J. W. *Erlich's Blackstone.* New York: Capricorn, 1959.

Foley, Henry. *Records of the English Province of the Society of Jesus.* 7 vols. in 8. London: Burns and Oates, 1877–1883.

Fox, Charles James. *Appendix to a History of the Early Part of the Reign of James the Second.* London: Miller, 1808.

Fox-Davies, Arthur Charles. *A Complete Guide to Heraldry.* London and Edinburgh: Nelson, 1929.

F[uller], R[obert]. *Missale Romanum Vindicatum; or, The Mass Vindicated from D. Daniel Brevents Calumnious and Scandalous Tract.* N. p., 1674.

Fuller, Thomas. *The Church History of Britain.* London: John Williams, 1655.

[G. T.] *A Letter in Answer to Two Main Questions of the First Letter to a Dissenter.* London: M. T., 1687.

Geyl, Pieter. *The Netherlands in the Seventeenth Century, 1609 to 1648.* 2d ed. London: Benn/New York: Barnes and Noble, 1966.

Ginsburg, Christian D. *The Song of Songs and Coheleth, Translated from the Original Hebrew, with a Commentary, Historical and Critical.* 1857. Reprint, New York: KTAV, 1970.

Goldie, Mark. "Sir Peter Pett, Sceptical Toryism, and the Science of Toleration." In *Persecution and Toleration*, ed. W. J. Sheils. Oxford: Ecclesiastical History Society/Basil Blackwell, 1984.

[Gother, John]. *An Agreement between the Church of England and Church of Rome, Evinced from the Concertation of Some of Her Sons with Their Brethren the Dissenters*. London: Henry Hills, 1687.

———. *Good Advice to the Pulpits, Deliver'd in a Few Cautions for the Keeping Up the Reputation of Those Chairs, and Preserving the Nation in Peace*. London: Henry Hills, 1687.

———. *Reflections upon the Answer to the Papist Misrepresented*. [London], 1686.

———. *Papists Protesting against Protestant-Popery*. London: Henry Hills, 1686.

The Great Case of Toleration Stated, and Endeavoured to Be Resolved in Order to Publick Security and Peace. London: Andrew Sowle, 1688.

Grey, Anchitell. *Debates of the House of Commons from the Year 1667 to the Year 1694*. London: D. Henry and R. Cave, 1763.

Guild, William. *Loves Entercours between the Lamb and His Bride, Christ and His Church; or, A Clear Explication and Application of The Song of Solomon*. London: Ralph Smith, 1658.

Hague, Dyson. *The Story of the English Prayer Book*. 2d ed. London and New York: Longmans Green, 1930.

Hale, Sir Matthew. *Historia Placitorum Coronae*. 2 vols. London, 1736.

Halifax, George Savile, Marquis of. *The Complete Works of George Savile, First Marquess of Halifax*. Edited by Walter Raleigh. Oxford: Clarendon Press, 1912. Reprint, New York: Augustus M. Kelley, 1970.

Harpsfield, Nicholas, LL.D. *A Treatise on the Pretended Divorce between Henry VIII and Catharine of Aragon*. Edited by Nicholas Pocock. Westminster, U.K.: Camden Society, 1878.

[Harrington, James, the Younger]. *Some Reflexions upon a Treatise Call'd "Pietas Romanas and Parisiensis" Lately Printed at Oxford*. Bound with his tract, *A Vindication of Protestant Charity*. Oxford: At the Theatre, 1688.

Hart, W. H. *Index Expurgatorius Anglicanus*. London: J. R. Smith, 1872.

Harth, Phillip. *Contexts of Dryden's Thoughts*. Chicago: University of Chicago Press, 1968.

Hartmann, Cyril. *Clifford of the Cabal*. London: Heinemann, 1937.

Hay, Malcolm V. *The Enigma of James II*. London and Glasgow: Sands, 1938.

Heylyn, Peter. *Aerius Redivivus; or, The History of the Presbyterians Containing the Beginnings, Progresse, and Successes of That Active Sect. From the Year 1536 to the Year 1647*. 2d ed. London: Christopher Wilkinson and Thomas Archer/ Oxford: John Crosley, 1672.

[Heywood, Samuel]. *The Right of Protestant Dissenters to a Compleat Toleration Asserted; Containing an Historical Account of the Test Laws, and Shewing the*

Injustice, Inexpediency, and Folly of the Sacramental Test, as Now Imposed, with Respect to Protestant Dissenters. 2d ed. London: J. Johnson, 1789.

The History and Proceedings of the House of Lords, 1660–1697. Vol. 1 of 8 vols. London: Timberland, 1742.

Hooker, Robert. *Ecclesiastical Polity.* 2 vols. Edited by Ernest Rhys. London: Dent/New York: Dutton, 1922.

Hopkins, David. *John Dryden.* Cambridge, London, and New York: Cambridge University Press, 1986.

[Hubert, William]. *The Puritan Convert.* N. p., 1676.

Hume, David. *The History of England.* London: Baynes, Priestley, 1822.

An Important Query for Protestants: Viz. Can Good Com Out of Galilee? London: G. L. and J. H., 1688.

Indulgence to Tender Consciences Shewn to Be Most Reasonable and Christian. By a Minister of the Church of England. London: Henry Hills, 1687.

James II. *The Life of James the Second King of England Collected Out of Memoirs Writ of His Own Hand.* 2 vols. Edited by J. S. Clarke. London: Longman, 1816.

Jefferson, D. W. "The Poetry of 'The Hind and the Panther.'" *Modern Language Review* 79 (1984): 32–44.

[Johnson, Samuel, or "Julian"]. *A Letter from a Freeholder, to the Rest of the Freeholders of England.* London, 1689. Printed in *A Seventh Collection of Papers Relating to Parliaments and the Penal Laws and Tests.* [N. p.], 1689.

Johnson, Samuel. *Lives of the English Poets.* 2 vols. Edited by Arthur Waugh. London: Oxford University Press, 1961.

———. *A Dictionary of the English Language.* London, 1755. Reprint, New York: Arno Press, 1979.

Johnston, Nathaniel. *The King's Visitatorial Power Asserted.* London: Henry Hills, 1688.

Jones, J. R. *The Revolution of 1688 in England.* New York: Norton, 1972.

Jusserand, J. J. *Angleterre, Vol. 2: 1666–1690.* From the series, *Recueil des Instructions données aux ambassadeurs et ministres de France depuis les Traités de Westphalie jusqu'à la Révolution Française.* Paris: E. de Boccard, 1929.

Kenyon, J. P. *The Popish Plot.* London: Heinemann, 1972.

———. *Robert Spencer, Earl of Sunderland.* London: Longmans, 1958.

James Kinsley. "Dryden's Bestiary." *Review of English Studies,* n.s., 4 (October): 331–36.

Langhorne, Richard. *Richard Langhorn's Memoires, with Some Meditations and Devotions of His, During His Imprisonment.* N. p., 1679.

Latin Hymns Sung at the Church of Saint Hugh Letchworth. Translated by Adrian Fortescue. 1913. Reprint, Harrison, N.Y.: Roman Catholic Books, n. d.

The Lay-Mans Answer to the Lay-Mans Opinion. London, 1687.

Le Clerc, Guillaume. *Le Bestiaire: Das Thierbuch des Normanischen Dichters Guillaume Le Clerc.* Edited by Dr. Robert Reinsch. Leipzig: O. R. Reisland, 1892.

L'Estrange, Roger. *A Brief History of the Times*. London: R. Sare, 1688.

———. *A Further Discovery of the Plot*. London, 1680.

Littledale, Richard Frederick. *A Commentary on The Song of Songs, from Ancient and Medieval Sources*. London: Joseph Masters/New York: Pott and Amery, 1869.

Lloyd, John. *The Song of Songs; Being a Paraphrase upon the Most Excellent Canticles of Solomon in a Pindarick Poem*. London: Henry Faithorne and John Kersey, 1682.

Lloyd, William. *An Answer to the Bishop of Oxford's Reasons for Abrogating the Test*. London, 1689.

Locke, John. *A Letter Concerning Toleration*. 1689. Edited by James H. Tully. Indianapolis, Ind.: Hackett, 1983.

Luther, Martin. "Lectures on The Song of Solomon." Translated by Ian Siggins. In *Luther's Works*, vol. 15 of 54 vols. Edited by Jaroslav Pelikan. St. Louis: Concordia, 1972.

Maccubin, Robert P., and Martha Hamilton-Phillips, eds. *The Age of William III and Mary II*. Williamsburg, Va.: College of William and Mary/New York: Grolier Club/Washington, D.C.: Folger Library, 1989.

Macpherson, James. *Original Papers; Containing the Secret History of Great Britain . . . to Which Are Prefixed Extracts from the Life of James II as Written by Himself*. 2 vols. London, 1775.

Matter, E. Ann. *The Voice of My Beloved: The Song of Songs in Western Medieval Christianity*. Philadelphia: University of Pennsylvania Press, 1990.

[Maurice, Henry]. *The Project for Repealing the Penal Laws and Tests*. [London, 1688].

McDonnell, Kilian, O.S.B. *John Calvin, the Church, and the Eucharist*. Princeton, N.J.: Princeton University Press, 1967.

McFadden, George. *Dryden the Public Writer, 1660–1685*. Princeton, N.J.: Princeton University Press, 1978.

Miller, John. *James II: A Study in Kingship*. London: Wayland, 1978.

———. *Popery and Politics in England, 1660–1688*. Cambridge: Cambridge University Press, 1973.

Milton, John. *Complete Prose Works of John Milton*. 8 vols. Edited by William Alfred et al. New Haven, Conn.: Yale University Press, 1962–1982.

Miner, Earl. *Dryden's Poetry*. Bloomington: Indiana University Press, 1967.

———. *The Restoration Mode from Milton to Dryden*. Princeton, N.J.: Princeton University Press, 1974.

The Ministers Reasons for His Not Reading the Kings Declaration, Friendly Debated by a Dissenter. London: G. Larkin, 1688.

[More, Henry]. *A Brief Discourse of the Real Presence of the Body and Blood of Christ*. London: Walter Kettilby, 1686.

Mountagu, Richard. *Appello Caesarem*. 1625. Reprint, Amsterdam: Theatrum Orbis Terrarum/New York: Da Capo, 1972.

Myerson, George. *The Argumentative Imagination: Wordsworth, Dryden and Coleridge.* Manchester, U.K.: Manchester University Press/New York: St. Martin's Press, 1992.

A New Test of the Church of England's Loyalty. London: N[at] T[ompson], 1687.

North, Sir Roger. *Examen; or, An Enquiry into the Credit and Veracity of a Pretended Complete History . . . All Tending to Vindicate the Honour of the Late King Charles the Second, and His Happy Reign, from the Intended Aspersions of That Foul Pen.* London, 1740.

Nusteling, Hubert P. H. "The Netherlands and the Huguenot Emigrés." In *La Révocation de l'Edit de Nantes et les Provinces-Unies,* ed. J. A. H. Bots and G. H. M. Posthumus Meyjes. Amsterdam and Maarssen: APA Holland University Press, 1986.

Origen. *Origen, Spirit and Fire: A Thematic Anthology of His Writings.* Edited by Hans Urs von Balthasar. Translated by Robert J. Daly, S.J. Washington, D.C.: The Catholic University of America Press, 1984.

Osborn, James M. *John Dryden: Some Biographical Facts and Problems.* New York: Columbia University Press, 1940.

Parker, Samuel, Bishop of Oxford. *Reasons for Abrogating the Test Imposed upon All Members of Parliament Anno 1678 Oct. 30.* London: Henry Bonwicke, 1688.

——. *History of His Own Time.* 1686. Translated from the Latin by Thomas Newlin. London: Charles Rivington, 1727.

——. *Religion and Loyalty.* London, 1686.

Paston, James. *A Discourse of Penal Laws in Matters of Religion.* London: For the author, 1688.

Pastor, Ludwig Freiherr von. *History of the Popes, Vol. 32: 1676–1700.* Edited by Dom Ernest Graf, O.S.B. London: Kegan Paul, 1940.

Patrick, Symon. *A Paraphrase upon the Books of Ecclesiastes and The Song of Solomon.* London: Richard Royston, 1685.

Payne, Henry. *An Answer to a Scandalous Pamphlet Entituled A Letter to a Dissenter Concerning His Majesties Late Declaration of Indulgence.* London: N[at] T[hompson], 1687.

——. *The Persecutor Expos'd: In Reflections, by Way of Reply, to an Ill-Bred Answer to the Duke of Buckingham's Paper.* London: J. L. for the author, n. d.

——. *The Siege of Constantinople.* London: Thomas Dring, 1675.

[Penn, William]. *A Defence of the Duke of Buckingham's Book of Religion and Worship.* London: A. Banks, 1685.

——. *Good Advice to the Church of England . . . to Abolish the Penal Laws and Tests.* London: Andrew Sowle, 1687.

——. *A Letter from a Gentleman in the Country to His Friends in London, upon the Subject of the Penal Laws and Tests.* [London], 1687.

——. *A Perswasive to Moderation to Church Dissenters.* [London: Andrew Sowle, 1686].

———. *Some Free Reflections upon Occasion of the Public Discourse about Liberty of Conscience*. London: Andrew Sowle, 1687.

———. *Three Letters Tending to Demonstrate How the Security of This Nation against All Future Persecution Lys in the Abolishment of the Present Penal Laws and Tests*. London: Andrew Sowle, 1688.

Plain Dealing Concerning the Penal Laws and Tests Delivered in a Dialogue between a Country Man and a Citizen. 1688.

Physiologus. Translated by Michael J. Curley. Austin: University of Texas Press, 1979.

Pocock, J. G. A. *The Ancient Constitution and the Feudal Law: A Study of English Historical Thought in the Seventeenth Century*. Cambridge: Cambridge University Press, 1957.

Poems on Affairs of State, 1660–1678. Vol. 1 of 7 vols. Edited by George de F. Lord. New Haven, Conn.: Yale University Press, 1963.

Pope, Marvin H. "Notes to the Song of Songs." In vol. 7C of the 44-volume *Anchor Bible*. Garden City, N.Y.: Doubleday, 1977.

Pulton, Andrew, S.J. *A Full and Clear Exposition of the Protestant Rule of Faith, with an Excellent Dialogue Laying Forth the Large Extent of True Protestant Charity against the Uncharitable Papists*. [London]: N.p., c. 1687.

Quarles, Francis. *Sions Sonets. Sung by Solomon the King and Periphras'd by Fra. Quarles*. London: W. Stansby for Thomas Dewe, 1625.

Rapin de Thoyras, Paul. *The Metallick History of the Reigns of King William III and Queen Mary, Queen Anne, and King George I. Being a Series of Near Four Hundred Medals, with the Explication of the Devises, Inscriptions and Legends*. Vol. 3 of *Tindal's History of England*. London: John and Paul Knapton, 1747.

Ronalds, Francis S. *The Attempted Whig Revolution of 1678–1681*. Totowa, N.J.: Rowman and Littlefield, 1974.

Roper, Alan. *Dryden's Poetic Kingdoms*. London: Routledge and Kegan Paul, 1965.

Reidy, Maurice F. *Bishop Lancelot Andrewes, Jacobean Court Preacher*. Chicago: Loyola University Press, 1955.

Sander, Nicholas. *The Rise and Growth of the Anglican Schism*. Translated by David Lewis. 1877. Reprint, Rockford, Ill.: TAN, 1988.

Sasse, Hermann. *This Is My Body: Luther's Contention for the Real Presence in the Sacrament of the Altar*. Minneapolis, Minn.: Augsburg, 1959.

Sclater, Edward. *Consensus Veterum; or, The Reasons of Edward Sclater Minister of Putney, for His Conversion to the Catholic Faith and Communion*. London: Henry Hills, 1686.

Scott, Sir Walter. *The Life of John Dryden*. Vol. 1 of *The Works of John Dryden* in 18 vols. London: William Miller, 1808.

A Short Answer to His Grace the D. of Buckingham's Paper, Concerning Religion, Toleration and Liberty of Conscience. London: For S. G., 1685.

S[hute], G[iles]. *A New Test in Lieu of the Old One.* London: George Larkin, 1688.

————. *A New Naked Truth; or, The Sandy Foundation of the Sacramental Test Shaken, by a Warning-Piece Discharged from Heaven against All Sorts of Persecutors.* London: George Larkin, 1688.

Sibbes, Richard. *Bowels Opened; or, A Discovery of the Near and Dear Love, Union and Communion betwixt Christ and the Church.* 3d ed. London: John Clark, 1648.

Smith, William. *The Mysteries and Intrigues of the Popish Plot Laid Open: With Depositions Sworn before the Secretary of State.* London: For C. W., 1685.

Speck, W. A. *Reluctant Revolutionaries.* Oxford: Oxford University Press, 1988.

Spelman, Henry. *The History and Fate of Sacrilege.* London: John Hartley, 1698.

Spenser, Edmund. *The Complete Poetical Works of Spenser.* Boston: Houghton Mifflin, 1908.

Spurr, John. *The Restoration Church of England, 1646–1689.* New Haven, Conn.: Yale University Press, 1991.

Stillingfleet, Edward. *A Discourse Concerning the Idolatry Practised in the Church of Rome.* 2d ed. London: Henry Mortlock, 1672.

The Statutes at Large, from the Twelfth Year of King Charles II. to the Last Year of King James II. Inclusive. Edited by Danby Pickering. Cambridge and London: Charles Bathurst, 1763.

Stoppa, Giovanni Battista. *The Religion of the Dutch.* 1673. Translated by John Davies. London, 1680.

The Substance of a Speech Made by H-s L-she, Esq; In Debate on the Bill for Enabling Papists to Take Building Leases. Dublin, 1772.

Taaffe, Nicholas Viscount. *Observations on Affairs in Ireland from the Settlement in 1691.* London: W. Griffin, 1766.

Tisdall, William. *The Case of the Sacramental Test Stated and Argu'd.* Dublin: Daniel Tompson, 1715.

Thorp, Willard. "Henry Nevil Payne, Dramatist and Jacobite Conspirator." In *The Parrott Presentation Volume*, ed. Hardin Craig. Princeton, N.J.: Princeton University Press, 1935.

Topsell, Edward. *Topsell's Histories of Beasts.* Edited by Malcolm South. Chicago: Nelson-Hall, 1981.

Turner, F. C. *James II.* New York: Macmillan, 1948.

Walker, Obadiah. "Animadversions upon the Reply to the Two Discourses Concerning the Adoration of Our B. Saviour in the Holy Eucharist." Appendix to Abraham Woodhead's *A Compendious Discourse.* Oxford, 1688.

Ward, Charles. *The Life of John Dryden.* Chapel Hill: University of North Carolina Press, 1961.

Weiss, Charles. *Histoire des refugiés protestants de France.* Paris: Charpentier/London: Jeffs, 1853.

Wilcocks, Thomas. *The Work of That Late Reverend and Learned Divine, Mr. Thomas Wilcocks.* London: John Haviland, 1624.

Wild, Robert. *A Letter from Dr. Robert Wild to His Friend Mr. J. J. upon Occasion of His Majesty's Declaration for Liberty of Conscience.* London: T. Parkhurst et al., 1672.

William of St. Thierry. "Exposition on The Song of Songs." In *The Works of William of St. Thierry.* 2 vols. Translated by Mother Columba Hart, O.S.B. Shannon, Ireland: Irish University Press, 1970.

John Wilson. *Jus Regium Coronae; or, The King's Supream Power in Dispensing with Penal Statutes: More Particularly as It Relates to the Two Test-Acts of the Twenty-Fifth, and the Thirtieth of His Late Majesty, King Charles the Second; Argu'd by Reason, and Confirm'd by the Common, and Statute Laws of This Kingdom.* London: Henry Hills, 1688.

Winn, James Anderson. *John Dryden and His World.* New Haven, Conn.: Yale University Press, 1987.

Wolf, J. B. *Louis XIV.* New York: W. W. Norton, 1968.

[Abraham Woodhead]. *Considerations on the Council of Trent, Being the Fifth Discourse Concerning the Guide in Controversies.* N. p., 1671.

———. *Dr. Stillingfleet's Principles, Giving an Account of the Faith of Protestants, Considered by N. O.* Paris: Christian et Guillery, 1671.

———. *Two Discourses Concerning the Adoration of Our B. Saviour in the Eucharist. The First: Animadversions upon the Alterations of the Rubrick in the Communion-Service in the Common-Prayer-Book of the Church of England. The Second Discourse, The Catholicks Defence, for Their Adoration of the Body and Blood of Our Lord, as Believed Really and Substantially Present in the Holy Sacrament of the Eucharist.* Oxford, 1687.

Zwicker, Steven N. *Politics and Language in Dryden's Poetry.* Princeton, N.J.: Princeton University Press, 1984.

Index

Ancient Faith and Modern Freedom in John Dryden's The Hind and the Panther *was* composed in ITC Galliard by Generic Compositors, Stamford, New York; printed on 50-pound Glatfelter Supple Opaque Recycled Natural and bound by Thomson-Shore, Inc., Dexter, Michigan; and designed and produced by Kachergis Book Design, Pittsboro, North Carolina.